Ornament of Precious Liberation

Ornament of Precious Liberation

Gampopa

Translated by Ken Holmes

EDITED BY Thupten Jinpa

FOREWORD BY His Holiness the Karmapa

Wisdom

Wisdom Publications
199 Elm Street
Somerville, MA 02144 USA
wisdompubs.org

Library of Congress Cataloging-in-Publication Data
Names: Sgam-po-pa, 1079–1153, author. | Holmes, Ken, translator. | Thupten Jinpa, editor.
Title: Ornament of precious liberation / Gampopa ; translated by Ken Holmes ; edited by Thupten Jinpa.
Other titles: Dam chos yid bźin gyi nor bu Thar pa rin po che'i rgyan. English
Description: Somerville, MA : Wisdom Publications, 2017. | Series: Tibetan classics. | Includes bibliographical references and index.
Identifiers: LCCN 2016022658| ISBN 9781614294177 (pbk. : alk. paper) | ISBN 1614294178 (pbk. : alk. paper)
Subjects: LCSH: Bodhisattva stages (Mahayana Buddhism)—Early works to 1800. | Religious life—Mahayana Buddhism—Early works to 1800. | Mahayana Buddhism—Doctrines—Early works to 1800.
Classification: LCC BQ4330 .S513 2017 | DDC 294.3/42—dc23
LC record available at https://lccn.loc.gov/2016022658

ISBN 978-1-61429-417-7 ebook ISBN 978-1-61429-432-0

21 20 19 18 17
5 4 3 2 1

Cover design by Jess Morphew. Cover painting Urgyen Gyalpo.
Interior design by Gopa&Ted2, Inc. Set in Diacritical Garamond Pro 10.7/12.7.

Wisdom Publications' books are printed on acid-free paper and meet the guidelines for permanence and durability of the Production Guidelines for Book Longevity of the Council on Library Resources.

This book was produced with environmental mindfulness.
For more information, please visit wisdompubs.org/wisdom-environment.

Printed in the United States of America.

Contents

THE KARMAPA

Foreword

When we consider the life and achievements of Lord Gampopa, it is self-evident that he was extraordinary and highly talented. Nine hundred years ago in the snow land of Tibet, few people had such great capacity. Tibetan Buddhism in general and the Dakpo Kagyü in particular owe him a profound debt of gratitude.

Before he renounced the life of a householder to become a monk, he was an accomplished physician, widely respected not just for his knowledge and ability to heal but also for his compassion and his concern for the welfare of others. In addition, he was a devoted husband and a loving father, a good human being. After his ordination at the age of twenty-five, he focused his mind on the Dharma.

There were many different lineages at that time in Tibet. Some only practiced the sutra teachings, others were purely tantric, and there was much mutual suspicion. The genius of Lord Gampopa was to bring together these seemingly conflicting traditions. Having established a strong base in the sutra tradition of the Kadampas, he met the great yogi Milarepa and received the instructions on the six yogas and mahāmudrā that had been passed down from the great Indian mahāsiddhas Nāropa and Maitripa. Gampopa was able to unite these two traditions, weaving them into a seamless path to liberation in what is known as "the confluence of mahāmudrā and Kadam."

Milarepa himself acknowledged Gampopa's greatness when he predicted that future generations would not call his own lineage the practice lineage of Milarepa but would call it Dakpo Kagyü. Of the three Kagyü forefathers, Gampopa was the only one to be ordained. Marpa the Translator and Milarepa were lay practitioners. When Gampopa, following the instructions he had received from Milarepa, settled at the remote Daklha Gampo hermitage, a large community of meditators gradually gathered around him, and thus Gampopa established the first monastery of the Dakpo Kagyü.

Gampopa's own teaching practices became the root from which developed the distinctive system that all the Dakpo Kagyü schools follow to this day. Students first studied the lamrim teachings on the stages of the path from the Kadam tradition, and then they were allowed to study mahāmudrā and other tantric practices. Hence, the extant lineages within the Dakpo Kagyü—the Drikung, Drukpa, Karma Kamtsang, Taklung, and Barom—resemble the branches of a family tree, and Lord Gampopa is our common ancestor. The *Ornament of Precious Liberation* is our great family treasure and our shared inheritance. It is my aspiration that through this text the different traditions of the Dakpo Kagyu will rediscover their common ancestry and become a joyous and harmonious family once more.

We should consider reading Gampopa's *Ornament of Precious Liberation* as unlike reading other books. This text has the power of a direct transmission from master to student. Gampopa himself promised that in the future those who were unable to meet him personally should not despair, because reading his two texts *Ornament of Precious Liberation* and *Jewel Garland of the Supreme Path* would be identical to receiving the teachings directly from him.

Finally, I would like to commend Ken and Katia Holmes for bringing Gampopa's words directly to English speakers. Though there are several earlier translations of *Ornament of Precious Liberation*, this translation is the most readable and faithful, and the extensive footnotes will be of help to practitioners and scholars alike.

The Seventeenth Karmapa Ogyen Trinley Dorje,
Dharamsala

Editor's Preface

The text in this volume has a long and rich history in the world of Tibetan Buddhism. Gampopa's *Ornament of Precious Liberation* remains to this day the quintessential understanding of the Buddhist path to enlightenment in the Kagyü school of Tibetan Buddhism. Trained in the Kadam teachings stemming from the Bengali master Atiśa as well in the Mahāmudrā instructions of Marpa Lotsāwa and his famed disciple Milarepa, Gampopa presents in his work a unique blending of two important streams of Tibetan spiritual instructions.

The step-by-step instructions developed in this work continue to guide and elevate the attentive reader and practitioner of Tibetan Buddhism today. Imbued by Gampopa with so much insight and helpful instruction, it is not surprising that this manual was considered a classic of Buddhist literature in Tibet. With this new translation, students and teachers of Tibetan Buddhism will have a chance to directly engage with the insights and instructions of a great spiritual master. For the general reader, it offers an opportunity to appreciate the richness of the Tibetan tradition and its creative synthesis of the vast corpus of classical Indian Buddhist teachings.

As the founder and director of the Institute of Tibetan Classics and editor of the present volume, it has been an honor for me to be part of this important translation project, which first appeared as part of an anthology of three path texts in *Stages of the Buddha's Teachings*, volume 10 of *The Library of Tibetan Classics*. I thank Ken Holmes for translating Gampopa's words into elegant English with such care and diligence. I thank my wife, Sophie Boyer-Langri, for her countless contributions to the work of the Institute. I would like to express my heartfelt thanks to Tsadra Foundation, who generously funded the direct costs of this translation project. The Hershey Family Foundation has supported the Institute of Tibetan Classics during its first decade, for which I am deeply grateful. I would also like to acknowledge the Ing Foundation for its generous patronage of the Institute since 2008. Finally, I thank the Scully Peretsman Foundation for supporting my own work, enabling me to edit this precious volume.

It is my sincere hope that this translation will be of benefit to many people. Through the efforts of all those who have been involved in this noble venture, may all beings enjoy peace and happiness.

Thupten Jinpa

Translator's Introduction

The work translated in this volume is the well-known *Ornament of Precious Liberation* by Gampopa Sönam Rinchen (1079–1153). It has been familiar to Western readers for over fifty years as *The Jewel Ornament of Liberation*, thanks to the translation by Herbert Guenther, which was so welcome and excellent for its time.[1] The text presents Gampopa's explanation of the essential elements involved in a gradual ascent of the bodhisattva path, from the beginner level up to the final awakening of supreme buddhahood. Gampopa was a founding master of the Kagyü tradition and is famous within it as the one who integrated the spiritual and literary legacy of the Kadam school.

Ornament of Precious Liberation is the main textbook for the study of Mahayana Buddhism in the Kagyü monastic schools and colleges. It is seen as a meditator's textbook, inasmuch as it is not an eloquent, scholarly masterpiece or an elaborate discussion but a need-to-know manual of essentials for a meditator. The language is down to earth and direct. The eminent twentieth-century Tibetan scholar Kyapjé Kalu Rinpoché, recognized as an authority by lamas of all Tibetan schools, presented this text as an enlightened being's (i.e., Gampopa's) overview of the vast scriptures of nontantric Buddhism and commented, "Even if you want to spend the rest of your life meditating in a cave, you must know Gampopa's *Ornament of Precious Liberation* by heart and you must understand Maitreya's buddhanature teachings." In this work, Gampopa carefully picks out the most salient points on each topic and, more importantly, provides students with an overall Dharma framework of topics into which subsequent studies can easily be slotted. Gampopa is always careful to back up his statements or summaries with quotations from the two main Indian Mahayana lineages. Although this is a textbook for Vajrayana meditators, the work remains exclusively a Mahayana treatise except for one or two minor references to his guru Milarepa and to the practice of Mahāmudrā.[2]

The writing, like most such texts, is not, and is not meant to be, an immersive read, unless one is already intimate with the terrain. Meanings are not elaborated. The discursive work is left to the Dharma master who teaches it. Once learned by heart as an *aide-memoire*, however, it provides teacher and student alike with an instant, multi-tiered reference for the structure of the bodhisattva path.

Tenrim

This work is a manual of the "stages of the doctrine," or *tenrim* (*bstan rim*), in the tradition of the Kadam monastery of Sangphu.[3] The tenrim genre aims at leading students to transform their outlook and lives by internalizing a series of ascending spiritual truths through a series of preparatory reflections, beginning with the preciousness of their human birth and then moving on to its precariousness—the contemplation of mortality turning students' minds away from the things of this life. Reflecting on the consequences of harmful deeds that will be experienced at the time of death and in the life to come inspires a strong desire to ensure that one's future birth is in a pleasant realm. Then, reflecting on the drawbacks of life in all realms in the wheel of existence (*samsara*), even human and divine ones, inspires students to desire liberation (*nirvana*). Yet personal liberation for oneself alone is also not a perfectly satisfactory solution. The student is encouraged to strive compassionately for the highest spiritual goal—the perfect awakening of a buddha in order to benefit all living beings. Such altruistic aspirations and practices are characteristic of the bodhisattva, and the bodhisattva practices leading to buddhahood are the main subject of this text, practices for developing such qualities as universal compassion and the highest insight into the nature of reality. The treatise ends with a chapter extolling the virtues of a buddha's awakening, the highest destination on the path.

Readers of Tibetan Buddhist manuals on beginning practice will be familiar with the preliminary contemplations described above, which parallel the so-called *four thoughts that turn the mind*, four contemplations that inspire a person to reject worldly life and pursue spiritual practice: the reflections on (1) the difficulty of finding a well-endowed human existence and on (2) the impermanence of life (which together turn the mind away from this life and toward future lives); and the reflections on (3) the defects of samsara and on (4) the workings of karmic causality (which together induce the mind to reject samsara and desire liberation). Many beginners' manuals in Tibetan Buddhist literature draw on these contemplations and proceed in a graduated manner through the specific practices.

Tenrim works largely descend from Atiśa. Unlike most lamrim works, tenrim texts do not frame their presentation around the three spiritual capacities, although they may certainly mention these three types of beings. Tenrim texts are Buddhist manuals that expound the "stages" (*rim pa*) of the Mahayana "doctrine" (*bstan pa*). Works of this genre were first transmitted via students of Atiśa (982–1054) at Sangphu Neuthok Monastery south of Lhasa. The earliest major text of the tenrim genre we have today is the *Great Treatise on the Stages of the Doctrine*, or simply *Great Tenrim*, of Drolungpa Lodrö Jungné (eleventh–twelfth centuries). Drolungpa's work was perhaps the most extensive compendium of Buddhist teachings attempted by a Tibetan when it first appeared.

Gampopa Sönam Rinchen

Gampopa, also known as Dakpo Rinpoché, was born in 1079 in the Dakpo district of central Tibet.[4] He originally trained as a physician, hence the other common title he is known by, Dakpo Lhajé ("Doctor of Dakpo"). He began his adult life as a married layman and only began intensive religious practice after experiencing the shock of the sudden deaths first of his children and then of his beloved wife when he was still in his early twenties. After extensive studies in other traditions, he eventually became a foremost disciple of Jetsun Milarepa (1040–1123). He had received full monastic ordination at the age of twenty-five and had sought out tantric initiations in Lower Dakpo from the master Maryul Loden. He had also studied intensively in Phenyul under masters of the Kadam tradition such as Jayulpa, Nyukrumpa, and Chakri Gongkhawa. Jayulpa (or Jayulwa) Shönu Ö (1075–1138) was a student of Chengawa Tsultrim Bar (1038–1103), and Nyukrumpa was in the lineage of Geshé Naljorpa Chenpo (1015–78). Following significant dreams, Gampopa left these teachers to seek out (with difficulty) Milarepa, from whom he received the Kagyü key instructions, especially those on "inner heat" (*gtum mo*), which he intensively and very successfully practiced for thirteen months in 1110–11. After meditating for an additional three years, he attained awakening. He returned to see

Milarepa twelve years later (1123), but the master had just passed away. As instructed by his guru Milarepa, he continued a primarily contemplative life in solitude at Daklha Gampo for some years, but his karma inexorably drew talented disciples to him, and thus naturally began, as predicted for him there by Milarepa, his time as a guru and Dharma master.

For his multitude of disciples, Gampopa established the first Kagyü monastery at Daklha Gampo. It is not for nothing that virtually the entire Kagyü lineage in Tibet calls itself the Dakpo Kagyü (literally, "teaching lineage of Dakpo") in his honor. The broad-spectrum Buddhism he taught was nurtured by four main disciples, including the Karmapa and his subsequent lineage of reincarnations. The so-called four major and eight minor Kagyu lineages trace themselves back to him and stem from those main disciples.[5]

The chapter on Gampopa in the *Hundred Thousand Songs of Milarepa* by Tsangnyön Heruka (1452–1507) tells more about his life story and indicates his spiritual standing as a tenth-level bodhisattva who had "served thousands of buddhas" before his birth in Tibet. It also identifies him as the person predicted by the Buddha in the *King of Meditation Sutra* to perpetuate the teachings of that sutra at a later age, appearing as a doctor in Tibet. Those teachings, on the absolute nature of reality and particularly of one's own mind, are known in the Kagyü tradition as Mahāmudrā and constitute its greatest treasure. Gampopa is seen as being the reincarnation of Candraprabhakumāra, the main interlocutor of the Buddha in that sutra.

He became the perfect heir, through Milarepa, to the Marpa Kagyü twin lineages of first the Mahāmudrā teachings of the great adept Saraha and secondly the highest yoga tantra practices gathered by the Indian great tantric adept (*mahāsiddha*) Tilopa.[6] Gampopa was also, as we have seen, an accomplished scholar within the early Kadam tradition. Thus, in Gampopa, we find a fusion of three elements. First, he was an exemplary monk, and Dakla Gampo Monastery was the start of monasticism within the Kagyü lineage. Second, through his mastery of the Kadam tradition, he was a great exponent of Indian Mahayana Buddhism, transmitting both of its major streams—those from Nāgārjuna and Asaṅga. Third, he was a main tantric disciple of the famous yogi Milarepa and holder of the tantras and Mahāmudrā teachings mentioned above, that Milarepa's guru, Marpa, had so meticulously sought in three major journeys to India.

The great Indian master Nāropa had predicted that the Kagyü lineage descending from his disciple Marpa would, like the offspring of the divine raptors the garuḍas, go from strength to strength over the generations. This proved true in the way its later masters integrated into it other lineages of teachings, compared often to new tributaries joining a river and strengthening its flow. In this context, Gampopa is famous among the earlier Kagyü hierarchs for his work integrating monasticism and the bodhisattva teachings of the Kadam tradition. However, Gampopa's case is not so much one of bringing to the Kagyü what was not already present but one of codifying and then establishing those particular elements of Dharma for the Kagyü tradition.

Unlike the earlier Kadam master Atiśa, Gampopa was neither a reformer nor a restorer. Contemporary Kagyü masters, such as Khenchen Thrangu Rinpoche and Khenpo Lhabu, make it clear that it would be a serious misunderstanding to think that the teachings in the *Ornament* were newly inserted into the Kagyü lineage by Gampopa. A thorough knowledge that the deities of highest yoga tantra are intricate, perfect symbols (*brda*) is implicit to the "view" needed for their practice. What they symbolize by literally putting a face on them are primarily the basic Buddhist teachings of Abhidharma and Mahayana, meaning that an excellent grasp of those teachings is required of a tantric meditator and especially of a master. Marpa had to have mastered those nontantric aspects of Dharma while in India for his tantric practice to be successful. His two main teachers there, Nāropa and Maitripa, had indeed been eminent scholars earlier in their lives. Although Marpa's Dharma heir Milarepa is seen romantically by many these days as a poet and a simple hermit, no one knows just how much of the doctrinal Dharma inheritance Marpa had passed on to him in their years together before the latter set off to his famous twelve years of solitary retreat. Milarepa's teaching songs about topics like the six perfections betray a "master class" quality that only someone sufficiently learned could have. Milarepa's heir, Gampopa, unlike his predecessors who had relatively small followings, is said to have attracted more than fifty thousand disciples to the mountain retreat where he first practiced in solitude. This gave him the ideal opportunity to lay solid and broad-based Dharma foundations for the Kagyü lineages that would stem from him. In particular, this work embodies the Mahayana material he presented as being what Kagyü followers need to know, both for its own sake and, very importantly, for the sake of their practice of tantra.

Ornament of Precious Liberation

Like the *Great Tenrim* of Drolungpa, which probably preceded it by a few decades, *Ornament of Precious Liberation* (*Dam chos yid bzhin gyi nor bu thar pa rin po che'i rgyan*) is a systematic exposition of the bodhisattva's path. In its overall structure, it is both more penetratingly and more broadly conceived than Drolungpa's work, though it omits none of Drolungpa's main topics. Its structure thus may represent an original plan conceived or adapted by Gampopa. He confirms his connection with Atiśa's tradition by quoting Atiśa's *Lamp for the Path to Awakening* prominently numerous times.

Within the Kagyü tradition, masters often speak of Gampopa's three key works. This one, his longest, is a tenrim, whereas his short stanza the *Four Dharmas* (*chos bzhi*) is traditionally explained at some length, through oral tradition, as a lamrim, presenting the three types of Dharma practitioners. His middle-length work, *Jewel Garland of the Supreme Path* (*Lam mchog rin chen 'phreng ba*), is a compendium of his personal advice (*man ngag*) concerning all levels and vehicles of practice. They are held to be the short, middling, and long versions of his overview teachings, as opposed to his specialized texts.

Gampopa divides his treatise into six main topics:

1. The prime cause for attaining highest awakening: the buddha nature (*tathāgatagarbha*)
2. The corporeal ground for achieving awakening: the precious human existence
3. The contributing condition that impels one to achieve it: the Dharma master
4. The means for achieving it: the instructions of the Dharma master
5. The result that is so achieved: the bodies (*kāya*) of buddhahood
6. The enlightened activities that follow the attainment of buddhahood, i.e., the spontaneous benefitting of living beings through buddha activities free from conceptual thought

To expound these topics in more detail, Gampopa divides his treatise into twenty-one chapters, one for each of those six main sections except for section 4, to which he devotes sixteen chapters. This is justified by the fact that section 4 contains the general instructions—the bodhisattva's perfections and so forth. We should note that, unlike earlier tenrim authors, Gampopa expounds the prime cause—buddha nature—as his first chapter. Gampopa also includes at the end of his treatise a distinct section on the enlightened activities that manifest spontaneously for one who attains buddhahood.

The six topics are causally related and can be illustrated through the oft-used metaphor of a plant. The whole genetic code determining the result is contained in the *prime cause*, the seed of buddha nature. Nothing else on earth has that. The seed needs to be planted in the right *ground*, a precious human existence, so as to germinate properly. The Dharma master is like the sunlight, warmth, rain, and nutrients that are *contributing conditions* triggering and nourishing the germination of the seed. The chemical interaction that determines the transformation is the *means*, the teachings suitable for each disciple. The full result comes with the *fruition* of enlightenment, and *enlightened activity* provides all the nourishment to beings and disperses the seeds for its own replication. Gampopa, in short, gives us the ultimate gardening manual.

Acknowledgments

I shall ever be indebted to Khenpo Tsultrim Gyamtso Rinpoché for first taking me carefully through Gampopa's entire text, term by term, idea by idea, on three separate occasions, and to Khenchen the Ninth Thrangu Rinpoché for his subsequent clarifications over many months of revision as he taught it *in extenso* in Kagyu Samye Ling. Most of all, I am grateful to Katia Holmes, whose years of devoted work on this text produced the initial draft that formed the basis for our first published translation, under the title *Gems of Dharma, Jewels of Freedom* in 1995. I was delighted then to bring to fruition the task that the Sixteenth Gyalwang Karmapa had entrusted to us but that ill health prevented her from completing. Since then, I am grateful that the support of the Institute of Tibetan Classics under the guidance of Thupten Jinpa and with funding from the Tsadra Foundation has allowed me to bring the translation to its present form. The excellent work of their teams on the Tibetan text, sourcing each quotation, comparing editions, and researching so many points, has truly impressed me and added a vital dimension to this translation beyond my best hopes. Every credit to them. I am delighted now for this opportunity to take this work forward, bringing it to a wider public and contributing to the never-ending duty of us translators to one day render perfectly Gampopa's thought in English.

Ornament of Precious Liberation

A Wish-Fulfilling Gem of Sublime Dharma

Gampopa Sönam Rinchen

Author's Preface

I prostrate to Youthful Mañjuśrī.[7]

Having paid homage to the buddhas, their spiritual heirs,
  the sublime Dharma,
and also to the gurus who are the root of all these,
I will now write, through the gracious kindness of revered Milarepa,
this *Gem of Precious Dharma, a Wish-Fulfilling Jewel* for both my own
  and others' benefit.

Generally, phenomena can be subsumed into the two classes of samsara and nirvana. That which is known as *samsara* is, by nature, emptiness, taking the form of illusions and characterized by suffering. That which is known as *nirvana* is also, by nature, emptiness, taking the form of the exhaustion, then disappearance, of the illusions and characterized by liberation from all suffering.

Who is deluded by these illusions of samsara? All sentient beings of its three realms.

On what are the illusions based? The illusions are projected onto emptiness.

What causes the delusion? It occurs through great ignorance.

In what way do the illusions manifest? Their illusions take the form of the experiences of the six classes of beings.

What would be a suitable metaphor for such an illusion? This resembles the illusion experienced in one's sleep and dreams.

Since when have these illusions been happening? Since time without beginning.

What is wrong with them? One experiences nothing but suffering.

When will the delusion become pristine awareness? It does so when highest enlightenment is reached.[8] Those who think that illusion may dissolve on its own should be aware that samsara is renowned for being endless.

Having, in the above way, carefully considered samsara in terms of it being an illusion, the extent of its suffering, its duration, and that it is not self-dispelling, strive in all earnestness and with great diligence, from this very moment onward, to attain unsurpassable enlightenment.

What exactly is needed to strive so? The synopsis[9] is:

> **Prime cause, basis, condition, means, results, and activity: by these six general key terms should the wise know peerless enlightenment.**

This means that one needs to know (1) the **prime cause** for highest enlightenment, (2) the beings whose existence forms a **basis** for achieving it, (3) the **condition** that incites that attainment, (4) the **means** by which it is attained, (5) the **results** of it being attained, and (6) the enlightened **activity** once there has been such attainment. These will be explained, in the above order, as being the following:

> The prime cause is buddha nature.
> The basis is a most precious human existence.
> The special condition is the Dharma master.
> The means is the Dharma master's instruction.
> The results are the bodies of perfect buddhahood.
> The activity is to nonconceptually fulfill the welfare of beings.

This is merely an outline of the main structure of this text. What follows is a detailed explanation of each point.

Part I. The Prime Cause

1. Buddha Nature

The line "The prime cause is buddha nature" states the following. As mentioned above, you need to gain freedom from the deluded nature of samsara and to attain highest enlightenment. However, you might well wonder, "Even if we or other ordinary people[10] like us were to try very hard, how could we ever possibly attain enlightenment?" In truth, anyone who practices with great effort cannot fail to reach enlightenment. Why? Because all forms of conscious life, including ourselves, possess its prime cause. Within us is buddha nature. The *King of Meditation Sutra* states:

> Buddha nature totally permeates all beings.[11]

The shorter *Great [Passing into] Nirvana Sutra* says:

> All sentient beings possess buddha nature.[12]

Further, the longer *Great [Passing into] Nirvana Sutra* says:

> Just as butter, for example, exists in milk as something totally permeating it, so does buddha nature permeate all sentient beings.[13]

The *Ornament of Mahayana Sutras* also states:

> Suchness is the same
> for all and everyone; it is that which is pure.
> Since this is the Tathāgata,
> all beings are endowed with this essence. MSA 10:37

If this is so, you may wonder why sentient beings are endowed with buddha nature. It is because: (1) dharmakāya, emptiness, pervades all beings, (2) the universal essence (*dharmatā*), suchness (*tathatā*), is without differentiation, and (3) every sentient being has the potential to become a buddha. This is just what is stated in the *Uttaratantra*, where it says:

> Because the Buddha's body pervades all,
> because suchness is without differentiation,
> and because they possess the potential,
> every living being at all times has buddha nature. RGV 1:28

To explain the first reason, "dharmakāya, emptiness, pervades all beings," here the Buddha is embodied in the dharmakāya, and the dharmakāya is emptiness. Since emptiness is something pervading all sentient beings, it follows that all those beings have the essence of buddhahood. The second reason, "the universal essence, suchness, is without differentiation," means that whether it be in terms of good and bad, great and small, or higher and lower, there is no difference between the universal essence in buddhas and the universal essence in sentient beings. Thus sentient beings possess the buddha essence. That "every sentient being has the potential to become a buddha" is explained through the five ways in which they stand in respect to enlightenment potential. These are outlined in the following synopsis:

> **Those with enlightenment potential can be summed up as belonging to five groups: those with severed potential, undetermined potential, śrāvaka potential, pratyekabuddha potential, and those with the Mahayana potential.**

Those with **severed potential** are characterized by six traits, such as lacking a sense of shame in public, having no dignity in private, lacking compassion, and so forth. The great master Asaṅga has said of them:

> Though seeing what is wrong with samsara, they are not in the least put off by it.
> Though hearing about the qualities of enlightened beings, they feel not the slightest faith in them.
> Without conscience and shame, and devoid of even a little compassion, they feel not the slightest regret for the unwholesome acts in which they fully indulge.

> Through compounding those six shortcomings, they are far from
> ready for enlightenment.[14]

It also says in the *Ornament of Mahayana Sutras*:

> It is certain that some are solely engaged in what is harmful.
> Some are constantly destroying whatever is good.
> Others lack those virtues conducive to liberation.
> They are devoid of anything that could in any way be
> wholesome. MSA 4:11

Although those who have the above traits are said to have severed potential, this refers to their having to pass an exceedingly long time in samsara and does not mean that they have definitively cut off any chance of achieving enlightenment. Provided that they make the effort, they can attain enlightenment. It says of this in the *White Lotus of Great Compassion Sutra*:

> Ānanda! Were someone lacking the fortunate circumstances for nirvana merely to cast a flower up in the sky, visualizing the Buddha, then that person thereby possesses the fruit of nirvana. I declare that person to be one who will reach nirvana and who will penetrate to its furthest end.[15]

The lot of those with **undetermined potential** depends on the circumstances. Those who train under śrāvaka spiritual teachers, become involved with śrāvakas, or come across śrāvaka scriptures will place their trust in the śrāvaka way and, having entered that way, will actually become śrāvakas themselves. Likewise, those who encounter pratyekabuddha or Mahayana circumstances will embrace the pratyekabuddha or Mahayana ways.

Those with **śrāvaka potential** fear samsara, believe in nirvana, and have limited compassion. The scriptures say:

> Seeing the sufferings of samsara, they are afraid;
> they manifestly aspire for nirvana;
> they are not interested in working for the welfare of sentient beings:
> those who bear these three characteristics have the śrāvaka
> potential.[16]

In addition to the above three characteristics, those with **pratyekabuddha potential** have enormous self-confidence, keep quiet about their teachers, and are loners. It is said:

> Grieved by samsaric existence, keen for nirvana,
> weak in compassion, exceedingly confident,
> secretive about their teachers, and loving solitude:
> these the wise should recognize as having the pratyekabuddha potential.[17]

Although the above two groups—those with śrāvaka potential and those with pratyekabuddha potential—may enter these two vehicles and attain their respective results, what they achieve is not true nirvana. At the time of their achievement they will, on account of a latent ignorance, acquire and exist in a subtle mental body brought about by their former untainted karma. They will be convinced that the state of untainted profound absorption they enjoy *is* nirvana and that they *have* attained nirvana.

One might object, "If this is not real nirvana, it would be inappropriate for the Buddha to teach these two paths." It is, in fact, entirely appropriate for the Buddha to teach them as he did. Let us consider the following example. Some merchants from Jambudvīpa[18] set out to the far-off oceans to obtain precious gems. At one point in their journey, they felt so tired and downhearted while crossing a great wilderness that they began to think they would never manage to get the jewels, and they contemplated turning back. However, through his magical powers, their leader created a great illusory citadel where they were able to rest and recuperate.

Like the merchants in this story, beings of weak resolve will feel overwhelmed when they learn of the tremendous wisdom of the buddhas, and they may feel that the task of achieving it is too daunting and far beyond the capacity of the likes of them. On account of the awe they feel, they will either never undertake the task of enlightenment or they will give up easily. By teaching the two paths of the śrāvaka and pratyekabuddha, the Buddha enables them to attain the refreshing, healing state of a śrāvaka or pratyekabuddha. In the *Lotus Sutra* it says:

> Likewise all the śrāvakas are
> under the impression that they have attained nirvana.

The Buddha tells them that
this is not nirvana but a respite.[19]

When they have rested and refreshed themselves in the state of a śrāvaka or pratyekabuddha, the Buddha knows it is time to encourage them to achieve full enlightenment. How is this done? The Buddha inspires them through perfect body, pure speech, and wisdom mind. Light rays stream from his mind. By these beams merely touching their mental bodies, śrāvakas and pratyekabuddhas are awakened from their untainted meditative concentration. Then the Buddha manifests his own perfect physical presence and declares the following with his pure speech: "O monks! By merely doing what you have done, the task is not accomplished and the work is not yet done. Your nirvana is not nirvana. Monks! Now approach the Tathāgata and pay heed to what he says; understand his instruction." That he motivates them thus is taught in the verses of the *Lotus Sutra*:

O monks! I therefore tell you today
that by this alone you will not attain nirvana,
and that for you to gain the pristine awareness of the omniscient ones,
you must give rise to a noble and mighty wave of effort.
By so doing, you will achieve all-knowing pristine awareness.[20]

Through being exhorted in this way, śrāvakas and pratyekabuddhas will cultivate the great bodhicitta.[21] Having conducted themselves as bodhisattvas for countless ages, they will become buddhas. Thus it is stated in the *Sutra on Going to Laṅka* as well. In the *Lotus Sutra* it states:

Those śrāvakas who have not attained nirvana will all, through having practiced the bodhisattva way of life, become buddhas.[22]

The synopsis for those with **Mahayana potential** is the following:

Mahayana potential is summed up through six topics: its categories, their essential characteristics, its synonyms, the reasons it is particularly outstanding, the forms it takes, and its signs.

First, there are two main **categories**: the potential as it exists naturally and the potential as something properly attained.

Second is an analysis of the **essential characteristics** of each of these. The *potential as it exists naturally*, since time without beginning, is the innate capacity of suchness to give rise to enlightened qualities. The *potential as something properly attained* is the capacity of one's former cultivation of virtue to give rise to enlightened qualities. Both these aspects of Mahayana potential make a readiness for enlightenment.

The **synonyms** for this are *potential, seed, element*, and *essential nature.*[23]

The **reasons** it stands far above the other forms of potential are as follows. The śrāvaka and pratyekabuddha potentials are lesser ones, because to realize them, only the afflictions need be eliminated. The Mahayana potential is outstanding because its total realization involves eliminating both obscurations.[24] This makes the Mahayana potential peerless, better than all the others.

The different **forms** of Mahayana potential are its *activated* and *dormant* states. When the potential has been activated, its signs are manifest and "the results have been properly attained." While it is dormant, the signs are not manifest and "the results have not [yet] been properly attained."

What activates the potential? Freedom from adverse conditions and the support of favorable ones activate it. While their contraries prevail, it remains dormant.

There are four adverse conditions: (1) birth in an unfavorable existence, (2) a lack of good inclinations,[25] (3) involvement in aberrant ways, and (4) being flawed with obscurations.

There are two favorable conditions: (1) externally, there are Dharma teachers, and (2) within, there is a proper mental attitude, aspiring to what is wholesome and so forth.

The **signs** [or evidence] of this potential are found in the *Ten Dharmas Sutra*, where it describes the indications of its presence:

> Just as one infers the presence of fire through smoke
> and that of water through the presence of waterfowl,
> likewise the potential of the bodhisattva mentality
> is detected by means of its signs.[26]

What are these signs? Naturally and without contrivance, such beings are peaceful in what they do and say, their minds have little deceit or hypocrisy, and they are loving and joyful in their relations with others. As it says in the *Ten Dharmas Sutra*:

> Never rough or rude,
> beyond deceit and hypocrisy,
> and full of love for all beings:
> they are the bodhisattvas.[27]

Further, they engender compassion toward all beings before entering into any activity. Genuinely aspiring to Mahayana Dharma, they undertake difficult tasks with forbearance that is never discouraged by the enormity of the undertaking, and they practice most properly and excellently that which generates virtue and has the nature of the perfections. It says in the *Ornament of Mahayana Sutras*:

> Compassion prior to action,
> aspiration as well as forbearance,
> and engaging perfectly in virtues:
> these should be recognized as signs of their potential. MSA 4:5

The above means that of the five types of potential, the Mahayana one is the most direct cause for buddhahood. The śrāvaka and pratyekabuddha potentials are also causes for attaining buddhahood but remoter ones. The undetermined potential is sometimes a direct cause, sometimes a remote cause. The severed potential is considered a very remote cause but not a total breach of the possibility of enlightenment; it is therefore an exceedingly far-removed cause for it.

Thus we have seen that, due to having one or another of these types of potential, sentient beings possess buddha nature, and this has also been demonstrated through the three reasons. The actual way they possess it can be exemplified by the way silver is present in silver ore, the way sesame oil is present in sesame, or the way butter is present in milk. Just as it is possible to obtain the silver that is in ore, the oil that is in sesame seeds, and the butter that is in milk, so it is possible to attain the buddhahood that is in all sentient beings.

This concludes the first chapter, concerning the prime cause, of this *Ornament of Precious Liberation, a Wish-Fulfilling Gem of Sublime Dharma.*

Part II. The Basis

2. A Precious Human Existence

Given that all sentient beings have buddha nature, can the five types of nonhuman beings—hell beings, hungry spirits (*preta*), and so forth—achieve buddhahood? They cannot. The excellent type of existence that provides a working basis for achieving buddhahood is known as a *precious human existence*, meaning someone who materially has *freedoms* combined with *assets* and who mentally has the three kinds of *faith*. The synopsis of the explanation of this is the following:

> **The very best basis is summed up in five points: freedoms, assets, conviction, aspiration, and clarity. Two of these are material and three are mental.**

They are **freedoms** inasmuch as the person is free from eight unfavorable conditions. According to [Prajñākaramati's *Commentary on the Guide to the Bodhisattva Way of Life*, in his summary of what is found in the] *Attention to Mindfulness Sutra*:

> The eight unfavorable states are to be
> a hell dweller, a hungry spirit, an animal,
> a barbarian, a long-living god,
> someone with fixed aberrant views, one born in a time without
> a Buddha,
> or a person with severe difficulty in understanding.[28]

Why are these states deemed unfavorable for the attainment of enlightenment? Hell is unsuitable because the very character of its experience is constant suffering. The hungry spirit state is unsuitable because of its mental anguish. The animal state is unsuitable because of its generalized benightedness. These three states are also devoid of a sense of dignity or regard for others.[29] Such beings do not really have any possibility of practicing Dharma because the above conditions render their general way of existing inappropriate for it.

The "long-living" gods are those without cognition. Because their stream of consciousness, along with its related mental activities, is in a state of suspension, they do not have the possibility of practicing Dharma: their mind is incapable of applying itself to it. Apart from these particular gods, all desire-realm gods live long compared to humans, and so could also be included in this category.

In fact, all the gods are in an unfavorable condition due to their attachment to the well-being of their situation. This makes them unsuited because they are unable to strive for virtue.[30] In this respect, the relatively limited degree of manifest suffering present in human life is a [helpful] quality, inasmuch as it fosters rejection of samsara, quells pride, gives rise to compassion for other beings, and makes us shun unwholesome action and appreciate virtue. This is also mentioned in *Guide to the Bodhisattva Way of Life*:

> There are further virtues to suffering:
> world-weariness helps dispel arrogance,
> compassion will well up for those in samsara,
> and one will shun nonvirtue and delight in virtue. BCA 6:21

The above explains why those four [nonhuman] sorts of existence simply do not have the freedom to work toward enlightenment. But neither do some forms of human existence: barbarians, because of the improbability of their interacting with spiritual teachers; those with fixed aberrant views, because of the difficulty they have in understanding virtue to be the cause of rebirth into better states and of liberation; those born in a world without a Buddha, because of the absence of teachings on what is and what is not to be done; and those with severe impediments, because these make them unable to understand the Dharma teachings explaining which things are worthwhile and which things are harmful.

The "very best freedom" is to be free from the above eight.

There are **ten assets**: five are personal and five are other-related. The *five personal assets* are described as:

> To be human, born in a central land, with complete faculties, free from having committed the worst of actions, and having appropriate trust.[31]

[1] "To be human" means to have been born the same as other humans, with male or female organs. [2] To have been born in a "central land" means birth in a place with accessible holy beings. [3] To have "complete faculties" means that you have the intellectual faculties needed for the actual practice of virtue, suffering from neither a severe learning difficulty nor a severe communication impediment. [4] "Free from having committed the worst of actions" means you have not committed the actions of immediate consequence[32] in this life. [5] "Appropriate trust" means confidence in all those wholesome things that truly merit trust—the noble teachings declared by the Buddha as a way of taming the mind.

The *five other-related assets* are: (6) a Buddha has manifested in the world, (7) the noble Dharma has been taught, (8) the teachings of noble Dharma are still extant, (9) there are those who follow them, and (10) loving kindness can be developed due to others.[33]

Someone possessing these ten personal and situational factors is called "a person with the very best assets." Where these two—the freedoms and the assets—are complete, that is the precious human existence. Why is it called "precious"? It is so termed because, being rarely encountered and exceedingly beneficial and useful, its qualities are comparable to those of a wish-fulfilling gem.

It is *rarely encountered*. It says in the *Bodhisattva Collection*:

> It is difficult to be born human,
> and then difficult to stay alive.
> The noble Dharma is a rare thing to obtain,
> and it is also rare for a buddha to manifest.[34]

Furthermore, it says in the *White Lotus of Great Compassion Sutra*:

> It is not easy to come by a human existence. A person possessing the finest freedoms is also rarely encountered, and it is difficult, too, to find a world in which a Buddha has appeared. Further, it

> is not at all easy to aspire to what is virtuous, nor is it easy to find most perfect aspiration.[35]

It also says in the *Marvelous Array Sutra*:

> It is rare to encounter that which is free from the eight unfavorable circumstances. It is rare, too, to be born human. It is also rare to obtain the very best form of freedom, in its plenitude. It is rare, too, for a Buddha to manifest. It is also rare not to have deficient faculties. It is rare, too, to be able to study the Buddha-dharma. It is also rare to be in the company of holy beings. It is rare, too, to find truly qualified spiritual teachers. It is also rare to be able to practice properly that which has been taught so purely. It is rare, too, to maintain a truly right livelihood, and rare, in the human world, to earnestly do what is in accord with Dharma.[36]

Furthermore, it says in *Guide to the Bodhisattva Way of Life*:

> These freedoms and assets are exceedingly rare. BCA 1:4A

What could exemplify this rarity, for whom is it so rare, and just why it is such a rare thing? *Guide to the Bodhisattva Way of Life* gives an analogy:

> On account of it being like that,
> the Buddha has said that to be human is as rare
> as a turtle putting its neck through the hole
> of a wooden yoke floating on a turbulent ocean. BCA 4:20

Where does this quotation come from? In the most excellent scripture it says, among other things:

> Were this vast land to be transformed into water, and were someone to set afloat a single one-holed wooden yoke to be driven in the four directions by the winds, a poor-sighted turtle might take thousands of years [to surface and put its head through it].[37]

For those born in the lower states of existence, this [precious human existence] is very hard to obtain. The rarity is due to causality, since the principal cause for obtaining an existence with freedoms and assets is a prior accumulation of merit in the continuum of lives. Once born into the lower realms, a being constantly does nothing but wrong and does not know how to develop virtue. For this reason the only ones born in the three lower realms who can attain a human existence are those who have built up relatively little evil, or those who have created karma that will have to be experienced but in some later life.

It is *exceedingly beneficial and useful*. It says in *Guide to the Bodhisattva Way of Life*:

> Concerning the attainment of making an able human life meaningful . . . BCA 1:4B

The "able human life" renders the Sanskrit term *puruṣa*,[38] a word [for a human life] connoting power or ability. A human existence endowed with the freedoms and assets is this "able human life," because it has the strength or ability to attain higher rebirth and ultimate good. Further, since there are three levels of this ability, there will be three corresponding categories of powerful human potential. Thus it says in *Lamp for the Path to Awakening*:

> One should know there to be three types
> of human ability: lesser, middling, and best. BP 2AB

Those with the lesser type of powerful human potential have the ability to achieve human or divine rebirth by avoiding descent into the lower states. Thus it says:

> A person described as someone with lesser ability
> is one who, through whatever means,
> strives for personal welfare and aspires
> merely to worldly well-being. BP 3

Those with the middling human ability are able to attain a state of peace and well-being by liberating themselves from samsara:

Someone who turns away from worldly happiness,
turns away from unwholesome action,
and strives for personal peace alone
is referred to as the "middling" type. BP 4

Those with the highest human ability are capable of attaining buddhahood for the benefit of sentient beings:

Those who, having understood their own suffering,
aspire to totally eradicate
the entire suffering in every being
are most excellent individuals. BP 5

Master Candragomin has also commented on the great benefit and use of a precious human existence, saying:

There are those who would reach the end of the ocean of rebirth
and, further, plant the virtuous seed of supreme enlightenment.
Their qualities far exceeding those of a wish-fulfilling gem,
how could such people engage in fruitless tasks?

The Sugata's path, found by a human
with such great strength of mind,
cannot be attained by gods, nāgas, demigods, garuḍas,
knowledge holders, kiṃnaras, and uragas.[39] ŚI 63–64

This human existence endowed with freedom and assets gives the ability to relinquish nonvirtue, cross samsara's ocean, tread the path of enlightenment, and attain perfect buddhahood. Therefore such an existence is far superior to those of gods, nāgas, and the like. It is something even better than a most precious wish-fulfilling gem. Because this human existence endowed with freedoms and assets is hard to obtain and of such great benefit, it is called "most precious."

Although it is so hard to obtain and of such tremendous benefit, it is *very easily destroyed*. This is because there is nothing that can perpetuate the life force, there are many causes of death, and the flow of moments never ceases. Thus it says in *Guide to the Bodhisattva Way of Life*:

> It is not right to contentedly think,
> "At least I won't die today."
> It is without doubt that at one time or another
> I will be annihilated. BCA 2:58

Thus, through its rarity, fragility, and real purpose, this physical existence should be considered a boat for doing whatever is needed to find a haven from the ocean of samsara. Thus it says:

> Making use of this vessel of able human life,
> get free from the mighty river of suffering.
> Since such a craft will be hard to come across in the future,
> don't fall into confusion: there is no time for sleep! BCA 7:14

Considering this existence as a steed to be ridden, do whatever must be done to get free from the hazardous path of samsara and suffering. Thus it says:

> Having mounted the steed of a pure human existence,
> gallop away from the hazardous paths of samsara's suffering.[40]

Considering this physical existence as a servant, make it do wholesome tasks. Thus it says:

> This human existence should
> be employed in service [of others]. BCA 5:66

The *three types of faith*: In order to act in such a way, faith is needed. It is said that without faith, noble qualities will not develop in a person. Thus the *Ten Dharmas Sutra* says:

> The noble qualities will not arise in someone without faith,
> just as a green shoot will not emerge from a scorched seed.[41]

The *Flower Ornament Sutra* also says:

> Those of worldly disposition with little faith
> will be unable to know the buddhas' enlightenment.[42]

Therefore, you should cultivate faith. As the Buddha teaches in the *Vast Manifestation Sutra*:

> Ānanda, cultivate faith; this is what the Tathāgata asks of you.[43]

What exactly does *faith* mean? When analyzed, it has three aspects: faith as conviction, faith as aspiration, and faith as clear joy.

Faith as conviction arises from contemplating actions and their consequences, the truth of suffering, and the truth of suffering's origin. *Conviction* means being convinced that the consequence of virtuous action is to experience well-being in the desire realm,[44] the consequence of nonvirtuous action is to experience misery in the desire realm, and the consequence of unwavering karma is to experience well-being in the form and formless realms. It means being convinced that through the power of karma and afflictions, explained as the *truth of all origination*, you will obtain the five contaminated aggregates, explained as the *truth of suffering*.

Faith as aspiration is to consider highest enlightenment as something very special indeed and to ardently study how it can be attained.

Faith as clear joy[45] is something stable that emerges with respect to its object, the Three Jewels—being a joyful clear mind that has devotion and respect for the most precious Buddha as teacher of the path, for the most precious Dharma as that which is the path itself, and for the most precious Sangha as the companions who practice the path. Thus it says in the *Treasury of Higher Knowledge*:

> What is faith? It is confidence in karma and its results, the [four] truths, and the most precious ones. It is aspiration and it is lucidity of mind.[46]

Further, it says in the *Precious Garland*:

> Whoever, despite temptation, anger, fear, or confusion,
> never strays from Dharma
> is said to possess faith.
> Such a person is a wonderful vessel for the highest good. RA 1:6

"Not to stray from Dharma despite temptation" means not to abandon Dharma out of craving. You would not renounce it despite temptations of food, wealth, consorts, kingdoms, or any enticement intended to persuade you to give up the Dharma.

"Not to stray from Dharma despite aggression" means not to abandon Dharma out of hostility. For example, you would not relinquish a Dharma way of life for the sake of [fighting] someone who had not only harmed you greatly in the past but is also harming you greatly in the present.

"Not to stray from Dharma despite fear" means not to abandon Dharma out of fear. For instance, even faced with the threat that, were you not to abandon Dharma, three hundred fierce warriors would cut five ounces of flesh from your body every day, you would still not relinquish it.

"Not to stray from Dharma despite confusion" means not to abandon Dharma out of ignorance. For instance, even though people might argue convincingly that cause and effect, the Three Jewels, and so forth are false, and thereby throw your Dharma into question, still you would not relinquish it.

Someone who can maintain conviction when faced with these four types of situations is a person with faith. Such faith makes one ideally suited to achieving liberation. Such faith will create countless benefits, including giving rise to the mentality of the best of beings, eliminating the unfavorable, sharpening and brightening the faculties, ensuring the nondegradation of moral discipline, removing afflictions, taking one beyond domains of experience marred by evil, enabling one to encounter the way of liberation, gathering a vast store of virtue, making one see many buddhas, and causing the buddhas' blessing to be received. As it says in the *Jewel Lamp Dhāraṇī Sutra*:

> The mental attitude of a great being induces
> faith in peerless enlightenment—
> faith in the enlightened beings and their teachings
> and trust in the activity of the bodhisattvas.[47]

This and more is said. Further, it is taught that all the buddhas, the blessed ones, will appear before a person of faith. The *Bodhisattva Collection* says:

> Thus the buddhas, the blessed ones, having recognized them as being worthy vessels of the Buddhadharma, will appear before them and will most properly teach them the way of the bodhisattva.[48]

Thus a "most precious human existence," having two sets of qualities (the freedoms and assets) as well as three mental qualities (the aspects of faith), is the proper basis for achieving peerless enlightenment.

This concludes the second chapter, concerning the basis, of this *Ornament of Precious Liberation, a Wish-Fulfilling Gem of Sublime Dharma.*

Part III. The Condition

3. Relying on the Dharma Master

Now to explain the line "The special condition is the Dharma master." Even with the very best *basis*, it will be very difficult to progress along the path to enlightenment without the encouragement of a good Dharma master, who represents the *condition* [for enlightenment]. The difficulty is due to the strength of ingrained habits—unwholesome tendencies fashioned by former harmful actions. Therefore one needs to rely on[49] Dharma teachers. The synopsis is:

> **Relying on Dharma masters is treated through five points: justification, the different kinds, the specific characteristics of each kind, how to rely, and its benefits.**

The necessity of relying on Dharma masters is **justified** in three ways: scripturally, logically, and through analogy.

For the *scriptural justification*, it says in the *Verse Summary of the Perfection of Wisdom*:

> Good disciples devoted to their teachers should
> always rely on wise and skillful Dharma masters.
> Why? Because from this will emerge the qualities of the wise.
> RS 15:1C–2A

In the *Perfection of Wisdom in Eight Thousand Lines* it says:

> Thus realized bodhisattvas who wish to genuinely and totally awaken to peerless, utterly pure, and perfect enlightenment should from the very outset seek out, rely on, and serve Dharma masters.[50]

For the *logical justification*, the reasoning is: given that you wish to attain omniscience [subject], you need to rely on Dharma masters [predicate], because by yourself you do not know how to accrue spiritual wealth or how to dispel your obscurations [reason]. The buddhas of the three times are an example substantiating this assertion. The pratyekabuddhas are an example of the contrary.

The above is explained as follows. For us to achieve perfect buddhahood, all forms of spiritual wealth will need to be accrued, and that accrual depends on Dharma masters. Furthermore, we will need to rid ourselves of all the obscurations, summarized in terms of the afflictions obscuration and the knowledge obscuration. Their removal is also dependent on Dharma masters.

The *justification by analogy* is that a Dharma master is like a guide when traveling an unknown path, like an escort when in a dangerous land, and like a ferryman when crossing a mighty river.

The first example is that of a *guide*. Traveling in unfamiliar lands without a guide, you risk going in the wrong direction or making a longer or shorter detour. But if there is a companion guide, there are none of these risks, and the destination can be attained without a single wasted step. Like this, if there is no good Mahayana Dharma teacher when setting out on the path to peerless enlightenment and heading for that state, then there is the danger of mistakenly taking an aberrant path or, even without straying that gravely, of making the greater detour of the śrāvakas or the lesser detour of the pratyekabuddhas. When accompanied by good Dharma teachers, who are like guides, there is no longer this danger of taking a completely wrong path, or of a large or small detour, and the citadel of omniscience will be reached. Thus it says in the *Instructions for Liberation of Śrī Saṃbhava*:

> Leading you along the path that reaches the farther shore, a good master is like a guide.[51]

The second example is that of the *escort*. In dreaded places there are harmful things such as bandits, thieves, wild animals, and the like. Going to such places without an escort is dangerous for possessions, for physical safety, and even for life itself. When accompanied by a powerful escort, however, we pass through without mishap. Similarly, without a Dharma master to act as an escort on the path to enlightenment, accruing spiritual wealth, and heading for the citadel of omniscience, we risk having our wealth of virtue plundered by that band of thieves [that consists of] ideas and mental afflictions within and harmful forces and misleading influences without. There is even the risk of our life in the happier realms being cut short. Therefore, it is said:

> As soon as that gang of robbers and thieves, the afflictions,
> find the opportunity,
> they will steal virtue
> and put an end to life in the higher states. BCA 5:28

Never straying from the Dharma master who is like an escort, the wealth of virtue will not be lost, existence as a being in the higher realms will not be cut short, and the citadel of omniscience will be attained. Therefore it says in the *Instructions for Liberation of Śrī Saṃbhava*:

> All the merit of a bodhisattva is protected by the Dharma master.[52]

One also reads in the *Instructions for Liberation of Upāsikā Acalā*:

> Good Dharma masters are like an escort because they ensure our safe passage to the state of omniscience.[53]

The third example is that of a *ferryman*. Crossing a mighty river, you may be securely aboard the boat, but if there is no ferryman, you cannot reach the other shore, and the boat may sink or be swept away by the currents. With a ferryman and through his striving, however, the other shore will be reached. Likewise, when trying to traverse the ocean of samsara without Dharma masters who are like ferrymen, you may well be aboard the ship of Dharma yet drown in samsara or be carried off by its currents. Thus it is said:

> When there is no oarsman,
> the vessel will not reach the other shore.
> Even if one may be accomplished in all,
> yet without a master, existence will be endless.[54]

Staying on board with the ferryman-like Dharma master, nirvana—the dry land of the far shore of samsara—will be attained. Therefore it says in the *Marvelous Array Sutra*:

> Delivering us from the ocean of samsara, the Dharma master is like a ferryman.[55]

Thus one really needs to rely on Dharma masters, who are like guides, escorts, and ferrymen.

The second point examines the **different kinds** of Dharma master. There are four: (1) the Dharma master as a specific individual, (2) the Dharma master as a bodhisattva who has attained the levels (*bhūmi*), (3) the Dharma master as an emanation body (*nirmāṇakāya*) of a buddha, (4) the Dharma master as an enjoyment body (*saṃbhogakāya*) of a buddha.

These correspond to the personal situation. Since one is totally unable to rely on buddhas or bodhisattvas while still a beginner in the Dharma, a Dharma master in the form of a specific individual is relied upon. When most of the action-related obscurations have been purified, one is able to rely on a Dharma master who is a bodhisattva on the levels. From the topmost stage of the path of accumulation onward, one can rely on a Dharma master in the nirmāṇakāya form of a buddha. Once the bodhisattva levels are attained, it is possible to rely on a Dharma master in the saṃbhogakāya form of a buddha.

Which of these four types is kindest to us? At the outset, when still in the dark pit of action and affliction, were we to try to rely on Dharma masters of the three latter types, we would not even be capable of seeing their faces; it is only due to our path being illuminated by the lamp held aloft by teachers who are specific individuals that we will eventually encounter them. Therefore, masters in the form of specific individuals are the kindest.

The third point concerns the **specific characteristics** of each of these four kinds of Dharma masters.

Buddhas embody the highest, most complete form of purification because they have eliminated both sorts of obscuration. They also embody the highest, most complete form of pristine awareness because they possess the two forms of knowledge.

Dharma masters as bodhisattvas on the levels will have whichever degree of purification and pristine awareness is appropriate to their particular level, from the first to the tenth. Of particular import are bodhisattvas of the eighth to tenth levels, for they have ten powers enabling them to nurture others: powers related to life, mind, requisites, karma, birth, aspiration, prayers, miracles, pristine awareness, and Dharma:

1. *Power over life* is the ability to stay in a world as long as wished.
2. *Power over mind* is the ability to enter stably into meditative absorption, just as is wished.
3. *Power over requisites* is the ability to shower an immeasurable rain of precious objects on beings.
4. *Power over karma* is the ability to rearrange karmic results in terms of dimension, state, type of existence, and mode of birth that might otherwise be experienced in other states.
5. *Power over birth* is the ability to take birth in the desire realm yet to always maintain profound meditative concentration and not experience any sort of degeneration, remaining completely unsullied by the evils of that state.
6. *Power over aspiration* is the ability to transform the elements—earth, water, and so forth—into one another, as wished.
7. *Power of prayer* is the ability to pray or compose prayers in a way that will most properly accomplish the well-being of oneself and others; also the power to make prayers become realities.
8. *Power over miracles* is the ability to demonstrate countless miracles and supernatural feats in order to kindle aspiration in beings.
9. *Power of pristine awareness* is knowledge that encompasses, in the best possible way, the ultimate meaning of Dharma, of key points, of the true sense of words, and of bodhisattva prowess.
10. *Power of Dharma* is the ability to teach beings that which is suited to them, in just the right amount. This is achieved by presenting all the different nouns, terms, and characters of Dharma, in the various sutras and other teachings, in such a way that their sole speech is understood by each in his or her own language and in a totally satisfying way that makes sense.

Dharma masters as specific individuals have as their characteristics qualities described sometimes as eightfold, fourfold, or twofold. Of those with eight qualities, *Bodhisattva Levels* says:

> Concerning the above, if one has eight things, then one should be known as a bodhisattva who is completely qualified as a Dharma master. What are the eight? They are: (1) to have a bodhisattva's moral discipline, (2) to be learned in the bodhisattva scriptures, (3) to have realization, (4) to be kind and loving to one's followers, (5) to be fearless, (6) to be forbearing, (7) to be of untiring mind, and (8) to know how to use words.[56]

Of those with four qualities the *Ornament of Mahayana Sutras* says:

> Broad based, eliminators of doubt,
> worthy of recollecting, and teaching the two natures:
> such are the very best
> of bodhisattva teachers. MSA 13:5

This means that: (1) their teaching is very broad based because they have studied many things; (2) they can remove others' doubts because they themselves have superb discerning awareness; (3) their speech is worthy of recollection because their deeds are those of holy beings; and (4) they teach the two natures: the characteristics of the completely defiled and of the utterly pure.

Of those with twofold qualities *Guide to the Bodhisattva Way of Life* says:

> Even should it cost your life,
> never forsake a qualified Dharma master,
> who is (1) skilled in the meaning of Mahayana
> and (2) maintains the noble bodhisattva discipline. BCA 5:102

The fourth point is **how to rely on** the Dharma master skillfully. Once someone has connected with such Dharma masters, there are three ways of relying on them: (1) by showing respect and rendering service, (2) by cultivating the relevant reverence and devotion, and (3) by personal Dharma practice and earnestness.

The first of these [has two parts]. *Showing respect* is accomplished by prostrating to them, rising quickly [when they enter], bowing to them, circumambulating them, speaking at the appropriate time with a loving mind, looking at them again and again with an insatiable mind, and so forth. This was exemplified by the way that Maṇibhadra, a powerful merchant's son, related to his teacher. It says in the *Marvelous Array Sutra*:

> Gaze insatiably at your Dharma master. Why? Dharma masters are rarely seen, rarely manifest, and are seldom met with.[57]

Relying on Dharma masters by *serving* them is accomplished by catering to their needs. This means providing them with food, clothing, bedding, seating, medicines when they are unwell, funds, and the like, in a way that accords with the Buddhist teaching. This is to be done without heed for one's own life or physical well-being, as exemplified by the realized being Sadāprarudita. In the *Instructions for Liberation of Śrī Saṃbhava* we read:

> A buddha's enlightenment is attained by serving Dharma masters.[58]

The second way is to rely on them by [cultivating] *reverence and devotion*. Having established the concept that the teacher is a buddha, whatever the teacher says is taken to be instruction, never to be transgressed, to be followed in constancy and with the cultivation of reverence, devotion, and joyous trust. This was exemplified by the way master scholar Nāropa relied on his guru. It says in the *Mother of the Conquerors*:

> Earnestly cultivate reverence for Dharma masters, follow them, and have joyous trust.[59]

Besides this, wrong ways of thinking about the personal conduct of masters should be abandoned, because their conduct is in fact their skillful technique at work. Instead, cultivate the noblest devotion for it. This was exemplified in the biography of King Anala.[60]

The third way to rely on masters is by *Dharma practice and earnestness*. There are three steps to Dharma practice in this respect: first to study Dharma under the masters' guidance, then to contemplate its significance, and finally to make it a reality in practice.

Do these earnestly; that is what will be most satisfying for the teacher. Thus the *Ornament of Mahayana Sutras* says:

> The firm one who practices just as instructed
> will surely please the mind. MSA 18:12CD

When someone's Dharma master is satisfied, that person will attain buddhahood. It says in the *Instructions for Liberation of Śrī Saṃbhava*:

> By satisfying the master, the enlightenment of all the buddhas will be attained.[61]

As far as requesting Dharma teachings from one's Dharma masters is concerned, there are three phases: the preparation, the actual instruction, and the conclusion. The preparation is to have the bodhisattva motivation when requesting the teachings. During the actual instruction, consider yourself to be like a patient, the Dharma to be like medicine, the teacher to be like the physician, and the earnest practice of Dharma to be the best and quickest way to recovery. The conclusion is to avoid the three mistakes of being like an upturned container, a leaky container, or a contaminated container.[62]

The fifth point is about the **benefits** of relying on Dharma masters. In the *Instructions for Liberation of Śrī Saṃbhava* we read:

> Child of noble descent! A bodhisattva who is most properly nurtured by a good Dharma master will not fall into the lower states. A bodhisattva who is totally protected by a Dharma master will not be swayed by corrupting friends. A bodhisattva who is perfectly trained by a Dharma master will not abandon the bodhisattva way. A bodhisattva who is most excellently sustained will completely transcend the activities of ordinary people.[63]

The *Perfection of Wisdom* [*in Eight Thousand Lines*] also says:

> A realized bodhisattva who is most properly nurtured will swiftly attain peerless, totally pure, and perfect enlightenment.[64]

This concludes the third chapter, concerning Dharma masters, of this *Ornament of Precious Liberation, a Wish-Fulfilling Gem of Sublime Dharma.*

Part IV. The Means: The Dharma Master's Instruction

4. The Impermanence of Conditioned Existence

We have the *cause*, buddha nature. Furthermore, because samsara has existed since time without beginning, at some point we must already have had the *basis*, a precious human existence, through which we met the *condition*, the Dharma master. What prevented us from becoming buddhas then? It was the harmful mistake of falling under the sway of four blockages that stopped us, and those like us, from attaining buddhahood.

The *four impediments that have prevented the attainment of buddhahood* are: (1) attachment to the experiences of this life, (2) attachment to worldly well-being in general, (3) attachment to the well-being of peace, and (4) ignorance of the means by which buddhahood is achieved. What can eliminate these four impediments? They are eliminated by heeding the instruction of Dharma masters and by putting those instructions into practice.

What does those masters' advice consist of? Here is the synopsis:

> **All the Dharma masters' instruction can be condensed into four topics: meditation on impermanence; meditation on samsara's faults and on actions and their consequences; meditation on love and compassion; and the teachings concerning the cultivation of bodhicitta.**[65]

This means that the Dharma masters' instruction comprises advice on (1) how to meditate on impermanence, (2) how to meditate on the defects of samsara and on actions and their consequences, (3) how to cultivate love and compassion, and (4) how to cultivate bodhicitta.

These act as remedies as follows.[66] Meditation on impermanence counteracts attachment to the experiences of this life. Meditation on the defects of samsara counteracts attachment to worldly well-being in general. The meditations on love and compassion counteract attachment to the well-being of meditative peace. The teachings on cultivating highest enlightenment counteract ignorance of how to attain buddhahood.

These cover all teachings—from taking refuge up to the meaning of the two types of absence of self-entity, or from the five path phases and the ten bodhisattva levels down through all the teachings on bodhicitta. Some of these topics form the basis for bodhicitta, some are its objective, some are the rituals connected with bodhicitta development, some are advice pertinent to bodhicitta, some concern its qualities and benefits, and some present its results. There is no Mahayana topic that is not included in the bodhicitta teachings. Hence all those forms of instruction stem from the Dharma master: they depend on the Dharma master. Therefore the *Marvelous Array Sutra* says:

> The Dharma master is the very source of all the teachings of virtue.

and

> Omniscience depends on the instruction given by Dharma masters.[67]

Meditation on impermanence

Of these, I first present impermanence, which is the remedy that counteracts attachment to the experiences of this life.

In general, every composite thing is impermanent. Therefore the Buddha taught:

> O monks! All composites are impermanent.[68]

How exactly are they impermanent? What is accumulated will eventually dwindle, what is built up will eventually disintegrate, what comes together will eventually part, and what lives will eventually die. Quoting the *Collection of Aphorisms*:

> The end of all accumulation is dispersal,
> the end of construction is disintegration,
> the end of meeting is parting,
> and the end of life is death. UV 1:22

How to meditate on this is explained through the synopsis:

> **Meditation on impermanence is well summarized in three topics: its categories, the meditation techniques, and the benefits of having meditated on it.**

First, the **categories** are two: the impermanence of the world and the impermanence of sentient beings. The first of these, the impermanence of the world—the outer vessel—has two subcategories: gross impermanence and subtle impermanence. The second, the impermanence of sentient beings—the inner essence—also has two subcategories: the impermanence of others and the impermanence of oneself.

Second, the **techniques for meditating** on these will be discussed in two parts: that of the world and that of its beings. For the world, first we consider its *overall impermanence.*

There exists nothing, from the wind mandala below [as its basis] up to the four levels of meditative concentration [of the form realm] above, that will not change, that is permanent by its very nature, or that has lasting materiality. At times, everything below the first level of concentration is destroyed by fire. At times, everything below the second level of concentration is destroyed by water. At times, everything below the third level of concentration is destroyed by wind. As these things occur, when there is destruction by fire not even ashes are left, just as when oil is consumed by flame. When there is destruction by water, there is not even sediment left, just as when salt is dissolved by water. When there is destruction by wind, nothing remains, just as when powder is blown away. Therefore the *Treasury of Higher Knowledge* says:

> There will be seven [destructions] by fire followed each by water;
> thus after seven by water,
> there will be seven by fire;
> finally there will be destruction by wind. AK 3:102

The fourth level of concentration will not be destroyed by fire, water, or air. The beings in that state are subject to death and transmigration, and therefore it ends automatically [at their death]. Thus it says:

> The celestial abodes of the impermanent arise and disintegrate
> along with the conscious beings that inhabit them. AK 3:101

Also, the destruction of this universe by fire, at a certain point, is foretold in the *Questions of the Layman Vīradatta Sutra*:

> After one eon, this world,
> the nature of which is space, will become space;
> even the mountains will burn away totally and be destroyed.[69]

The *subtle impermanence* of the environment is that of the flux of the four seasons, the rising and setting of the sun and the moon, and moment-to-moment change.

Let us consider the first of these. Due to the powerful influence of the coming of spring, our environment, the world, changes as follows. The land becomes soft and ruddy in color, and the trees, grasses, and plants bud. However, this is but the manifestation of a transitory period. Due to the powerful influence of the coming of summer, the land becomes predominantly deep green, and leaves and branches grow on the trees, grasses, and plants. This, too, is but the manifestation of a transitory period. Due to the powerful influence of the coming of autumn, the land then hardens and is predominantly golden. Its trees, grasses, and plants bear fruit. This, too, is but the manifestation of a transitory period. Due to the powerful influence of the coming of winter, the land becomes frozen and whitish, and the trees, grasses, and plants are dried up and brittle. This, too, is but the manifestation of a transitory period.

Now let us consider impermanence in terms of the rising and setting of the sun and moon. The power of day breaking makes our environment, the world, become light and bright. The power of night falling makes it disappear into darkness. These are also signs of impermanence.

Finally, let us consider impermanence in terms of moment-by-moment change. Our environment, the world of one small instant of time, does not persist into the next instant of time. It gives the impression of remaining the same, yet in fact something similar has taken its place, as exemplified by cascading water.

The second technique of meditation contemplates the *impermanence of* the inner essence, *sentient beings*, first considering the impermanence of others and then one's own impermanence.

The *impermanence of others*: All conscious beings in the three realms are impermanent. It says in the *Vast Manifestation Sutra*:

> The three realms are impermanent, like autumn clouds.[70]

One's own impermanence is based on understanding that "I also have no power to remain in this life and must go on to another." The way to understand this is twofold: (1) by examining your own existence and (2) by applying to yourself what is observed of others' existences. The way to meditate on the first of these is as follows: meditate on death, on the specific characteristics of death, on the exhaustion of life, and on separation.

Meditation on death is to contemplate "I will not stay long in this world and will soon be moving into the next."

Meditation on the specific characteristics of death involves contemplating the thought "This life force of mine will be used up, respiration will stop, and this body will take on the appearance of a corpse, while this mind will be obliged to wander off to another life."

Meditation on the exhaustion of life is to contemplate: "Since a year ago, a year has passed, and now my life is precisely that much shorter. Since a month ago, a month has passed, and now my life is precisely that much shorter. From yesterday until today, a day has gone by, and now my life is precisely that much shorter. A moment has just gone by, and my life is precisely that much shorter." It says in *Guide to the Bodhisattva Way of Life*:

> Without ever stopping for even a day or a night,
> this life is constantly on the wane.
> Because what is left diminishes and disappears,
> how could the likes of me not die? BCA 2:39

Meditation on separation is to contemplate: "The friends and relatives, wealth and possessions, body, and so forth that I have at present and that I value so much will not always be able to accompany me. Soon will we be parted." As it says in *Guide to the Bodhisattva Way of Life*:

> By not knowing that I would have to leave
> everything behind and depart . . . BCA 2:35

Alternatively, one could engage in the ninefold way of meditating on death. The ninefold technique is centered on three main contemplations: "I will certainly die," "The time of death is indefinite," and "When I die, nothing whatsoever can accompany me."

There are three reasons *it is certain one will die*: (1) No one previously has escaped death. (2) The body is a composite phenomenon. (3) Life is consumed from moment to moment.

1. It is certain I will die because there was no one in the past who did not die. The great master Aśvaghoṣa said:

> If ever you see or hear about someone
> on earth or in the upper realms
> who is considered immortal,
> doubt it![71]

Therefore even "seers of truth"[72] cannot find a place to go to escape death and encounter immortality. They will all die, not to mention the likes of us! It is said:

> Even the great rishis endowed with
> five types of clear cognition who travel far through space
> would be unable to travel to some place
> where they can enjoy immortality.[73]

Besides this, even realized beings such as pratyekabuddha or śrāvaka arhats had to leave their bodies in the end. What, then, for the likes of us! Therefore it says in the *Collection of Aphorisms*:

> When even the pratyekabuddhas
> and the śrāvakas [disciples] of the buddhas
> have to quit their bodies,
> what need is there to speak of ordinary beings? UV 1:25

Besides this, if even the totally purified, utterly perfect emanation body (*nirmāṇakāya*), adorned with the marks and signs of a supreme being, whose very nature was like a vajra, had to leave behind his body, then so much the more is it true of ordinary folk like us. The great master Aśvaghoṣa said:

> If even the vajra bodies of the buddhas,
> adorned with the special marks and signs, are impermanent,
> then there is no point even mentioning
> other beings' bodies, which are like plantain trees.[74]

2. It is certain I will die because my body is something composite. Any composite whatsoever is impermanent, and every composite is destructible by nature. The *Collection of Aphorisms* says:

> Alas, all composites are impermanent,
> characterized by birth and decay! UV 1:3

Hence, since this body is not noncomposite but composite, it is impermanent, and so it is certain that it will die.

3. It is certain I will die because life is consumed from moment to moment. Life gets closer to death with the passing of each instant. If this is not obvious, let us consider examples that bear some similarity: an arrow shot by a strong archer, a torrent cascading over the edge of a steep cliff, and a prisoner being led to the place of execution and imminent death.

The first example is that of an arrow shot by a strong archer. Not halting even for an instant at any one place in space, it speeds swiftly to its target. Life, too, never stands still even for an instant and heads swiftly toward death. As is said:

> An arrow loosed from a bowstring
> by a mighty archer never hovers
> but speeds to its target;
> human life is like that, too.[75]

The second example is that of a torrent cascading over the edge of a steep cliff. Its waters tumble down without pausing even for an instant. Likewise, it is extremely clear that human life is unable to pause. This is found in the *Crown Jewel Dhāraṇī Sutra*, where it says:

> Friends, this life passes as swiftly
> as water gushing over a waterfall.
> Immature beings, unaware of this and living unskillfully,
> proudly intoxicate themselves with sense pleasures.[76]

Furthermore, the *Collection of Aphorisms* says:

> It flows on like the current
> of a mighty river, never turning back. UV 1:33CD

The third example is that of a prisoner being led to the place of execution, whose every step brings death closer. We are just like that. In the *Noble Tree Sutra* it says:

> Just like a prisoner being led to the place of execution,
> whose every step brings him closer to death.[77]

The *Collection of Aphorisms* also says:

> Just as those on their way to execution
> draw closer to their death
> with every step that is taken,
> so it is with the life force of humans. UV 1:14

There are three reasons why *the time of death is not definite*: (4) The lifespan is uncertain. (5) The body has no single vital essence. (6) There are many possible causes of death.

4. The time of death is not definite because lifespan is uncertain. Although the lifespan is fixed for some other sentient beings and for human beings in other parts of the cosmos, the lifespan of ordinary people in this world is not definite. In the *Treasury of Higher Knowledge* it says:

> Here it is not definite: ten years at the end
> and inestimable at the beginning. AK 3:78

Just how it is indefinite is explained in the *Collection of Aphorisms*:

Some will die in the womb,
some when they are born,
some when they can only crawl,
some when they can run,
some when aged, some when young,
and some in the prime of life.
Eventually they all go. UV 1:9–10

5. The time of death is indefinite because the body has no single vital essence. This body has no solid, enduring essence, only its thirty-six impure substances. Thus *Guide to the Bodhisattva Way of Life* says:

Using the scalpel of discerning awareness,
first dissect yourself mentally,
peeling away the layer of skin
and going through the flesh to the skeleton.

Having even dissected the bones
and gotten to the marrow,
examining carefully, ask:
"What is there that could be its vital essence?" BCA 5:62–63

This is what we ourselves ought to investigate.

6. The time of death is not definite because there are many potential causes of death. There is nothing that could not become a cause of death, either for me or for someone else. It says in the *Letter to a Friend*:

There are many things that damage life.
As life is more unstable than an air bubble in water,
it is a wonder that in-breaths give way to out-breaths
or that anyone awakens from sleep. SU 55

There are three contemplations on how, once dead, *nothing can accompany you*: (7) wealth and objects cannot accompany you, (8) friends and relatives cannot accompany you, and (9) your own body cannot accompany you.

7. Wealth and objects cannot accompany you after death. *Guide to the Bodhisattva Way of Life* says:

> Although you may have obtained so many things,
> and have used and enjoyed them for a long time,
> you depart naked and empty-handed,
> as though robbed by thieves. BCA 6:59

Not only do wealth and possessions not accompany you at death, they also harm both this life and the next. They harm this life on account of the suffering caused through quarrels over them, having to protect them from theft, and enslavement to them. The ripening of karma planted in this way harms future lives, taking one to the lower states.

8. Friends and relatives cannot accompany you at death. As it says:

> When the time comes to die,
> children will not be a refuge,
> nor father and mother, nor friends and loved ones.
> None could be your refuge.[78] UV 1:41

Not only do relatives and friends not accompany you at death, they also harm both this life and the next. They harm this life through the anguish of worrying about their well-being and their lives. The full karmic ripening of these fears spoils your future lives by taking you to the lower realms.

9. Your own body cannot accompany you at death, nor can its physical qualities do so. No strong or courageous person can turn death away, no swift athlete can outrun it, and no eloquent speaker or negotiator can dissuade it. That would be like trying to prevent or delay the sun from setting behind a mountain: no one can.

The physical substance of the body cannot accompany you either. *Guide to the Bodhisattva Way of Life* says:

> Your body, which you have clothed and fed
> at the expense of great hardship, will be unable to help you:
> it will be eaten by jackals or birds, be burned by fire,
> rot in water, or be buried in a grave.[79]

Not only can your body not accompany you, as just explained, it also harms both this life and the next. It injures this life through the great sufferings that occur when it cannot bear sickness, heat, cold, hunger, or thirst, or when there is fear of being killed, bound, or beaten. [Actions related to] these misfortunes will drag you into the lower states in future lives.

The second way [of contemplating your own impermanence] is by *observing what happens to others and applying it to yourself.* This means that when actually witnessing others die, hearing of their deaths, or recollecting people dying, you imagine this happening to you and then meditate accordingly.

Applying to yourself the deaths of other people you have witnessed dying is done as follows. Think of those closely related to you who were strong at first, of healthy complexion, feeling happy, and never giving a moment's thought to death, yet who were then stricken by fatal illness. Their bodily strength waned, they could not even sit up, their complexion lost its luster, becoming pallid and dry, and they suffered distress. There was no way to cure the pain or lessen the emotional burden. Medicines and examinations were of no more help, and even religious ceremonies and special prayers could not make them better. They knew that they were going to die and that nothing could be done to prevent it. Surrounded by their remaining friends, they ate their last meal and spoke their last words. Evoking these images, think: "I, too, am of the same nature. I will also be subject to this. I, too, have these characteristics and have not transcended this particular phenomenon."

Then, from the moment the breath stopped, that person's body was considered unfit to stay even a day in the very place that had been the beloved home from which the person could not bear to part. Once the corpse was laid on a bier, swathed, and bound, it was lifted up and carried out of the house. At that moment some embraced it and clung to it, some wept and wailed, some fainted and were overcome with grief. Yet others remarked, "This dead body is simply the likes of earth and rock, and you are small-minded to carry on as you do!" Contemplating such scenes as a corpse making its one-way journey over the threshold, think: "I, too, am of the same nature. . . ."

Then, contemplating the corpse once it has been left in the charnel ground, where it is ripped apart by jackals and dogs, decomposed by insects, and where there are the disintegrated remains of skeletons, think: "I, too, will be like this...."

The way to apply to yourself the instances of other peoples' deaths that you have heard about is as follows. Whenever people say, "Such and such a person died," or "There is a corpse in such and such a place," think, as above: "I, too, am like that...."

The way to apply to yourself the instances of other peoples' deaths that you recollect is as follows. Think about all the people—some elderly, some young, and some lifelong friends—who have died in your area, town, or in your own house. Bearing their deaths in mind, think, as above, "I, too, am like this...," and reflect on how, before too long, you will also go that way. In the sutras it says:

> Since no one knows which will come first—
> tomorrow or the next life—
> it makes sense to strive for what has meaning in the next life
> and not put a lot of effort into what is just for tomorrow.[80]

The third point discusses the **benefits** of meditating on impermanence. By understanding that all composite things are impermanent, strong craving for this life will be countered. Further, the seed of trust will be planted, diligence will be reinforced, and this will be an important factor in realizing sameness, since it quickly frees the mind from attraction and rejection.

This concludes the fourth chapter, concerning the impermanence of composite phenomena, of this *Ornament of Precious Liberation, a Wish-Fulfilling Gem of Sublime Dharma.*

5. The Suffering of Samsara

One might feel, "What does it matter if there is impermanence and death, since I'll be reborn anyway? In that next life I could experience the very finest that being human or divine has to offer. That is fine by me!" To think thus is to be attached to the pleasures of cyclic existence (*samsara*). As the remedy for this I shall explain how to become familiar with the defects of samsara. The synopsis is:

> **The defects of samsara are covered by three topics: the suffering of conditioned existence, the suffering of change, and overt suffering.**

These three sufferings can be explained through metaphors: the suffering of conditioned existence is like uncooked rice, the suffering of change is like cooked rice mixed with poison, and overt suffering is like stomach pains due to eating the poisoned rice. The three sufferings can also be explained in terms of their character. The suffering of conditioned existence has a neutral feeling, the suffering of change has a feeling of pleasure about it, and overt suffering actually feels like suffering. The three sufferings can also be explained in terms of their essential characteristics, as follows.

First, the **suffering of conditioned existence**: We suffer merely through having taken on [a human life composed of] the aggregates, to which suffering is inherent. Ordinary people do not feel this suffering of conditioned existence and can be compared to people stricken by raging fevers, who are insensitive to trivial physical ills like an itchy ear. Stream-enterers and the other three types of emancipated being [i.e., once-returners, nonreturners, and arhats] can perceive this suffering of conditioned existence. They can be compared to someone virtually cured of the fever and hence now quite aware of minor aches and pains. A small hair put on the palm of the hand causes neither discomfort nor pain, but that same hair in the eye will cause great irritation and unpleasantness. Similarly, ordinary people are insensitive to the suffering of conditioned existence, whereas realized beings are greatly distressed by it. As it says in the *Commentary on the Treasury of Higher Knowledge*:

> When a single hair in our palm enters into our eyes,
> it engenders discomfort and pain.
> The childish, akin to the palm, do not recognize
> the suffering of conditioned existence.
> The noble ones, akin to the eyes, perceive
> conditioned existence as suffering.[81]

Second, the **suffering of change** is so called because all the pleasures of samsara, whatever they may be, will eventually change into suffering. As it says in the *White Lotus of Compassion Sutra*:

> The divine realms are a cause for suffering to arise. The human realms are also a cause for suffering.[82]

Hence even those who attain the human status of a universal monarch (*cakravartin*) will, in time, change and find themselves in a state of suffering. It says in the *Letter to a Friend*:

> Even a universal monarch will,
> in the course of time, become a servant. SU 69CD

Furthermore, even someone who achieves the physical form and the experiences of Indra, lord of the gods, will eventually fall from that state, first dying, then transmigrating. It says:

> Even having become Indra, worthy of offerings,
> you fall back to earth through the power of karma. SU 69AB

Besides this, the likes of the king of the gods, Brahma, who has transcended sensual desire and attained the felicity of evenly resting in meditative concentration, will also eventually fall. It says:

From the pleasures of being Brahma, free of desires,
you'll have to put up with the unceasing suffering
of being fuel in the Hell of Relentless Agony. SU 74B–D

The third point is that of suffering as **overt suffering.** This comprises the significant and quite obvious sufferings experienced above and beyond that of having a life composed of aggregates to which suffering is inherent. They are to be known through two categories: those of the lower states of existence and those of the higher states.

The *sufferings of the lower states of existence* are those of the three lower states: hells, hungry spirits, and animals. Each is to be understood through four points: their respective subcategories, locations, sufferings experienced, and lifespan.

The hells. The subcategories are: the eight hot hells, the neighboring hells, the eight cold hells, and the occasional hells, making eighteen types in all.

The [eight] hot hells. Where are these hot hells? They are situated beneath Jambudvīpa, for there are many who go from here to there. In the very lowest live the sentient beings of Relentless Agony Hell. Above them, working upward, are the Exceedingly Hot, Hot, Great Wailing, Wailing, Gathering and Crushing, Black Line, and Reviving hells, respectively. Therefore the *Treasury of Higher Knowledge* says:

Twenty thousand [leagues] beneath here
is Relentless Agony,
with seven other hells above it. AK 3:58

The reason for their names will be given, as well as a general explanation for the sufferings endured in those places. The first is the Reviving Hell, where beings are bound, immolated, and hacked to death by each other. Subsequently, a cold wind blows to revive them, and the process resumes. This continues relentlessly throughout their stay there.

In the Black Line Hell, a black line is traced on the body, which is then sawed with blazing saws and chopped with flaming, red-hot axes. As it says:

Some are cut up with saws,
others chopped up by unbearably sharp axes. SU 78CD

In the Gathering and Crushing Hell, beings are gathered between mountains and also crushed and squeezed in iron presses. In the first instance, mountains in the form of rams' heads come together, crushing the trapped beings. The hills then draw apart, and a cold wind arises to restore the people to their former condition. They are crushed and restored time after time. The *Letter to a Student* says:

> Two terrifying long-horned rams as big as mountains,
> crush all the bodies gathered between them and grind them to
> powder. ŚI 45

Some are squeezed between iron presses, their blood squirting out like four rivers. It says:

> Some are ground like sesame seeds,
> others milled to dust like fine flour. SU 78AB

Beings in the Wailing Hell scream with terror as they are burned. Beings in the Great Wailing Hell scream even louder. In the Hot Hell beings are tortured by fire and the like. Boiling metal poured into their mouths burns their viscera, and they are pierced through with one-pointed spears from the anus to the top of the head. In the Exceedingly Hot Hell they are tortured even more than this. Without skin, they are burned by molten metal poured down their throats so that fire comes out their orifices. Then they, too, are pierced—by tridents that puncture the soles of the feet and the anus and penetrate up through the top of the head and the shoulders. It says:

> Similarly, some are forced to drink
> a blazing liquid of molten metal
> while others are impaled
> on blazing iron stakes bearing many spikes. SU 79

Relentless Agony (Avīci) Hell is a blazing iron building, twenty thousand leagues (*yojana*) in height and breadth, within which are copper and iron cauldrons several leagues wide, into which are poured molten bronze and iron that are kept boiling by unbearable fires coming from the four directions. It says:

> Some are cast head first into iron cauldrons
> and boiled up like rice soup. SU 82CD

It is so named because the suffering there is unremitting.

The lifespans of hell beings are taught as:

> In the first six, starting with the Reviving Hell,
> a day and night is equivalent to the life of the sense-dimension gods,
> and hence their lifespans are calculable
> working from the lifespans of those gods. AK 3:82

The lifespan of the class of the Four Great King gods is equivalent to a day and night in the Reviving Hell. Thirty days make a month, and twelve months make a year. Reviving Hell beings live for five hundred of their own years. This makes their lifespan 1,620 billion human years.

In a similar way, lifespan in the Black Line Hell is calculated according to that of the gods of the Heaven of the Thirty-Three. Since beings can live for up to a thousand hell years, their lifespan is the equivalent of 12,990 billion human years.[83] Correlating the Gathering and Crushing Hell with the Aggression-Free god realm then, since beings can be there for two thousand hell years, their lifespan is the equivalent of 100,680 billion human years.[84] Correlating the Wailing Hell with the Joyful god realm then, since beings can stay there for four thousand hell years, their lifespan is the equivalent of 844,420 billion human years.[85] Correlating the Great Wailing Hell with the Delighting in Creation god realm then, since beings can stay there for eight thousand hell years, their lifespan is the equivalent of 6,635,520 billion human years. Correlating the Hot Hell with the Rulers of Others' Creations god realm then, since beings can stay there for sixteen thousand hell years, their lifespan is the equivalent of 51,084,010 billion human years.[86] Those in the Exceedingly Hot Hell can remain there for half an intermediate cosmic eon, and those in the Relentless Agony Hell for a whole intermediate cosmic eon. As it says:

In the Exceedingly Hot, a half, and in the Relentless Agony,
a whole intermediate cosmic eon. AK 3:83

The neighboring hells. These are situated in the four cardinal directions around the eight hells mentioned above. The first of these is the Glowing Coals Hell, where there are knee-deep glowing coals. As beings there take a step, seeking escape, the flesh, skin, and blood are completely burned off their legs when they put their feet down, yet restored as they lift them up again. That is the first additional hell. Nearby is the Impure Swamp of Putrefied Corpses Hell, infested by white worms with black heads. With sharp, hard, pointed mouths, they enter the flesh, penetrating to the bone. This is the second additional hell. Nearby is the Great Razor Highway Hell, where beings are molested by a forest of sword-like leaves, terrifying large black dogs, and iron trees with lacerating leaves and branches, on which perch ravens with iron beaks. This is the third additional hell. Nearby is the Most Extreme River, full of boiling lye in which beings are cooked. They are prevented from leaving the river by beings who stand along the banks brandishing weapons. This is the fourth additional hell. It says about these:

Besides the eight there are sixteen others,
in the four cardinal directions from them:
the Glowing Coals, a Swamp of Putrefaction,
the Razor Highway, and so on, and the River. AK 3:39

You may wonder whether the guardians of the hells—who appear to be humans or ravens with iron beaks—are actual sentient beings. The Vaibhāṣika schools hold them to be sentient beings, whereas the Sautrāntika schools say they are not. The Yogācāra schools and the lineage transmission of Marpa and Milarepa hold them to be manifestations of their perceiver's own mind, due to former evils enacted. *Guide to the Bodhisattva Way of Life* accords with this interpretation:

Who could have created the beings there
and their hellish weapons for such purposes?
Who made the burning iron ground,
and from what are the fires generated?

> The Great Sage has said that all these sorts of things
> are due to the existence of an unwholesome mind. BCA 5:7–8AB

The eight cold hells. These are: (1) the Cold Sore Hell, (2) the Burst Cold Sore Hell, (3) the Chattering Teeth Hell, (4) the Sneezing Hell, (5) the Alas! Hell, (6) the Hell Where Frostbitten Skin Cracks in the Shape of an Utpala, (7) the Hell with Cracks Like a Lotus, and (8) the Hell with Cracks Like Giant Lotuses. It is said:

> There are eight cold hells: the Cold Sore Hell and the others.
> AK 3:59

They are located beneath this Jambudvīpa, directly beneath the hot hells. Below is a general outline of the sufferings experienced in those states and an explanation of their names.

In the first two hells, the cold is so unbearable that the beings have cold sores or [in the second] festering cold sores. The next three are named after the sounds and cries that beings there are heard to make due to the unbearable cold. The last three derive their names from the bodily changes that take place: in the sixth the skin turns blue with cold and cracks open in fivefold or sixfold cracks, looking like an utpala flower; in the seventh it has turned from blue to red, and the cracks have ten or more lips, like a lotus; and in the last the skin is violently inflamed and split into a hundred or more flaps, like an open, giant lotus.

How long does the lifespan of these beings last? Just as an example, the Bhagavan Buddha stated the following:

> O monks, here is an example. Say a storehouse able to hold eighty bushels of sesame seeds, like those of this land of Magadha, were to be filled with such seeds. If once every hundred years one grain were to be removed, then after a certain period all the eighty bushels of that Magadha sesame would eventually be emptied from that store. I could not tell you which of the two—that period of time or the lifespan of those in the Cold Sore Hell—would be the longer. O monks! The lifespan in the Open Cold Sore hell is twenty times that of the Cold Sore Hell.

> O monks! The lifespan in the Great Open Lotus Hell is twenty times that in the Open Lotus Hell.[87]

Master Vasubandhu taught this in a briefer form:

> The lifespan in the Cold Sore Hell
> [approximates] the time it would take to empty a store of sesame seeds
> by removing just one seed every hundred years.
> The lifespan in the others increases by a factor of twenty. AK 3:84

Therefore the lifespan in the Cold Sore Hell is the time it would take to empty a full sesame store; that of the Open Cold Sore Hell is that multiplied by twenty; that of the Chattering Teeth Hell is that multiplied by four hundred; that of the Sneezing Hell is that multiplied by eight thousand; that of the Alas! Hell is that multiplied by 160,000; that of the Utpala-Wound Hell is that multiplied by 3,200,000; that of the Lotus-Like Wounds is that multiplied by 64,000,000; and that of the Great Lotus Wounds is that multiplied by 1,280,000,000.

The occasional hells. These are created by the karma of one or two people or many people, and depend on the specific action performed. They take many different forms and have no definite location. Some of these hell beings live in rivers, some in the hills, and some in desolate areas or yet other places. Some are in subterranean realms. Some are in the human realm, such as those seen by the realized Maudgalyāyana. Likewise some are in destitute places, like those seen by Saṅgharakṣita.[88] Their lifespan is not fixed.

This concludes the explanation of hell beings' sufferings.

Hungry spirits. There are two categories: the king of the hungry spirits—Yama, lord of the dead—and the scattered spirits.

As for their habitats, Yama, the ruler of the hungry spirits, lives some five hundred leagues beneath this Jambudvīpa world. His scattered subjects have no set location, living in deserts and the like. There are three types of the latter: those that have an external eating or drinking impediment, those that have an internal impediment, and those with a general eating or drinking impediment.

The sufferings endured are as follows. Some anguished spirits have supernatural powers and experience almost god-like splendors. However, those with an external eating or drinking impediment see food and drink as pus and blood. They cannot eat or drink it because they perceive themselves as being prevented from so doing by other beings. Those with an internal impediment are not prevented by others from ingesting the food but are themselves unable to do so. It is said:

> Some have a mouth the size of a needle but a belly
> the size of a mountain. Anguished with hunger,
> those with the strength to look for food cannot find
> a morsel even among rubbish. SU 92

Among those with an eating and drinking impediment there are two types: fire garlands and filth eaters. As soon as the first type ingests food or drink, they are burned by it, as if by fire. The second eat excrement, drink urine, and cut off their flesh to eat. This was seen in a wilderness by Koṭikarṇa.[89]

How long does the lifespan of a hungry spirit last? A month of human time is the equivalent of a day and night of hungry spirit time. This enables us to calculate how long, in human terms, they live, because their lives last five hundred of their years.[90] It is said:

> . . . hungry spirits live
> for five hundred [years]: a day being a month. AK 3:83

Animals. There are four main categories: many-legged ones, quadrupeds, bipeds, and the legless.

Their habitat can be water, open land, or forest, but the majority live in the oceans.

The sufferings they experience are those of enslavement and being slaughtered and butchered when exploited by humans, or being eaten by each other in the wild. It says of domesticated animals:

> Powerless, they are exploited:
> beaten, kicked, chained, and goaded. SU 90CD

And of wild animals it is said:

> They are those slaughtered for their pearls, wool,
> bones, blood, flesh, or hides. SU 90AB

Concerning those living in the great oceans:

> They eat whatever is in front of the face.[91]

Animal lifespan is not fixed. The longest living continue for up to an intermediate cosmic eon. It says:

> The lifespan of animals is an eon, at most. AK 3:83

This concludes the section on the sufferings of the lower states.

The *sufferings of the higher states of existence* are considered in three areas: humans, demigods, and gods.

Humans. Humans experience eight principal sufferings. It says in *Nanda's Abiding in the Womb*:

> Likewise birth is a suffering, aging is a suffering, sickness is a suffering, death is a suffering, to be separated from what one likes is a suffering, to encounter what one dislikes is a suffering, to strive after and obtain what one wants is a suffering, and also to undergo hardship in order to maintain what one has is a suffering.[92]

The first of these is the *suffering of birth*, which also serves as the source of all the others. Although four possible modes of birth[93] are taught, most humans are born from a womb. When that is the case, various sufferings occur in the period starting from the intermediate state (*bardo*) and continuing until a womb is entered. In general, bardo beings have certain supernatural abilities. They are able to move through space and to see remote birth states through a type of divine vision. This leads to the subjective experience of four types of hallucinations generated by the force of former actions, such as the stirring of a mighty wind, a heavy fall of rain, a darkening of the sky, and the presence of frightening sounds made by hordes of people.

Then, according to how good or bad the person's karma is, the following distorted perceptions will come to arise: "I'm entering a celestial palace," "I'm going on top of a multistory building," "I'm approaching a throne," "I'm entering a thatched hut," "I'm going into a house made of leaves," "I'm slipping in between blades of grass," "I'm entering a forest," "I'm going through a hole in a wall," or "I'm slipping in between straws."

Furthermore, seeing from afar the future parents in sexual embrace, [the bardo being] heads toward them. Beings who have accumulated a great store of merit and who will have a high rebirth see a celestial palace, multistory building, or the like and head for it. Those with a middling store of merit who will have a middling rebirth see the grass-thatched hut and so forth and head toward that. Those who have gathered no merit and who will have a low rebirth see the hole in the wall and so forth and head toward that. Having reached there, one who is to be born a boy will feel attracted to the mother and averse to the father, whereas one who is to be born a girl will feel attraction for the father and aversion toward the mother. By these feelings of attraction and aversion, the bardo consciousness becomes fused with the impure substances of the parents.[94]

It is taught that from that moment on, thirty-eight weeks will be spent in the womb.[95] It is also taught that some spend eight months, some nine, and some ten. Some spend an indefinite period, and there are even some who spend up to sixty years in the womb.[96]

During the first week in the mother's womb, it is just like being cooked and fried in a hot cooking pot, due to the consciousness combined with the physical constituents causing experiences of unbearable suffering. This stage of the embryo, called the *ovoid,* is in form like rice jelly or yogurt.

In the second week in the mother's womb, the "all-touching" energy stirs. Its contact with the mother's womb makes the four elements become manifest. This is called the *oblong* and is like curds or churned butter in appearance.

In the third week in the mother's womb, the "activator" energy stirs the womb, making the four elements further consolidate. This is known as the *lump* and looks like a metal spoon or an ant.

Likewise, in the seventh week spent in the mother's womb, the "twister" energy arises. Its effect on the child in the womb causes formation of the two arms and two legs. The suffering undergone during this period is as though one strong person were pulling out the limbs while another was using a rolling pin to spread out the body.

Likewise, in the eleventh week spent in the mother's womb, the "orifice-forming" energy occurs. Its effect on the child in the womb is to cause the nine bodily orifices to appear. The suffering at that time is like that of a fresh wound being probed by a finger.

Furthermore, when the mother eats irregularly or eats predominantly cold food, one suffers as if one had been thrown naked onto ice. Very hot, sour, or spicy foods will create pain in a similar way. If the mother overeats, the pain is like that of being crushed between rocks. If she does not eat enough, the child also suffers, feeling as if it has been sent spinning through space. When she moves quickly, jumps or turns around sharply, or suddenly bends her body, the child is pained as though it were falling over a precipice. At times of violent intercourse, it suffers as though being beaten by thorny sticks.

In the thirty-seventh week, the child becomes aware of being in a womb, preceiving it as a dirty, foul-smelling, pitch-black prison. Completely fed up with it, the thought of leaving occurs. In the thirty-eighth week, the "flower-gathering" energy stirs the mother's womb, turning the fetus around toward the gateway of birth. The suffering at that time is like that of being placed upon a [rapidly rotating] iron machine.

Thus, as one develops during the pregnancy from a week-old embryo into a fully developed fetus, one is boiled and stirred around in the womb, as in a hot or even scalding pot; one is affected and shoved about by the twenty-eight different vital energies; and one is nurtured and developed by nutrients coming from the mother's blood and so forth. Therefore it says in *Nanda's Abiding in the Womb*:

> From the week-old embryo—the ovoid—
> a flesh bubble arises,
> and from this arises the oblong,
> the second-week embryo.
> This grows more solid,
> giving rise to the head and four limbs,
> and once the bones are well formed and connected,
> the body becomes complete.
> The cause of all this happening is karma.[97]

Then the "heading-downward" energy stirs, turning the head downward. The body leaves the womb, arms outstretched, experiencing pains that feel as though it were being drawn through an iron press. Some die in the process. Sometimes both mother and child die in childbirth.

At birth itself, when the child first has contact with surfaces, it suffers as though it has been thrown onto a bed of thorns. A little later, when wiped, it feels as though its skin is being peeled off and its body rubbed against a wall.

One's entire stay [in the womb] is as uncomfortable, confined, dark, and impure as just described: even if a really tough person were offered three measures of gold in return for putting up with being in that kind of an impure, filthy hole for just three days, could such a person manage it? The suffering of being in the womb is even worse than that. As it says in *Letter to a Student*:

> Stifled by unbearable smells and impurities,
> totally confined in utter darkness, staying in a womb is like being
> in hell
> because one has to put up with great suffering,
> while the body remains totally constricted. ŚI 19

Once convinced of this, think: "Who could possibly enter a womb even one more time?"

Although the *sufferings of aging* are also immeasurable, they can be summarized as tenfold: radical change in physique, hair, skin, complexion, abilities, prestige, quality of life, health, mental ability, and the life force itself.

1. There will be *marked physical change* as the body, previously strong and robust and holding itself erect, becomes bent, twisted, and needing to support itself with a stick.
2. There will be *marked change in hair.* Formerly jet black, it becomes white or is lost.
3. There will be *marked change in the skin*. Once as fine and smooth as Benares fine cloth or Chinese silk, it becomes coarse, lined, and heavily wrinkled, looking like braided copper bangles.
4. There will be *marked changes of complexion*. Once filled with

brightness and luster, like a freshly opened lotus, it now fades, becoming bluish or grayish, like an old, withered flower.

5. There will be *marked changes in ability and power*. The enthusiasm and ability that were previously enjoyed will change, as declining physical strength prevents the harder tasks from being undertaken and as mental decline takes away any enthusiasm for doing things. The sense faculties become blunt and lose their abilities, perceiving their objects in an unclear and confused way.
6. There will be *marked changes in prestige*. Although formerly praised and respected by others, the elderly wane in other people's esteem and become the object of inferiors' scorn. Even strangers find them unappealing, and they become the object of children's tricks and become a source of shame for their children and grandchildren.
7. There will be a *marked change in quality of life*. The pleasure given by possessions, food, and drink deteriorates. The body cannot feel properly warm, nor can the mouth find good taste in anything. There is a fancy for what is not available and difficulty getting others to get supplies or make food.
8. There will be *marked change in health*. Once stricken by old age, the greatest of ailments, there is suffering, for age brings on all the other diseases.
9. There will be a *marked change in mental ability*. Becoming senile and confused, the elderly forget almost immediately what has just been said or done.
10. When time is up, *life's end is reached*. Short of breath and starting to wheeze since all the component elements of the body have worn out, death is now at hand.

The *Vast Manifestation Sutra* says of all this:

> Old age turns a pleasant physique into an unpleasant one.
> Old age steals prestige and damages abilities and strength.
> Old age steals happiness and increases suffering.
> Old age is the maker of death and the robber of beauty.[98]

Although the *sufferings of sickness* are also immeasurable, they can be summed up as sevenfold: (1) being struck down by a powerful disease, (2) undergoing painful physical examinations, (3) having to take strong medicine, (4) being prevented from eating and drinking what is enjoyable, (5) having to follow the doctor's orders, (6) the diminution of wealth, and (7) fear of death. The *Vast Manifestation Sutra* says of this:

> Tormented by being prey to—and actually falling victim to—
> the sufferings of hundreds of maladies, they are like human
> ghosts.[99]

The *sufferings of death* are also countless. It says of them in the *Advice to a King Sutra*:

> Great King! Someone tormented like this, on the torture spike of death, is no longer so arrogant. Protectors, allies, or friends help you no more. Stricken by disease, the mouth is thirsty, the face changes, the limbs give way, you are unable to work, and you soil your body with saliva, snot, urine, and disgusting vomit, and you also wheeze noisily. The doctors abandon hope, and you sleep on your bed for the last time, sinking into the stream of samsara and becoming frightened of the lord of death's emissaries. The breathing stops, the mouth and nostrils gape. You leave this world behind and head for the next. It is the great departure, the entrance into deepest darkness, the fall over the greatest precipice, and the mighty ocean sweeping you away. Borne away by the winds of karma, you go to the place of no settling, and this without being able to take one iota of your possessions. Though you cry out "O Mother! O Father! Oh, my children!" there is, at that time, Great King, no other protector, no other refuge, no other ally, than Dharma.[100]

Then there is the *suffering of being separated from loved ones*. When father, mother, children, or friends die, there is immeasurable suffering, in the form of misery, grief, weeping, wailing, and the like.

The *suffering of encountering the unwanted* is the distress of conflict that occurs when meeting hated enemies. There are many sufferings, such as arguments, physical conflict, and so forth.

The last two types of suffering—the *strife of obtaining* and the *difficulty of maintaining*—are self-evident.

Demigods. Besides having suffering akin to that of the gods, the demigods also suffer from pride, jealousy, fighting, and quarrelling. It says:

> Demigods endure great mental torment because they are,
> by their very nature, resentful of the gods' splendors and enjoyments. SU 102AB

Gods. Gods of the desire realm suffer through having to fight off the demigods, through dissatisfaction due to their endless desires, and through losing their self-confidence. They also suffer by their limbs being severed and parts of their bodies being amputated, by being killed or expelled, and at the end of their lives, they suffer through death, losing their divine status and going to another existence. It is said:

> When death comes, divine child, five signs will appear: your clothes start to smell bad, flower garlands wither, your two armpits begin to sweat, foul smells arise from your body, and you begin to find seats uncomfortable.[101]

Gods of the form and formless dimensions do not have the above-mentioned sufferings. However, since they die, transmigrate, and do not have the power to remain in their state, they suffer through having to take birth in a lower state.

Likewise, once the good karma of humans or gods of any level is exhausted, they have to fall into states of suffering. Therefore the whole condition of samsara, the very nature of which is suffering, is like that of a house ablaze. To quote *Nanda's Abiding in the Womb*:

> Woe and alas! Because this immensity of self-perpetuating existence is ablaze, completely flaming, really burning, totally blazing, not even a few remain undefeated by it. What is this raging inferno? It is the fire of aggression, passion, and stupidity; the

> fire of birth, aging, and death; the fire of sorrow, lamentation, mental unhappiness, and unrest. Because these fires are constantly raging and blazing, no one escapes them.[102]

Knowing the sufferings of samsara to be just like that will, in itself, turn the mind away from the pleasures of worldly existence. To quote the scriptures, the *Meeting of Father and Son Sutra* states:

> Recognizing the sufferings of samsara,
> true weariness with it will arise,
> and fear of its three realms will
> stimulate a diligent abandoning of it.[103]

The great teacher Nāgārjuna has also said, in a similar vein:

> Since samsara is like that, there is no good birth
> as a god, a human, a hell being, a hungry spirit,
> or as an animal. So know rebirth to be
> a vessel for many harms. SU 103

This was the fifth chapter, explaining the sufferings of samsara, from this *Ornament of Precious Liberation, a Wish-Fulfilling Gem of Sublime Dharma.*

6. Karma and Its Effects

If you wonder what causes the sufferings described above, understand them to arise from tainted *karma* (actions). The *One Hundred* [*Stories*] *about Karma* says of this:

> Actions are of various kinds;
> those actions have created beings in all their variety.[104]

The *White Lotus of Great Compassion Sutra* says:

> The worlds have been made by actions. Their manifestation is due to actions. Sentient beings have been created by actions and have sprung from actions. Through action arises all their different types.[105]

The *Treasury of Higher Knowledge* says:

> The various worlds were generated by actions. AK 4:1A

If you wonder what exactly karma is, know that it falls into two areas: mental activity and activity set in motion by thought. The *Compendium of Higher Knowledge* says of this:

> What is karma? It is mental activity [itself] and mentally motivated action.[106]

The *Treasury of Higher Knowledge* says:

> *Karma* is intention and what is done because of that. AK 4:1B

Furthermore, in the *Fundamental Verses on the Middle Way* it says:

> The Supreme Sage has taught that *karma* means
> mental activity and that which is done because of thought.
> MMK 17:2

You may wonder what these two actually are. "Mental activity" means the actions of mind. "That which is done" means whatever physical and verbal activity has been intended and provoked by mind. The *Treasury of Higher Knowledge* says:

> Intention is mental activity;
> what it generates is physical and verbal activity. AK 4:1CD

The following synopsis outlines actions and the results they generate:

> **Actions and their consequences are summed up through six points: their categories, characteristics, ownership, apportionment, inflation, and ineluctability.**

First are its **categories**: (1) nonvirtuous actions and their effects,[107] (2) virtuous actions and their effects, (3) the action of unwavering karma and its effect.

The second point concerns the **characteristics** of these three.

Nonvirtuous actions and their effects. Although generally speaking there are very many sorts of nonvirtuous actions, they can be summarized as the *ten nonvirtues*. Three are physical: killing and so forth. Four are verbal: lying and so forth. Three are mental: avarice and so forth. Each of these is itself treated through three points: its categories, its results, and some particular instances.

Killing has three categories: killing through desire and attachment, killing through anger and aversion, and killing through confused ignorance. The first of these is to kill for the sake of meat, hides, and so forth; for sport or financial gain; or to safeguard yourself or loved ones. The second is to murder those you feel aversion for, on account of grudges or competition and the like. The third is done in order to make offerings.

The results of killing are also threefold: the ripened result, the result corresponding to the cause, and the dominant result. The ripened result is rebirth as a hell being. The result corresponding to the cause is that even if you are reborn human, you will have a short life and many sicknesses. The dominant result is to be reborn in an ill-fated and unattractive land.

The particular instance—the most heinous among all forms of killing—is to kill an arhat who is also your father.

Stealing has three categories: stealing by force, stealing by stealth, and stealing through cheating or fraudulence. The first of these is to steal with needless violence; the second is to steal unnoticed, by burglary and the like; and the third is to cheat through corrupt weights and measures.

Of the three types of result, the ripened result is rebirth as a hungry spirit. The result corresponding to the cause is that even if reborn human, you experience poverty. The dominant result is to be reborn in a place where there is much frost and hail.

The worst case of stealing, the most pernicious act, is to take wealth belonging to your guru or to the three precious refuges.

Sexual misconduct has three categories: sex proscribed by family ties, sex proscribed by belonging to someone else, and sex proscribed due to religious factors. The first of these is intercourse with parents, siblings, and so forth [blood relations]. The second is intercourse with someone committed to another person or belonging to a monarch. The third includes five areas of improper intercourse because of organs involved, place, time, degree, or manner. *Inappropriate organs* refers to oral or anal intercourse. An *inappropriate place* is in the proximity of a guru, temple, stupa, or large gathering. *Inappropriate times* are those when lay precepts are being observed, during pregnancy, while the mother is breastfeeding, or during daylight hours. An *inappropriate degree* is five or more times consecutively. *Inappropriate forms* of intercourse are the likes of rape and anal or oral intercourse with a person of the same sex or with a hermaphrodite.

Of the three types of result, the ripened result is rebirth as a hungry spirit. The corresponding result is that even if reborn human, your partner will be like a hateful enemy. The dominant result is to be reborn in a very dusty land. The worst case is the pernicious act of having intercourse with your own mother who also happens to be an arhat.

Lying is of three types: lies that are your undoing, big lies, and trivial lies. The first of these are those of false gurus and involve pretense about spiritual accomplishment. The second are lies told with the intention to benefit oneself or to harm others. The third are lies that are neither beneficial nor harmful.

Of the three types of result, the ripened result is rebirth as an animal. The corresponding result is that, even if reborn human, you are denigrated by others. The dominant result is to have bad breath. The worst case is the pernicious act of lying to your guru when you have slandered the Tathāgata.

Divisive speech is of three types: vehement, insinuated, or via third parties. The first separates friends by direct slander; the second separates them through insinuations made in their presence; and the third does so through rumors.

Of the three types of result, the ripened result is rebirth in hell. The corresponding result is that, even if reborn human, you will be separated from friends. The dominant result is birth in a place where the landscape is erratic and dangerous. The worst instance among such divisive speech acts is the pernicious act of causing a schism in the Sangha.

Wounding speech is of three types: direct, insinuated, or via third parties. The first is to tell someone openly of their faults and weaknesses. The second means to say hurtful things, in a half-disguised manner mingled with jest, relevant to someone present. The third is to gossip about someone's faults or weaknesses to their friends and third parties.

Of the three types of result, the ripened result is rebirth in hell. The corresponding result is that, even if reborn a human, the sounds and words you hear will be disturbing. The dominant result is rebirth in a hot and arid place where there is much evil. The worst instance, the most pernicious act of all wounding speech, is to speak harshly to your father or mother or to a realized being.

Useless speech is of three types: deluded useless speech, useless worldly chatter, and true but useless speech. The first concerns the formulas and recitations of deluded belief systems. The second concerns silly talk, jokes, and the like. The third concerns attempts to explain Dharma to those lacking respect or an appropriate frame of mind.

Of the three types of result, the ripened result is rebirth as an animal. The corresponding result is that, even if reborn a human, the person's words will carry no weight. The dominant result is rebirth in a place where the seasons are completely erratic. The worst instance, the most pernicious type of useless speech, is that which distracts those who are practicing Dharma.

Avarice is of three types: avarice concerning your own things, other people's things, and those things that belong to neither you nor others. The first is a grasping attachment to family status, physical appearance, qualities, wealth, and possessions, thinking, "There is no one quite like me." The second is to covet the good things others possess, thinking, "If only this were mine." The third involves attachment to things that belong to no one, such as the precious substances buried in the earth, thinking, "If only I could own that."

Of the three types of result of avarice, the ripened result is to be reborn as a hungry spirit. The corresponding result is that even if reborn human, avarice will dominate the mind. The dominant result is rebirth in a place where the quality of food is poor. Of all the sorts of avarice, the most pernicious is the wish to steal the possessions of those who have truly renounced the world.

Malevolence is of three types: due to hatred, jealousy, or resentment. The first is to contemplate killing another because of hatred, as happens in times of war. The second, due to competition and the like, is to think about killing or harming another through fear of being surpassed. The third, due to long-standing resentment, is to contemplate killing or hurting someone who has previously wronged one, or the like.

Of the three types of result of malevolence, the ripened result is rebirth in hell. The corresponding result is that even if reborn human, hatred dominates your mind. The dominant result is rebirth in a place where the food is bitter and coarse. Of all types of malevolence, the worst instance and most pernicious act is to plan to commit one of the five acts that have an immediate consequence.[108]

Aberrant belief is of three types: aberrant beliefs about actions and their consequences, about the truth(s), and about the precious refuges. The first of these means not believing that virtuous and nonvirtuous actions produce their respective consequences—happiness and suffering. The second is to consider that the truth of cessation will not be obtained through practice of the truth of the path.[109] The third is to deprecate the three precious refuges, believing them to be untrue.

Of the three types of result of aberrant belief, the ripened result is rebirth as an animal. The corresponding result is that even if reborn human, stupidity and confusion dominate your mind. The dominant result is rebirth in a place without harvests. The worst instance and most pernicious act among aberrant beliefs is to become caught up in the "thorn-like" view.[110]

The above was a general explanation of the ripened results of such actions. Three kinds of ripened results of an action can be distinguished according to the affliction present, the frequency of action, or the person acted on:

1. If the actions were done through anger or hatred, rebirth in hell is more likely. If they were done through passion or attachment, rebirth as a hungry spirit is more likely. If they were done through stupidity and confusion, rebirth as an animal is more likely. Thus the *Precious Garland* says:

> Through attachment, you will become a hungry spirit,
> through anger, you will be cast into hell,
> and through confusion, you become an animal. RA 3:29

2. Innumerable nonvirtuous acts lead to rebirth in hell. A great deal of nonvirtuous acts lead to rebirth as a hungry spirit. A few such harmful actions lead to rebirth as an animal.

3. If the nonvirtuous act is committed against a very special person, there may be rebirth in hell. If committed against someone of medium importance, there may be rebirth as a hungry spirit. If committed against a lesser person, there may be rebirth as an animal.

The above was an explanation of nonmeritorious actions and their consequences. To quote the *Precious Garland*:

> Attachment, anger, ignorance, and the actions
> to which they give rise are nonvirtue.
> Nonvirtue brings all the sufferings
> and hence all the lower states of existence. RA 1:20AB AND 21AB

Virtuous actions and their effects. First, we consider the actions. The ten virtuous actions consist of renouncing the nonvirtuous ones and, furthermore, engaging in their counterparts, the things that should be done: protecting the lives of others, giving lavishly, maintaining pure sexual conduct, speaking the truth straightforwardly, dispelling discord among people and bringing them into harmony, speaking peacefully and sincerely in a way that pleases others, speaking in a way that is meaningful, reducing desires and being content with what one has, cultivating loving kindness and the like, and penetrating the highest meaning.

These actions have threefold consequences. The ripened result is rebirth in the human or divine planes of the desire realm. The corresponding result will be, for instance, that by abandoning harm to others and by protecting life, longevity is gained, and similarly for the other virtues. The dominant result is that by giving up killing you will be reborn in a very prosperous and powerful place, and so on and so forth, according to the virtue concerned.

The above was an explanation of beneficial actions and their consequences. The *Precious Garland* says:

> What is generated by non-attachment,
> non-anger, and non-delusion is virtue.
> Virtue brings all fortunate rebirths
> and happiness in all lifetimes. RA 1:20CD AND 21CD

The action of unwavering karma and its effect. Cultivating the meditative attainment creates causes that give rise to rebirth in similar meditative states. These meditative attainments consist of the eight preparatory absorptions, the eight actual absorptions, and the special meditative attainment. Their consequences—birth in the absorption [realms]—consist of the seventeen types of form-realm gods and the four types of formless-realm gods. The general condition for these causes and effects to occur is the practice of the ten virtues.

The first of the meditative concentrations is propelled by meditatively cultivating its obstacle-removing stage. This is the preparatory attainment that removes inability. It leads into the first completing concentration proper, which is a meditative absorption accompanied by investigation, sustained analysis, joy, and bliss. Through cultivating this, there will be rebirth among the gods of the [first two] Brahma realms. By then cultivating the special aspect of this concentration, there will be rebirth in the Great Brahma heaven.

The second meditative concentration is propelled by meditatively cultivating its obstacle-removing stage, the preparatory attainment. This leads into the second completing concentration itself—a meditative absorption accompanied by joy and physical well-being but in which concept and analysis have been abandoned. By cultivating this, there will be rebirth among the gods of the second concentration, in the Small Light, [Limitless Light, and Radiant] heavens.

It is likewise for the propelling meditative attainment for the third and fourth meditative concentrations. By cultivating the actual meditative absorption of the third completing concentration, in which there is physical well-being but mental joy is abandoned, there will be rebirth among the third concentration gods of the Lesser Virtue, [Limitless Virtue, and Complete Virtue] heavens.

By cultivating the actual meditative absorption of the fourth completing concentration, in which investigation, sustained analysis, joy, and bliss have all been left aside, there will be rebirth among the fourth concentration gods of the Cloudless Heaven and so forth [up to Akaniṣṭha, eight heavens in all].

What arises having these four meditative concentrations is meditation on the Sphere of Infinite Space. Cultivating this gives rise to rebirth as a god of the Sphere of Infinite Space. Transcending this leads to meditation on the Sphere of Infinite Consciousness, and cultivating this gives rise to rebirth as a god of the Sphere of Infinite Consciousness. Transcending this leads to meditation on the Sphere of Nothing Whatsoever, and cultivating this gives rise to rebirth as a god of the Sphere of Nothing Whatsoever. Transcending this leads to meditation on the Sphere of Neither Cognition Nor Absence of Cognition, and cultivating this gives rise to rebirth as a god of the Sphere of Neither Cognition Nor Absence of Cognition.

What exactly is meant by the phrase "transcending this"? It means that the subsequent stage represents a transcendence of the previous mind condition and moves toward another condition that is freer from desire and attachment.

Are the spheres of Infinite Space and so forth so called because limitless space itself [and the others] are the actual object of meditation? No. The first three are called Infinite Space and so forth because the mind is anchored by evoking terms such as "infinite space" and so on during the meditative attainment. Later, when the preparatory stage is over, there is no such anchoring of the mind. The last of the four is so called because of its diminished cognition. Although there is barely any lucid cognition, it cannot be said that there is absolutely none at all.

All the eight actual absorptions consist of single-pointed, virtuous mind. With these the cause and effects of unwavering karma have been presented. The *Precious Garland* says:

> Through the absorptions, the immeasurables, and the formless
> [states],
> the happiness of Brahma [heaven] and so forth is experienced.
> RA 1:24

Thus the three kinds of tainted action described above [i.e., nonvirtuous, virtuous, and unwavering] give rise to the substance of samsara.

The third point is [**ownership**—the fact] that actions determine your personal lot. The consequences of the actions that someone has done will be experienced by that person alone: they come to maturity in the aggregates of their doer and in no one else. In the *Compendium of Higher Knowledge* it says:

> What does it mean, "Actions determine your personal lot"? Because individuals experience the full maturation of actions they themselves have done, and because that [maturation] shares nothing in common with others, it is called "personal."[111]

Were this not the case, then karma could dwindle or become exhausted, or someone might receive evil consequences from acts committed by someone else. This is why the sutra says:

> The deeds committed by Devadatta will not come to maturity in the earth or in water and so forth. They will come to maturity solely in his very own aggregates and sense spheres. In those of whom else could they possibly come to maturity?[112]

The fourth point is [**apportionment**—the fact] that experiences due to action are strictly apportioned. Happiness or suffering is infallibly experienced as the respective consequence of virtuous or harmful action. By accumulating virtuous action, happiness will be experienced as a result. By accumulating harmful action, suffering will be experienced as a result. The *Compendium of Higher Knowledge* says of this:

> How will experience be apportioned? Subject to the ripened result of actions, a person experiences his own share that

> corresponds specifically to the virtuous or nonvirtuous actions that have been done.[113]

The *Shorter Sutra on Mindfulness* says:

> Through virtue, one attains happiness.
> Through nonvirtue, suffering occurs.
> This is the reason for teaching clearly
> the virtuous and nonvirtuous actions and their consequences.[114]

And in the *Questions of Surata Sutra*:

> From the seeds of spicy plants,
> spicy fruits will grow;
> and from sweet seeds,
> sweet fruits will come to grow.
>
> Wise and skillful people should know
> through this example the full consequence of
> evil to be like the spicy [fruit]
> and bright action to be like the sweet.[115]

The fifth point is [**inflation**—the fact] that great results can be created by a small cause. It has been taught that it is possible even for a single moment of evil action to cause you to experience an eon in the hells. In *Guide to the Bodhisattva Way of Life* it says:

> The Sage has said that whoever generates an evil mind
> against a benefactor such as the bodhisattva
> will stay in hell for as many eons
> as there were moments of evil mind. BCA 1:34

It is also said that a person will experience suffering for five hundred existences for each instance of bad speech uttered, and so forth. The *Collection of Aphorisms* says:

Even a small bad action
can generate much fear and considerable damage
in a future existence:
it is like poison that has entered the system. UV 28:25

It is also the case that even a small virtuous act can induce great consequence. The *Collection of Aphorisms* says:

Even doing a small wholesome act
can produce great happiness in future existences
and create great consequence,
like grains that produce the most abundant harvests. UV 28:26

The sixth point is [**ineluctability**, the fact] that karma never just fades away. Except for the case of action that has been properly remedied, results will not be lost or become any weaker [with time], even though the karma may not ripen for endless eons. Although you may have been in a state of ease for a considerable period, the result will be induced whenever you encounter the requisite circumstances, whatever they may be.

Being convinced about actions and their consequences, as explained above, and fearing the sufferings of samsara, then, as it is said:

Someone who turns away from worldly happiness,
turns away from unwholesome action,
and strives for their own peace alone,
that person is referred to as "middling." BP 4

A "middling" person who cultivates such an approach would be the likes of the seven daughters of King Kṛkin.[116] Thus it says in the *One Hundred [Stories] about Karma*:

The karmas of physical beings are
not lost or weakened even for a hundred eons.
Once they are established, their results will ripen
whenever the appropriate time comes.[117]

In the *Shorter Sutra on Mindfulness*, it says:

> Fire may become cold,
> the wind may be caught by a lasso,
> and the sun and moon may fall down,
> but the consequences of karma are infallible.[118]

This concludes the sixth chapter, concerning actions and their effects, from this *Ornament of Precious Liberation, a Wish-Fulfilling Gem of Sublime Dharma*.

7. Loving Kindness and Compassion

Now I present, as the antidote to counteract attachment to solitary peace, the practice of compassion. "Attachment to solitary peace" means longing only for one's own nirvana and lacking altruistic activity due to absence of loving concern for sentient beings. This is the Hinayana. As it is said:

> When personal welfare takes priority, thinking,
> "To really benefit myself, I must ignore
> all the various things that need to be done to help others,"
> then self-interest has taken control.[119]

When loving kindness and compassion become part of you, you have so much care for other conscious beings that personal liberation alone would be unbearable. Therefore you need to cultivate loving kindness and compassion. Master Mañjuśrīkīrti has said:

> A follower of the Mahayana should not be without loving kindness and compassion for even a single moment.[120]

and

> It is not anger and hatred but loving kindness and compassion that vouchsafe the welfare of others.[121]

The development of loving kindness

The first of these two topics is loving kindness. The synopsis for this subchapter is:

> **Limitless loving kindness is well summarized by six topics: its categories, its focuses, the form it takes, the means of cultivating it, its measure, and its qualities.**

First, there are three **categories**: (1) loving kindness focused on sentient beings, (2) loving kindness focused on the nature of things, and (3) loving kindness with no objective reference. It says of these in the *Akṣayamati Sutra*:

> Loving kindness focused on sentient beings is that of bodhisattvas first cultivating bodhicitta; loving kindness focused on the nature of things is that of the bodhisattva engaged in the deeds; and loving kindness without any objective reference is that of bodhisattvas who have attained the forbearance accepting phenomena as unborn.[122]

Second, explaining [only] the first category of loving kindness, the **focus** includes each and every sentient being. Third, the **form it takes** is that of a mind longing for [all sentient beings] to find happiness. Fourth, the **way to cultivate loving kindness** is as follows. Since gratitude is the root of love, bring to mind the kindness of sentient beings. In this respect, the person who has been kindest to you in this life is your own mother. In what way? She has been kind by creating your body, kind through undergoing hardships [on your behalf], kind by nurturing your life, and kind by teaching you the ways of the world. The *Perfection of Wisdom in Eight Thousand Lines* says:

> Why is this? Mothers gave birth to us, underwent hardships, kept us alive, and taught us all about the world.[123]

First consider *the kindness of nourishing your body*. This body of yours did not start out fully grown, with its flesh fully developed and with a healthy complexion. It developed gradually inside your mother, through the different embryonic and fetal stages, being gradually created and nourished by vital fluids from her very own flesh and blood. It grew thanks to nourishment from the food she ate. It came into being by her having to put up with all sorts of embarrassment, sickness, and suffering. Furthermore, generally speaking, it was she who helped make this body, which started out a tiny infant, into [its present] bulk as big as a yak.

Next, consider *the kindness of undergoing hardships*. You did not come into this world clothed, finely adorned, with money in your pocket and provisions for the journey. When you came into this unfamiliar place, where you knew no one and had nothing, the only wealth you had was your howling mouth and empty stomach. Your mother gave you food so that you would not go hungry, drink to keep you from thirst, clothes to fend off the cold, and wealth to keep you from poverty. It was not as though she just gave you things she no longer needed herself: she herself went without food, without drink, and without new clothes.

Furthermore, not only did she sacrifice her happiness as far as this existence is concerned, she also deprived herself of using her assets [as offerings] to provide for her own prosperity in future lives. In brief, without regard for her own happiness in both this life and the next, she devoted herself to rearing and caring for you, her child. Nor did she obtain what was needed easily and pleasurably. To provide for you she was obliged to do harm, to suffer, and to toil. She did harm by having to resort to fishing, killing animals, and so on to provide for you. She suffered because what she gave you was the fruit of trading, laboring in the fields, and so forth, wearing the late evening or early morning frost for her boots, the stars as a hat, riding the horse of her calves, beaten by the whip of the long grass, her legs exposed to be bitten by dogs and her face exposed to the looks of men.

She also treated this undefined person who had become her child with more love than her own father, mother, or lama, even though she knew not who this being was or what you would become. She looked at you with loving eyes, gave you her gentle warmth, cradled you in her arms, and spoke to you with sweet words, saying, "My joy! Ah my sunshine, my treasure! Coochie coochie, aren't you Mummy's happiness?" and so forth.

Next, consider *the kindness of keeping you alive*. It is not as though you were born as you are now, knowing how to feed yourself and endowed with the necessary ability to accomplish difficult tasks. When you were helpless, useless—a little worm unable to think—your mother did not discard you but did an inconceivable number of things to nurture your existence. She took you on her lap, protected you from fire and water, held you away from dangerous precipices, got rid of all sources of harm, and prayed for you. At those times when she feared for your life or health, she resorted to divinations, astrology, exorcisms, recitations of texts, special ceremonies, and so on.

Finally, consider *the kindness of teaching you the ways of the world*. At first you were not the clever, experienced, strong-minded person you are now.

Apart from being able to bawl out to other members of your family and flap your limbs about, you were ignorant. When you did not know how to feed yourself, it was she who taught you how to eat. When you knew not how to dress yourself, it was she who taught you. When you did not know how to walk, it was she who taught you. When you could not even speak, it was she who taught you, repeating "Mama," "Dada," and so on. Having taught you various crafts and skills, she helped you become a balanced being, strengthening your weaker points and introducing you to the unfamiliar.

Moreover, apart from being your mother in this life, she has also been your mother in previous lives, an inestimable number of times, due to the unending round of existences that has been going on since time without beginning. The *Beginningless Time Sutra* says:

> Were one person to set down a little jujube kernel for every piece of earth, stone, plant, or forest that there is in the world and a second person to count them, eventually a time would come when the count would be completed. Yet were we to try to count the number of times that one being has been our mother, it would be impossible.[124]

The *Letter to a Friend* says:

> If you reduced the earth to little balls the size of jujube kernels,
> their number would be less than that of the number of times any
> one being has been your mother. SU 68CD

Recalling the kindness shown by her in the ways described above every time she was your mother in the past and contemplating it all, you will recognize that her kindness has been absolutely immeasurable. Bearing this carefully in mind, cultivate as sincerely and as frequently as possible a loving, positive mind longing for her happiness.

Furthermore, every sentient being has been your mother, and they have all shown you the same kindnesses enumerated above. Just how many sentient beings are there? Sentient beings are as vast as space itself. The *Prayer of Excellent Conduct* says:

> Whatever the farthest end of space may be,
> that is the limit of sentient beings' existence.[125]

Therefore a sincere mind that longs to benefit and bring happiness to all beings throughout space is to be cultivated as much as possible. When that has arisen, it is true loving kindness. The *Ornament of Mahayana Sutras* says:

> A bodhisattva acts toward sentient beings
> as though they were an only child,
> with a love so great coming from the very marrow of the bones,
> and thereby wishes to benefit them continuously. MSA 14:20

Great loving kindness is benevolence so strong that it brings tears to your eyes and makes the hairs of your body stand on end. *Limitless loving kindness* occurs when you no longer discriminate between beings.

The fifth point is the [**measure** or] gauge of accomplishment. Loving kindness has been achieved when your sole wish is for others' happiness and your mind no longer yearns for personal happiness alone.

Sixth, the [**qualities** or] benefits of cultivating loving kindness are immeasurable. The *Candraprabha Sutra* says:

> The merit of limitless offerings made to the Supreme Being,
> even if they fill a hundred quadrillion buddhafields, does not
> equal the benefit
> derived from a benevolent mind.[126]

The good results generated by even an instant's practice of loving kindness are countless. The *Precious Garland* says:

> The merit of offering, three times a day, every day,
> three hundred pots of food
> cannot even begin to compare with that created
> by one tiny instant of loving kindness. RA 3:83

Until buddhahood is attained, you will be benefitted in eight ways by this practice. These are described in the *Precious Garland*:

> Even before you achieve liberation, you will derive
> these eight[127] benefits from loving kindness:
> you will be loved by gods and humans,

and they will also protect you;
your mind will be happy and full of joy;
you will not be harmed by either poison or weapons;
all your aims will be effortlessly accomplished;
and you will take rebirth in the Brahma realms. RA 84–85

The practice of loving kindness also affords excellent protection. This is illustrated in the story of Mahādatta.[128] It also affords excellent protection for others, as illustrated by the example of King Bāla Maitreya.[129] Once loving kindness has been attained, it will not be difficult to cultivate compassion.

The training in compassion

The synopsis for this subchapter is:

> **Limitless compassion is well summarized by six topics: its categories, its object of reference, the form it takes, the means of cultivating it, its measure, and its qualities.**

First, there are three **categories**: (1) compassion focused on sentient beings, (2) compassion focused on the nature of things, (3) compassion with no particular focus.

The first kind is compassion that arises through understanding the sufferings of beings in the lower states of existence. The second occurs when there is familiarity with the meaning of the four truths of the noble ones and hence understanding of both causes and consequences, thereby counteracting belief in permanent, concrete realities. Compassion arises through realizing how much other beings are unaware of karmic cause and effect and how they perceive things as concrete and lasting. The third kind of compassion occurs when meditative penetration has brought realization of the emptiness of all phenomena. Extraordinary compassion then arises toward sentient beings who believe in real existence. As it says:

When, through meditative equipoise,
a bodhisattva becomes perfected through practice,
compassion arises in particular toward
those gripped by the demon of believing in reality.[130]

Of these three, only the development of the first will be discussed here.

Second, this first type of compassion has every sentient being as its **focus**.

Third, the **form** it takes is that of a mind longing for [each sentient being] to become free from suffering.

Fourth, the **way to cultivate compassion** is through reflections based on the mother. You imagine her right here, in front of you, being cut up by some people and being beaten, boiled, or burned by others. Or perhaps her body is completely frozen with cold, to a point where is it covered with cold sores, blistered, and cracked open. If this were really the case, would you not experience compassion for her? Since it is a definite fact that those beings suffering in hell have also been our mothers and that they are currently enduring such sufferings, how can compassion not arise toward them, too? Cultivate actual compassion by contemplating in this way and by wishing those beings to be free from suffering and its causes.

Equally, were your own mother to be right in front of you, tormented by hunger and thirst, afflicted by disease and pain, full of fear, utterly terrified and completely disheartened, would you not experience profound compassion for her? It is certain that those hungry spirits who suffer torments like these have all been your own mothers. How can you not feel compassion? Contemplate this and wish them to be freed from their sufferings.

Equally, were your own mother to be right in front of you, old and withered by age, and yet other people nevertheless made her labor as a defenseless slave, beat her hard, killed or chopped her up alive, would you not experience great compassion? It is certain that those beings born as animals are subject to these sufferings and that they were formerly your very own mothers. How can you not feel compassion? Contemplate this and wish them to be free from suffering.

Equally, were your own mother to be right in front of you, blind and near the edge of a precipice a thousand miles deep, unaware of her danger and without anyone who could lead her away or cry out, "Hey, be careful of the abyss!" and then she started wandering toward the edge, would you not experience very great compassion? It is certain that gods, demigods, and humans are all three standing at the edge of the abyss that is the lower states of suffering. Unaware of cause and effect, they do not know that to avoid falling they must give up unwholesome action and practice virtue. Because they do not benefit from the support of a Dharma teacher, they fall into and experience the three lower realms. As it is then so hard to get out of those states, how can you not feel great compassion for them, since they, too, were formerly your own mothers? Contemplate compassion thus and wish them all to be free of suffering.

Fifth, the [**measure**, or] gauge of accomplishment, is that compassion has been achieved when the shackles of cherishing oneself more than others have been cast off and when there is a real, rather than merely verbal, desire that all beings may be liberated from suffering.

Sixth, the [**qualities** or] benefits of this practice are immeasurable. The *Section Discussing the Realization of the Lord of the World* [in the *Perfectly Gathering the Qualities of Avalokiteśvara Sutra*] says:

> Were one thing like all enlightened qualities in the palm of your hand, what would it be? Great compassion![131]

The *Perfectly Gathering the Qualities* [*of Avalokiteśvara*] *Sutra* says:

> O Blessed One! It is like this: wherever the precious wheel of the universal monarch goes, it is automatically accompanied by all his attendant hosts. O Buddha! Wherever the great compassion of the bodhisattva goes, all enlightened qualities accompany it.[132]

Also, it says in the *Sutra of the Tathāgata's Secrets*:

> O master of the secret teaching [Vajrapāṇi]! The root of pristine awareness that knows everything lies in compassion.[133]

As taught above, loving kindness is the wish for the happiness of all beings, and compassion is the wish for them all to be free from suffering. When these are present, a person can no longer find contentment in striving solely for the happiness of personal peace and is joyful at the prospect of attaining buddhahood so as to benefit all beings. Therefore love and compassion constitute the remedy to clinging to the well-being of mere peace.

Once loving kindness and compassion have arisen, others will be cherished more than oneself. It is said:

> Those who, having understood their own suffering,
> aspire to totally eradicate

all the sufferings in every being
are most excellent individuals. BP 5

Among those who have become such "excellent individuals" were the brahman Mahādatta and so forth.

This concludes the seventh chapter, concerning love and compassion, from this *Ornament of Precious Liberation, a Wish-Fulfilling Gem of Sublime Dharma.*

8. Taking Refuge

Now, as an antidote for ignorance of the means for attaining buddhahood, I present the factors associated with generating bodhicitta. For this, the synopsis is the following:

> **The development of supreme bodhicitta is covered through twelve topics: basis, nature, different types, aim, causes, source from which the vow is taken, ceremony, benefits, failings, causes for breakage, methods of restoration, and instructions.**

First topic: The basis for cultivation of bodhicitta

First, the sentient beings that constitute a suitable **basis** for the cultivation of bodhicitta are those who: (1) belong to the Mahayana, (2) have taken refuge in the three most precious refuges, (3) have taken one of the seven classes of prātimokṣa vows, and (4) have developed the aspiration aspect of bodhicitta.

Whereas to have taken refuge in the three precious refuges is the minimum requirement for a life becoming a suitable basis for aspiration bodhicitta, the above four conditions make that life also a proper basis for cultivating engaged bodhicitta.[134] Why is this? It is explained in *Bodhisattva Levels* that aspiration must precede actual practice, and it is explained in *Lamp for the Path to Awakening* that one needs to have taken refuge in order to develop aspirational [mind]. Furthermore, the latter text also states that you need one of the prātimokṣa vows as a foundation for the bodhisattva vow, and in the *Treasury of Higher Knowledge* it says that refuge is the basis on which the prātimokṣa vows are taken. Lastly, *Bodhisattva Levels* says that bodhicitta development cannot even occur in those who are not of the Mahayana type. Thus a combination of all these various factors must be present.

The first point is that there needs to be the Mahayana potential in general, and more particularly that this needs to have been awakened.[135] These points can be understood from the fuller explanation above.[136]

The second point concerns the need to have taken refuge. Should you seek refuge in powerful worldly deities, such as Brahma, Viṣṇu, Śiva, and so forth, or in powerful local forces such as gods or serpent spirits that inhabit mountains, rocks, lakes, ancient trees, and the like? These are not true refuges because none of them has the power to be a refuge. A sutra says of this:

> People of the world seek protection
> from the gods of the mountains and forests,
> from shrines and offering groves, and from sacred trees,
> but these refuges are not true refuges.[137]

Should you then perhaps seek refuge in your parents, friends, relatives, and so forth—those beings who care about you and are glad to help? In fact, these cannot be a refuge either. It says in the *Sutra of the Play of Mañjuśrī*:

> Parents are not your refuge;
> neither are loved ones or relatives.
> Subject to their own wishes,
> they abandon you and go where they please.[138]

Why are none of these able to provide refuge? Because to constitute a refuge, there must be no fear [of samsara] and there must be liberation from its sufferings. None of the above has transcended fear, and they are still subject to suffering. Other than buddhas, no one is definitively liberated from suffering. Other than Dharma, there is no way to achieve buddhahood. Other than the Sangha, there are none who can help us practice Dharma. Hence refuge should be sought in those three. It is said:

> Today, take your refuge in the Buddha,
> in the Dharma, and in the supreme community, the Sangha,
> for it is they who can dispel fear in the fearful
> and it is they who can protect the unprotected.[139]

Since they do possess the ability to protect, do not let yourself be devoured by doubt, wondering, "But can they really protect me once I have taken refuge in them?" The *Great [Passing into] Nirvana Sutra* says:

> One who has taken refuge in the Three Jewels
> will attain fearlessness.[140]

The synopsis explaining refuge in those three is:

> **Taking refuge is summarized through nine topics: categories, basis, source, duration, motivation, ceremony, function, instruction, and benefits.**

First, there are two different **categories** of refuge: general and particular.

Second, there are two types of person who form a **basis** for taking refuge: (1) those who constitute the general basis; people who fear samsara's sufferings and who conceive of the three precious refuges as deities, and (2) those who constitute the particular basis; people of Mahayana potential who have a relatively pure human or divine existence.

Third, there are also two **sources** of refuge:

1. *The general source*: The most precious Buddha is the Blessed One, awakened and complete, who has the most excellent purity, pristine awareness, and greatness of nature. The most precious Dharma has two aspects: the Dharma of teachings, comprising the twelve branches of [the Buddha's] supreme speech, and the Dharma as realization, comprising the truths of cessation and the path. The most precious Sangha is also twofold: the Sangha composed of worldly people, as a gathering of four or more full monks (*bhikṣu*) who have properly maintained their vows; and the most excellent Sangha, as the eight types of beings belonging to the four stages of result.[141]

2. *The special source*: This is explained as the source actually present, the source that is direct realization, and the ultimate source. For the *source actually present*, the Buddha is an image of the Tathāgata, the Dharma is the Mahayana scriptures, and the Sangha is the bodhisattva sangha. For the *source in terms of direct realization*, the Buddha is the one possessing the nature of the three bodies, the Dharma is the sublime Dharma of peace and nirvana, and the Sangha is bodhisattvas who have attained the levels of

sublime realization. The *ultimate source*, in terms of ultimate essence, is the Buddha alone. About this the *Uttaratantra* says:

> In ultimate terms the refuge for beings is
> the Buddha and the Buddha alone . . . RGV I:21AB

Why is the Buddha capable of providing the [only] totally dependable source of refuge?

> . . . because the Sage possesses the dharmakāya
> and in terms of the Sangha he is the ultimate sangha. RGV I:21CD

Sages (*muni*), free from generation and cessation, totally pure, and without desire, are the highest refuge because they possess the dharmakāya and because they are the ultimate achievement of the Sangha of the three vehicles, having attained the dharmakāya, the ultimate conclusion of total purity. This being the case, are the Dharma and the Sangha lasting refuges or not? The *Uttaratantra* says:

> The two aspects, Dharma and the assembly of noble ones,
> are not the supreme lasting refuge. RGV I:20CD

Why is it that they are not a lasting source of refuge? Of the two types of Dharma, the Dharma as teachings, being a collection of terms and an assembly of letters, is something to be abandoned once it has served its purpose, like a vehicle once the journey is done. Hence it is not a lasting refuge. As for the two aspects of Dharma as realization, the truth of the path is not a refuge because it is by its very nature unreliable, being impermanent on account of being a composite creation. The truth of cessation is not a lasting refuge because, according to the śrāvakas, it is a nonexistence—the end of a continuum—like the extinction of a flame. As for the Sangha, they themselves take refuge in the Buddha through fear of samsara and cannot constitute a supreme and lasting refuge because of having that fear. The *Uttaratantra* says:

> Because they are to be abandoned, unreliable,
> nonexistent, and endowed with fear:

> the two aspects, Dharma and the assembly of noble ones,
> are not the supreme lasting refuge. RGV 1:20

Therefore Master Asaṅga said:

> The inexhaustible refuge, the permanent refuge, the eternal refuge, the most elevated refuge is one and one only. What is it? It is the Tathāgata, the defeater of the enemy, the totally and utterly perfect Buddha.[142]

Well, then, does this not contradict what has been said above about the three refuges? The latter originated as a skillful means for guiding those training as Buddhists. The *Great Liberation Sutra* says:

> In brief, the refuge is one, but in terms of method it is three.[143]

How are these three refuges presented as skillful means? The *Uttaratantra* says:

> The three refuges are presented
> as teacher, teaching, and those training,
> in terms of the three vehicles, three activities,
> and in accordance with [diverse] aspirations. RGV 1:19

Thus the refuges are presented in terms of three qualities, three capacities, three modes of action, and three types of aspiration: (1) Emphasizing the qualities of the teacher, those of bodhisattva capacity, as well as those who aspire to actions that principally elevate the Buddha, take refuge in the Buddha saying, "I take refuge in the Buddha, the most sublime human." (2) Emphasizing the qualities of the teachings, beings of pratyekabuddha capacity, and those aspiring to act in a way that principally elevates the Dharma, take their refuge in the Dharma saying, "I take refuge in the Dharma, the most sublime of all that transcends desire and attachment." (3) Emphasizing the qualities of the trainees, those of śrāvaka capacity, and those who aspire to act in a way principally focused on the Sangha, take refuge in the Sangha saying, "I take refuge in the Sangha, the most sublime of communities."

Thus the above three points present the three refuges in terms of six types of person. The noble Buddha has taught that these are mere conventional realities, designed to help beings progress gradually through their respective courses of training.

Fourth, there are two possible **durations**. The *general duration* is to take refuge from the time [of the ceremony] onward for as long as one lives. The *special duration* is to take refuge from that time onward until the essence, enlightenment, is attained.

Fifth, there are two possible **motivations**. The *general motivation* is to consider personal suffering unbearable. The *special motivation* is to consider others' sufferings unbearable.

Sixth, there are two forms of **ceremony**, general and special. For the *general ceremony*, the refuge seeker first requests refuge from the teacher. Then the teacher either makes offerings to the three precious refuges as a prelude to the ceremony or, when there are no representations present, visualizes them in space and makes mental homage and offerings. Then the refuge seeker repeats the following three times, after the teacher, with utmost sincerity:

> All buddhas and bodhisattvas, please heed me, I pray. Master, please heed me, I pray. I, [so-and-so] by name, take refuge from now until I reach the essence—enlightenment—in the Buddha, the most sublime of all humans, in the Dharma, the most sublime of all that transcends desire, and in the Sangha, the most sublime of communities.

The *special ceremony* is in three parts: a preparation, the actual ceremony, and a conclusion.

The preparation involves first offering a mandala, together with flowers, to an appropriate preceptor, after which the preceptor is requested to confer refuge. Provided the supplicant is a suitable person and someone with Mahayana potential, the preceptor, having accepted the request, will, on the first evening, set up representations of the three precious refuges, arrange offerings, and explain both the benefits of taking refuge and the shortcomings of not doing so.

The actual ceremony takes place on the second evening. The supplicant first cultivates the notion that the [symbols of refuge] on the shrine are the real presence of the most precious refuges, and then pays homage and makes prostrations to them. The following words are then repeated three times, after the preceptor:

> All buddhas and bodhisattvas, please heed me, I pray. Master, please heed me, I pray. From this moment on, until the essence of enlightenment is reached, I, [so-and-so] by name, take my refuge in the buddhas, the blessed ones who are the most sublime humans. I take refuge in the Dharma that is peace and nirvana, the most sublime of all that is free from desire and attachment. I take refuge in the Sangha of realized bodhisattvas who are beyond turning back, the most sublime of communities.

Then, inviting the sources of refuge in terms of direct realization and imagining them to be really present, homage is paid to them and offerings made, thinking, "Whatever I do, you are aware of it." Following this, the refuge prayer, as above, is repeated.

> Next, in terms of the one-and-only essence as a source of refuge, homage is expressed, offerings are made, and refuge is taken in a way in which the three spheres[144] are totally pure. Since all phenomena have been, from the very beginning, without self-entity and without any truly existing nature, the Buddha, Dharma, and Sangha must be envisioned as also being thus. This is the inexhaustible refuge, the permanent refuge, the eternal refuge. Thus the *Questions of Nāga King Anavatapta Sutra* says: What is it to have taken refuge with a mind free from pollution? By knowing all phenomena not to exist, by not envisioning them as being form, as possessing characteristics, or as being something, but by envisioning them as being totally pure awakened realities,[145] refuge has been taken in the Buddha. By envisioning all phenomena as following after dharmadhātu,[146] refuge has been taken in the Dharma. By envisioning them in a way that is nondual and without conceptual elaboration, refuge has been taken in the Sangha.[147]

On the third evening, there is the concluding ceremony, during which thanksgiving offerings are made to the most precious sources of refuge.

Seventh, concerning the **function** of refuge the *Ornament of Mahayana Sutras* says:

> It is the highest refuge because
> it protects from all sorts of harm,
> from the lower states, from unskillful action,
> from the ego-view of the perishable composite,[148] and from lesser vehicles. MSA 10:7

The general refuge protects from all harms, from falling into the lower states, from ineffective courses of action, and from false beliefs about the self based on the perishable collection (the aggregates). The particular refuge protects from the lower paths as well.

Eighth, the **instructions** concerning refuge are ninefold: three common instructions, three particular instructions, and three specific instructions.

The three instructions *common* [to all three refuges] are: (1) to strive at all times to make offerings to the three precious refuges, at least dedicating the first mouthful of food when eating; (2) to never abandon the three precious refuges even should this cost life itself or involve personal loss; and (3) to develop the habit of repeatedly calling to mind the qualities of these three most precious things and taking refuge in them.

The three *particular* instructions are: (1) Having taken refuge in the buddhas, refuge need no longer be sought in any other divinity. In the *Great [Passing into] Nirvana Sutra* it says:

> The best of all those who love virtue are
> those who have taken refuge in the buddhas.
> They will never go soliciting
> refuge from other divinities.[149]

(2) Having taken refuge in the Dharma, harm should no longer be done to any sentient being. The sutra says:

> Having taken refuge in the noble Dharma,
> a person is removed from a mentality of harm and violence.[150]

(3) Having taken refuge in the Sangha, trust should not be placed in the misguided (*tīrthika*).[151] The sutra says:

> Those who have taken refuge in the Sangha
> will not side with the tīrthikas.[152]

The three *specific* instructions are: (1) Respect should be shown for images of the Tathāgata, whatever they may be, from a small image molded in clay upward, because they represent the real, most precious Buddha. (2) Respect should be shown for the volumes and collected works of scripture, from a mere letter of scripture upward, because they represent the most precious Dharma. (3) Respect should be shown for Buddhist garb, from a simple patch of yellow cloth upward, because it represents the most precious Sangha.

Ninth, eight [principal] **benefits** come from taking refuge: (1) A person becomes a Buddhist. (2) It is the basis for all the [other] precepts. (3) All evils formerly committed will be consumed. (4) Hindrances created by humans or nonhumans can no longer overwhelm [the person]. (5) All that is wished for will be achieved. (6) Great causal merit is accrued.[153] (7) The person will not fall into the lower states and (8) will soon become truly and perfectly enlightened.

The first point in this overall section on the persons whose lives constitute a basis for bodhicitta discussed the necessity of [having] Mahayana potential, [that is, belonging to the Mahayana fold]. The second concerned the need to have taken refuge, as explained above. The third point deals with the need to have taken one of the prātimokṣa commitments.

Prātimokṣa vows

There are four main types of prātimokṣa vows, which, when considered through the individuals [males and females] who take them, make eight categories. Of these, if you disregard the temporary precepts observed when fasting,[154] there are seven types. Whichever one of these seven is appropriate is adopted. The seven classes of prātimokṣa commitment are those of the monk, nun, novice monk, trainee nun, novice nun, ordained layman, and ordained laywoman.[155] *Bodhisattva Levels* says of these:

> The seven categories of those who have most properly adopted the precepts of prātimokṣa are these: those [observing] the moral discipline of the monk, nun, novice monk, trainee nun, novice nun, ordained layman, and ordained laywoman. According to their content, these precepts are those of laypersons or renunciates, as appropriate.[156]

Now, one might ask, "Why is it that one needs to have prātimokṣa vows as a prerequisite for generating the engaged bodhicitta?" They should understand this need for such vows as a basis [for engaged bodhicitta] in three ways: by simile, by scriptural authority, and by reason.

The first way is by *simile*. A place to which a great universal monarch is invited to come and stay should not be filled with impurities such as dung and rubbish. It should be an excellent dwelling place, spotlessly clean and decorated with many fine adornments made of precious substances and the like. It should be a pleasing place. Likewise, when someone is cultivating the great monarch bodhicitta and hoping for it to remain, the "place" where it can abide is not in a person who is not committed to avoiding wrong physical, verbal, and mental actions. It is not in one who is tarnished by the stains of evil. It is to be invited to reside in someone without the stains of physical, verbal, and mental evil, someone whose physical existence is properly adorned with the moral discipline of commitment.

The second way is by *scriptural authority*. In the bodhicitta section of the *Ornament of Mahayana Sutras* it says, "Its basis is extensive vows" (MSA 5:4). The temporary lay vows are of limited extent because they only last for a day and a night. Unlike this, the other seven classes are extensive commitments, and this is why those seven are taught as constituting the foundation for bodhicitta. Further, *Lamp for the Path to Awakening* states:

> Only those who have the lasting commitment
> in one of the seven classes of prātimokṣa vows
> are suitable for the bodhisattva vow;
> it is not so for others. BP 20

This is explained as meaning that you should observe whichever one of those seven types is appropriate.

The third way is by *logical necessity*. Through the prātimokṣa vows, you abandon harm to others along with its basis. Through the bodhisattva vows, you benefit others. There is no way in which you can benefit others without first renouncing harming them. However, according to some people, the prātimokṣa vows are not necessarily a prerequisite for giving rise to the bodhisattva vow because hermaphrodites, eunuchs, gods, and so on who are unable to take the prātimokṣa vows *are* able to give rise to bodhicitta. Some also assert that the prātimokṣa precepts cannot be a prerequisite because they expire at death, whereas the bodhisattva commitment does not.

If you wonder about these points, understand that the prātimokṣa precepts fall into three categories, determined by the attitude with which they are taken: (1) When these vows are taken because of a motivation to reach happiness in the three dimensions of existence, they are called *the moral discipline of vested interest.* (2) When they are taken with the wish of being rid of suffering forever, they are known as *the moral discipline of śrāvaka renunciation.* (3) When they are taken through a wish to achieve great enlightenment, they are called *the moral discipline of the bodhisattva vow.*

The first two of the above cannot be taken by hermaphrodites, eunuchs, gods, and the like. They finish at death and cannot be restored if damaged, and so they are not the foundation for the bodhisattva vow. The moral discipline of the bodhisattva vow can be taken by hermaphrodites, eunuchs, gods, and so on, is not lost at death, and can be restored if damaged. For these reasons it is the prerequisite for both taking and keeping the bodhisattva vow. Thus it says in the commentary to the *Ornament of Mahayana Sutras*:

> What is the foundation of that mentality? The vow of bodhisattva moral discipline is its foundation.[157]

Therefore prātimokṣa precepts are needed as a basis for giving rise to bodhicitta but are not necessarily required as a continuous basis for maintaining bodhicitta.

> This is a similar case to the meditative concentration vow being a necessary basis for giving rise to the untainted vow but not necessarily required for the latter's continuance.[158]

There is no need to take the bodhisattva prātimokṣa precepts through a special ceremony. If they have already been taken as part of śrāvaka training, they will still be extant when the mind has the special inspiration [of bodhicitta] and will automatically become the bodhisattva's prātimokṣa commitment, since the lesser motivation will have been abandoned but not the spirit of renouncing harming others.

Thus we have seen that someone who has Mahayana potential, who has taken refuge in the three most precious refuges, and who has taken whichever is appropriate of the seven classes of prātimokṣa vow is a suitable person for giving rise to bodhicitta.

This concludes the eighth chapter, concerning refuge and taking precepts, from this *Ornament of Precious Liberation, a Wish-Fulfilling Gem of Sublime Dharma.*

9. The Proper Adoption of Bodhicitta

Second topic: The essential nature of bodhicitta development

Having explored the first point, the basis for bodhicitta, at length, the second point defines the **essential nature** of bodhicitta development, which is a wish for utterly pure and perfect enlightenment so as to be able to benefit others. This is clearly defined in the *Ornament of Clear Realization*:

> Developing bodhicitta means wanting
> utterly perfect enlightenment for the sake of others. AA 1:18AB

Third topic: Types of bodhicitta

The **different types** of supreme bodhicitta are described in three ways: by simile, according to what demarcates levels, and according to their characteristics.

The *similes* typifying bodhicitta, from that of an individual person through to that of a buddha, were taught by Ārya Maitreya in the *Ornament of Clear Realization*:

> These are the twenty-two examples:
> earth, gold, the moon, fire,
> treasure, a jewel mine, an ocean,
> a vajra, a mountain, medicine, a Dharma master,
> a wish-fulfilling gem, the sun, a song,
> a king, a treasury, a highway,
> a carriage, a reservoir,
> melodious sounds,[159] a river, and a cloud. AA 1:19–20

These twenty-two similes cover bodhicitta from [initial] aspiration through to [final] dharmakāya. To relate these to the five phases of the path: (1) Bodhicitta endowed with aspiration is like the *earth*, for it serves as the foundation for all good qualities. (2) Bodhicitta endowed with commitment is like *gold*, for it will not change until enlightenment is achieved. (3) Bodhicitta endowed with profound commitment is like the waxing *moon*, for [with this] every virtuous quality will increase. These three constitute the beginner's stage, that is, the lower, middle, and higher sections of the path of accumulation.

(4) Bodhicitta endowed with integration is like *fire*, for it burns as its fuel the obstacles to the threefold wisdom, such as omniscience. This is encompassed by the path of application.

(5) Bodhicitta endowed with the perfection of generosity is like a *great treasure*, for it brings satisfaction to all beings. (6) Bodhicitta endowed with the perfection of moral discipline is like a *jewel mine*, for it acts as the supporting ground for precious qualities. (7) Bodhicitta endowed with the perfection of forbearance is like an *ocean*, for [with this] one remains untroubled by whatever unwanted things occur. (8) Bodhicitta endowed with the perfection of diligence is like a *vajra*, for one remains indestructible. (9) Bodhicitta endowed with the perfection of meditative concentration is like a *mountain*, for one remains unshaken by distractions posed by the mind's objects of attention. (10) Bodhicitta endowed with the perfection of wisdom is like *medicine*, for it pacifies the sicknesses that are the affliction and knowledge obscurations. (11) Bodhicitta endowed with the perfection of skillful means is like a *Dharma master*, for [with this] one never relents from bringing benefit to beings, no matter what the circumstances. (12) Bodhicitta endowed with the perfection of aspiration is like a *wish-fulfilling gem*, for [with it] one achieves whatever result is wished. (13) Bodhicitta endowed with the perfection of powers is like the *sun*, for it helps bring disciples to full maturity. (14) Bodhicitta endowed with the perfection of pristine awareness is like the *melody of Dharma songs*, for [with it] one gives disciples Dharma teachings that inspire them. These ten, mentioned above, correspond in their respective order to the ten bodhisattva levels, from the Joyous [the first level] to the tenth. Thus they lie within the sphere of the path of seeing and the path of cultivation.[160]

(15) Bodhicitta endowed with clear awareness is like a powerful *king*, for with it one benefits others with unimpeded power. (16) Bodhicitta endowed with the wealth of goodness and pristine awareness is like a *treasury*, for one

becomes a storehouse of many accumulations. (17) Bodhicitta endowed with the factors conducive to enlightenment is like a great *highway*, for with it one treads the way that all the noble ones have trod. (18) Bodhicitta endowed with great compassion and deeper insight is like a *carriage*, for with it one travels directly to one's goal, straying into neither samsara nor the mere peace of nirvana. (19) Bodhicitta endowed with *dhāraṇī*[161] and prowess is like a *reservoir*, for with it everything learned through study or otherwise is retained and not wasted. These five are encompassed by the special bodhisattva path.

(20) Bodhicitta endowed with the "beautiful garden of Dharma" is like listening to *melodious sounds*, for it makes those disciples keen on liberation eager to listen. (21) Bodhicitta endowed with the one and only way [traveled by all the buddhas] is like the flow of a great *river*, for with it one never deviates from the purpose of benefitting others. (22) Bodhicitta endowed with the dharmakāya is like a rain *cloud*, for on it depends the bringing about of the welfare of sentient beings, such as through demonstrating the deed of residing in Tuṣita Paradise. These last three points are encompassed within the stage of buddhahood. Thus the twenty-two [aspects of bodhicitta presented by means of similes] cover the entire path from the beginner's level through to buddhahood.

Classified in terms of *what demarcates levels*, bodhicitta is fourfold: (1) bodhicitta endowed with aspiration, (2) bodhicitta endowed with extraordinary intention, (3) bodhicitta in its full maturity, and (4) bodhicitta with obscurations eliminated. The first of the above corresponds to the levels of practice motivated by aspiration; the second applies to the first seven great bodhisattva levels; the third, to the eighth through tenth levels; and the fourth, to the level of buddhahood. Thus the *Ornament of Mahayana Sutras* says:

> Bodhicitta on the various levels is held
> to be accompanied by aspiration, pure extraordinary intention,
> full maturity,
> and the elimination of all obscurations. MSA 5:2

Classified in terms of *essential characteristics* bodhicitta is twofold: the ultimate bodhicitta and the relative bodhicitta. As the *Sutra Definitely Elucidating the Noble Intention* says:

> There are two aspects to bodhicitta: ultimate bodhicitta and relative bodhicitta.[162]

What, then, is ultimate bodhicitta? It is emptiness having compassion as its very essence, an unvacillating state that is lucidity, free of the extremes of conceptual elaboration. Therefore the sutra says:

> Of those, ultimate bodhicitta is that vivid clarity that transcends the world, without any extreme of conceptual elaboration, extremely clear, having the ultimate meaning as its object, unpolluted and unwavering, as still as a flame protected from the breeze.[163]

And what would relative bodhicitta be? Quoting the same sutra:

> Relative bodhicitta is the commitment, through compassion, to lead all sentient beings out of samsara.[164]

Of the two forms of bodhicitta mentioned above, it is stated in the *Ornament of Mahayana Sutras* (MSA 5:7–8) that ultimate bodhicitta is attained by realizing suchness, while relative bodhicitta arises through language in the form of adopting it [in a valid ritual]. Furthermore, the *Detailed Exposition of the Ornament of Mahayana Sutras* says:

> At what stage is there ultimate bodhicitta? From the first great bodhisattva level, the Joyous, onward.[165]

In terms of categories, relative bodhicitta has two aspects: *aspiration bodhicitta* and *engaged bodhicitta*. Thus *Guide to the Bodhisattva Way of Life* says:

> Bodhicitta can be summed up
> as being known through two aspects:
> the mind aspiring to enlightenment
> and the mind proceeding to enlightenment. BCA 1:15

There are many different explanations of the particularities of these two aspects of relative bodhicitta—aspiration and engagement. According to Master Śāntideva, of the tradition stemming from Ārya Mañjuśrī through

Master Nāgārjuna, *aspiration* is like a wish to go and comprises in reality all intentions longing for perfect buddhahood, whereas *engagement* is like the actual going and is in reality the practical application of all that will achieve buddhahood. Thus *Guide to the Bodhisattva Way of Life* says:

> Just as wanting to go and actually going
> are known to be different,
> so should these two be respectively
> distinguished by the wise. BCA 1:16

According to the great Serlingpa, of the lineage stemming from Ārya Maitreya through Master Asaṅga, aspiration is to make a promise committing oneself to the result, thinking, "For the benefit of all sentient beings I will attain perfect buddhahood," whereas engagement is to make a promise committing oneself to the cause, thinking, "I will train in the six perfections as the cause of buddhahood." In line with this interpretation, the *Compendium of Higher Knowledge* says:

> Those who develop bodhicitta are of two types: those who are not special and those who are particularly excellent. Of these, those who are not special think, "Oh, if only I could become totally enlightened in unsurpassable, totally pure, and perfect buddhahood." Those who are particularly excellent think, "May I totally accomplish the perfection of generosity . . . and so forth . . . through to the perfection of wisdom."[166]

Fourth topic: The focus of bodhicitta

Fourth, the **focus** of bodhicitta encompasses both enlightenment and the welfare of sentient beings. It says of this in *Bodhisattva Levels*:

> Hence bodhicitta is something focused on enlightenment and focused on sentient beings.[167]

Of these two, bodhicitta focused on enlightenment is that which is focused on striving for Mahayana pristine awareness. In the chapter in the *Ornament of Mahayana Sutras* concerning bodhicitta development it says:

> . . . likewise that which it is focused on is pristine awareness.
> MSA 5:3D

That which is focused on sentient beings does not mean focused on just one, two, or several beings. Space is pervaded, for as far as it stretches, by conscious life forms, and they in turn are permeated by karma and affliction. Wherever the latter pervade, suffering pervades also. Bodhicitta is developed to remove those beings' sufferings. Thus the *Prayer of Excellent Conduct* says:

> Whatever may be the limits of space,
> they are the limits of sentient beings.
> They are also the limits of karma and the afflictions,
> and they are the limits of my aspirations as well.[168]

Fifth topic: The causes of bodhicitta

Fifth, concerning the **causes for bodhicitta development**, the *Ten Dharmas Sutra* says:

> Such a mind will arise on account of four causes: insight into the benefits and qualities of such a mentality, faith in the Buddha, recognition of the sufferings of sentient beings, and proper encouragement from a Dharma teacher.[169]

Further, *Bodhisattva Levels* says:

> What are the four causes for that? (1) The first cause for the arising of the bodhisattva mind is that of possessing the very best potential. (2) The second cause for the arising of the bodhisattva mind is to be properly supported by the buddhas, bodhisattvas, and by Dharma teachers. (3) The third cause for the arising of the bodhisattva mind is to have compassion for sentient beings. (4) The fourth cause for the arising of the bodhisattva mind is fearlessness in the face of samsara's suffering and the sufferings of undergoing hardships, even though these may be long enduring, manifold, difficult to cope with, and without respite.[170]

In the *Ornament of Mahayana Sutras*, separate causes are mentioned for the generation of the two aspects of bodhicitta: (1) generation of a verbally arisen bodhicitta on the basis of having received it through a perfect ritual and (2) generation of ultimate bodhicitta. With respect to the first it says:

> Through the power of support, of the cause, and of the root,
> of learning, and of virtuous habits,
> it is taught that, respectively, stable and unstable bodhicitta
> and bodhicitta taught by others will emerge. MSA 5:7

The generation of "bodhicitta taught by others" refers to that which has arisen on the basis of others' revelatory speech (*vijñapti*) and is also known as "that which is properly received and occurs by means of words." This is relative bodhicitta. Within this there are those that arise through the power of *support*—that is, through the presence of a Dharma teacher. Then there are those that arise through the power of *cause*, meaning by the force of our natural potential; those that arise through the power of the *root* of virtue, meaning the activation of that potential; those arising through the power of *learning*, when the varieties and meaning of the Dharma are explained; and those that arise through the power of *virtuous habits*, through whatever has been routinely studied, directly understood, firmly adhered to, and so forth in this life.

Of the above, that which arose through the power of support is nonenduring, while those that arose through the power of the cause and the rest endure.

As to the cause for the arising of ultimate bodhicitta, it is said that:

> Having pleased well the perfect buddhas,
> and having gathered perfectly merit and wisdom,
> nonconceptual pristine awareness of reality arises;
> this is held to be the ultimate bodhicitta. MSA 5:8

That is, ultimate bodhicitta is generated through study of scriptures, practice, and realization.

Sixth topic: The source from which the vow is taken

The sixth point concerns the **source** from which the bodhisattva vow is adopted. There are two ways [of taking the vow]: one involving a preceptor and one without a preceptor. If it poses no obstacle to life or practice of purity, the aspirant should go to a preceptor, if one is available, and take the commitment personally, even if the latter is far away. The characteristic qualities of such teachers are (1) skill in the ritual ceremony for administering the vow, (2) having received the vow themselves and kept it unimpaired, (3) the ability to convey the meaning of the ritual's physical gestures and words, (4) a loving care for their disciples that is undefiled by the pursuit of material gain. Thus it says in *Lamp for the Path to Awakening*:

> Take the vow from a good master,
> possessing the very best characteristics.
>
> A good master should be known as someone
> skilled in the ceremony for taking the vow
> who has personally kept whatever the vow entails
> and gives the vow patiently and compassionately. BP 22CD–23

Bodhisattva Levels says:

> To be able to give the bodhisattva wish, the preceptor should be in accord with Dharma, have taken the vow, be skilled, know how to communicate the meaning of the ritual words, and know how to make the disciple understand.[171]

However, if such a lama resides close by but there is a possibility of some threat to life or to purity in going to him, then there is the "lama-less" method. For this, stand before an image of the Buddha and sincerely recite three times the words of the aspiration bodhicitta or the engaged bodhicitta vow, whichever is appropriate. Thereby you receive the aspiration or practice vow. Thus *Bodhisattva Levels* says:

> Should it happen that there is no such person with the requisite qualities, bodhisattvas properly go before an image of the

> Buddha and take the vow of bodhisattva moral discipline by themselves.[172]

If neither a preceptor nor a Buddha image is available, the words of the aspiration or engaged bodhicitta vow are recited three times in front of buddhas and bodhisattvas visualized as truly present, assembled in space before the aspirant. The *Compendium of Trainings* says:

> Further, should there be no such spiritual mentor, meditate that the buddhas and bodhisattvas dwelling in the ten directions are really present and take the vow through the strength of your own mind.[173]

Seventh topic: The ceremony

The seventh point explains the **ceremony** for adopting bodhicitta. Many ways and traditions of taking the bodhisattva vow have emerged, evolving from the specific styles of instruction of lineages originating from the great learned masters. Though there are many, the subject matter here concerns the two [main] traditions: Master Śāntideva's tradition, of the lineages passed down from Ārya Mañjuśrī to Master Nāgārjuna; and Master Serlingpa's tradition, of the lineages passed down from Ārya Maitreya to Master Asaṅga.

Master Śāntideva's tradition. This is the lineage passed down from Ārya Mañjuśrī to Master Nāgārjuna; it has a ceremony in three stages: (1) a preparation, (2) the actual ceremony [generating bodhicitta], and (3) a conclusion.

[Preparation]

The *preparation* is in six parts: (1) making offerings, (2) shedding past wrongs,[174] (3) rejoicing in virtue, (4) requesting the buddhas to teach the Dharma, (5) supplicating the buddhas not to abandon the world, and (6) dedicating the roots of virtue.

The first, *making offerings*, needs to be understood in terms of both recipients and the offerings themselves. The offerings are made to the most precious refuges. Since it is explained that making offerings to them creates the same merit whether or not you are actually in their presence, offerings are made both to those present and to those not actually present. Thus the *Ornament of Mahayana Sutras* says:

> With a mind filled with faith,
> offer robes and so forth to the buddhas,
> both in reality and with your imagination,
> in order to complete the two accumulations. MSA 18:1

As for the offerings, there are two types: surpassable and unsurpassable offerings. The *surpassable offerings* are also twofold: material offerings and the offering of realization.

Material offerings comprise prostrations, praises, material goods neatly and properly set out in the right order, and also the offering of things that belong to no one in particular. These can be actual things of good quality as well as creations of the imagination and the offering of your own body. Such offerings can be studied in detail in other works.

Realization as an offering entails offering Mahāmudrā[175] meditation on the deities' forms as well as the various arrays [of offerings] emerging from the profound meditative absorptions of the bodhisattvas.

Unsurpassable offerings are twofold: those that take place within what appears to be objective reality and those beyond objective reality. The first of these is bodhicitta meditation. As it is said:

> When a wise person cultivates bodhicitta,
> this is the highest offering he can make
> to the buddhas and their heirs.[176]

The second, offering that is beyond objective reality, refers to meditation on the absence of self-entity, which is the supreme offering. Therefore it says in the *Questions of the Devaputra Susthitamati Sutra*:

> Were a bodhisattva, desirous of enlightenment,
> to make offerings to the Buddha, the best of all humans,
> offering quantities of flowers, incense, food, and drink
> equal in number to the grains of sand on the banks of the
> river Ganges,

so doing for ten million cosmic ages,
and were another such bodhisattva to offer his training
in the teachings on no-self, absence of life force, and absence of personality,
along with the resulting achievement of being able to sustain clear lucidity,
it would be the latter bodhisattva who made the better offering.[177]

It also says in the *Lion's Roar Sutra*:

> Not to create ideas or descriptions is to make offerings to the Tathāgata. To be without adopting or rejecting and to penetrate that which is nondual is to make offerings to the Tathāgata. Friends, since the very character of the body of the Tathāgata is insubstantial, do not make offerings while conceiving it to be substantial.[178]

This concludes the section on making offerings.

The second [of the six parts of the preparation] is *shedding past wrongs*. Generally speaking, good and evil depend on the mind's motivation: mind is the master, and body and speech are its servants. The *Precious Garland* says:

> Since mind precedes all things,
> it is often said, "Mind is master." RA 4:73

Hence when the mind is motivated by a defiled state—desire, anger, and the like—people may commit the five acts with an immediate consequence, the five like them, or the ten negative actions. They may break vows or profound commitments or perhaps incite others to do such things. Even if they do not do these things personally, they may delight in the fact that others are perpetrating such evils. All the preceding are what is meant by the terms "wrong" and "nonvirtue." Not only those [manifestly wrong actions] but even Dharma activities such as study, contemplation, or practice that are motivated by a mind under the sway of passion, anger, and the afflictions also become nonvirtue. Thus the *Precious Garland* says:

> Attachment, anger, ignorance, and the actions
> to which they give rise are nonvirtue.
> Nonvirtue brings all the sufferings
> and hence all the lower states of existence. RA 1:20AB AND 21AB

Further, in *Guide to the Bodhisattva Way of Life*, it says:

> From nonvirtue will arise suffering.
> The correct thing to do, day or night and in every circumstance,
> is to contemplate one thing and one thing alone:
> How can I attain definitive release from this? BCA 2:63

This is the reason every wrong needs to be shed. Will calling wrongs to mind actually purify them though? Most definitely! The *Great [Passing into] Nirvana Sutra* says:

> Although a wrong may have been committed, subsequent remorse will put things right, in much the same way as certain precious substances restore water's clarity or as the moon retrieves her brilliance when emerging from clouds.[179]

and

> Hence it is by unburdening yourself of wrongdoings, with remorse and without dissimulation, that there will be purity.[180]

In what way exactly should you rid yourself of wrongdoings? By applying the four powers. Thus it says in the *Sutra Teaching the Four Qualities*:

> Maitreya! If bodhisattva mahāsattvas have these four things they will overcome evils that have been committed and established. What are these four? They are (1) the power of the thorough application of total remorse, (2) the power of thoroughly applying the remedy, (3) the power of renouncing harmful acts, and (4) the power of the support.[181]

First is the *power of the thorough application of total remorse*. This is to disclose sincerely and with ardent regret, in the presence of the refuges, wrongs done in the past. How to stimulate remorse? There are three ways: (1) by considering the pointlessness of those wrongs, (2) by considering fear, and (3) by considering the urgent need for purification.

[First,] *remorse by considering their pointlessness* is engendered by reflecting, "I have committed wrongs sometimes to subdue my enemies, sometimes to protect my friends, sometimes for the sustenance of my own body, and sometimes to accumulate material wealth. However, when I die and the time comes to move on to another life, my enemies and friends, my country and my body, and my wealth and possessions will not accompany me. Yet I shall be shadowed by the wrongs and obscurations created by my harmful actions; no matter where I am reborn these will rise up as my executioners." This is why the *Questions of the Layman Vīradatta Sutra* says:

> Father, mother, brothers, sisters, spouse,
> servants, wealth, and acquaintances
> cannot accompany those who die,
> but their actions do follow and trail after them.[182]

It also says:

> When great suffering comes,
> children and spouse offer no refuge.
> You experience the agony alone,
> and they cannot share your lot.[183]

Guide to the Bodhisattva Way of Life says:

> I must go, leaving everything behind.
> Unconscious of this,
> I commit various wrongs
> for the sake of the loved ones and those I dislike.
>
> However, those I love will cease to exist,
> those I dislike will cease to exist,
> and even I myself will cease to exist.
> In such a way, everything comes to the end of its existence.
>
> BCA 2:34–35

Thus we have committed wrongs for the sake of those four: friends, enemies, our body, and possessions. Those four will not accompany us for very long, yet on their account we have committed wrongs that bring much trouble and little benefit. Contemplating the reality of this, great remorse will arise.

There are those who think that even if wrong actions are of little benefit, they will not really bring harm to their doer. They should contemplate the second point: *remorse by considering fear*. Reflecting, "The consequence of wrong is fear," remorse will arise. Wrong actions result in three main times of fear: fear prior to death, fear when actually dying, and fear after death.

Prior to death, those who have committed wrongs will experience unbearable sufferings, feeling struck to their very marrow and so forth. It is said:

> As I lie on my bed,
> I may be surrounded by my friends and relatives,
> but it is I and I alone who will experience
> the feelings of life coming to its end. BCA 2:40

At the time of actual death, the result of wrongdoing is fear. The wrongdoer experiences the henchmen of the Lord of Death, black and horrible beings brandishing lassos, coming to place their lassos around his neck so as to lead him off to hell. Later others, bearing sticks, swords, and all sorts of weapons, torture and torment in many differing ways:

> When grabbed by Yama's henchmen,
> what use are relatives, what use are friends?
> At that time merit alone provides shelter,
> and merit have I not pursued! BCA 2:41

The *Letter to a Student* says:

> Having locked time's noose around our necks,
> Yama's ferocious henchmen prod us with sticks and drag us
> along. ŚI 34

A person who thinks "I won't be afraid of Yama's henchmen" should reflect as follows:

> Even those taken to a place
> where their limbs are to be hacked off
> become terror-stricken and dry-mouthed,
> their eyes bulging and bloodshot and the like.
>
> What need to mention my unspeakable horror
> when gripped by the fear that comes at the time of death
> and I am seized by the terrifying emissaries
> of the Lord of Death, vivid as if in flesh and blood? BCA 2:44–45

There will also be fear beyond death as a consequence of wrongdoing. Having descended into the great hells, the unbearable sufferings of being boiled, burned, and so on are experienced, and this is quite terrifying:

> Seeing hells depicted, hearing about them,
> thinking about them, reading about them, and seeing models—
> if these make people shudder with fear, what need is there to
> speak of
> those who actually experience the unbearable fruition of their acts
> [in the hells]. SU 84

Thus wrongdoing will come to be regretted by understanding the terrible fears that result from it.

Third is *remorse by realizing the urgent need for purification*. If you think that it will probably be all right to rectify wrongdoings at some later time, realize that it will not be all right at all and that atonement is needed urgently. Why? Because there is a distinct possibility that death will come before wrongs have been purified. It says:

> Before my wrongs are purified
> I may well come to die.
> Pray save me swiftly
> so that I am definitely released from my wrongdoings. BCA 2:32

If you think that somehow you will not die before misdeeds have been purified, then consider this: the Lord of Death will not bother in the least about how many misdeeds have or have not been purified. He will steal life away whenever the opportunity presents itself; the time of death is uncertain. Thus it says:

> It is wrong to feel so confident.
> My death will not wait for me to finish the things I have to do.
> As far as this ephemeral life is concerned,
> it matters not whether I am sick or healthy. BCA 2:33

Since those who do not realize the uncertainty of their lifespan are quite likely to die without having cleared up their misdeeds, all wrongs should be purified as quickly as possible. The risk is very real, so give rise to great remorse. When sincere remorse has been stimulated by the three contemplations described above, misdeeds should be admitted and purification requested in front of either the general or special sources of refuge.

Thus it has been taught that the power of total repentance will purify misdeeds, just as a plea from someone who cannot afford to repay a debt to a rich man may persuade him to wipe out that debt.[184]

There was once an evil person known as Aṅgulimāla. Even though he had committed grave misdeeds, killing 999 people, he managed to purify his evils and achieve the state of an arhat by practicing this power of the thorough application of total and utter remorse.[185] Thus it is said:

> Once someone who previously did not care
> later comes to learn to be heedful,
> he becomes beautified, like the moon breaking free from clouds,
> as was the case with Nanda, Aṅgulimāla, Ajātaśatru, and
> Udayana.[186] SU 14

Second [of the four powers] is the *power of thoroughly applying the remedy*. Virtuous actions are the remedy for misdeeds. They will consume impurities. Thus the *Compendium of Higher Knowledge* says:

> Actions with remedial power will prevent corresponding misdeeds from coming to unwholesome fruition by transforming the consequence into something else.[187]

In the *Treasury of the Tathāgatas*, it says that cultivating awareness of emptiness purifies misdeeds.[188] In the *Diamond Cutter Sutra*, it says that misdeeds will be purified by reciting the profound scriptures.[189] In the *King for Establishing the Three Commitments Tantra* and in *Questions of Subāhu Tantra*, it says that misdeeds will be purified by reciting mantras.[190] In the *Heap of Flowers Dhāraṇī*, it says that faults are purified by making offerings to the stupas of the Buddha.[191] It also says, in the section on buddha images,[192] that making images of the Buddha will purify misdeeds. Elsewhere it says that listening to teachings, reading or writing out the scriptures, and so forth—whichever one feels for the most—will also purify wrong actions. The *Basis of Vinaya* says:

> Whosoever has committed evil action
> but then annihilates it through virtue
> shines in this world
> like the sun or moon emerging from clouds.[193]

You may wonder, "If engaging in virtue is the antidote for evil, then do you have to do a quantity of good that is equivalent to the amount of bad previously done?" Not so. The *Great [Passing into] Nirvana Sutra* tells us:

> Even a single virtuous act overcomes many evils.[194]

and

> Just as a small vajra can destroy a mountain, a little fire can burn down a forest, or a minute amount of poison can kill beings, likewise a small beneficial action can overcome a great wrong. It is most efficacious![195]

The *Sutra of Golden Light* explains:

> Someone may have committed unbearable evils
> for a thousand ages,
> yet performing just one perfect purification
> will cleanse all their wrongs.[196]

Thus it has been taught that misdeeds will be purified by the power of thoroughly applying remedies. It is like someone who has fallen into a putrid swamp and, once out of the swamp, bathes and is anointed with perfumed oils.[197]

[For example] there was once a nobleman's son called Udayana. Even though he had killed his own mother, he managed, through this power of thoroughly applying the remedy, to purify himself of his misdeeds. He was reborn as a god and obtained the Dharma result of a stream-enterer.[198] [Thus, as already quoted:]

> Once someone who previously did not care
> later comes to learn to be heedful,
> he becomes beautified, like the moon breaking free from clouds,
> as was the case with Nanda, Aṅgulimāla, Ajātaśatru, and Udayana.
> SU 14

Third [of the four powers] is the *power of renouncing harmful acts.* In awe of the full consequences of karma, you desist from wrong henceforth, thinking,

> Guides of humanity, please [help me]
> remove these evils I have committed.
> These misdeeds are indeed bad.
> Never will I do them again. BCA 2:65

Thus it has been taught that the power of renouncing evil will purify misdeeds, just as diverting a dangerous river removes the threat from a town.[199] [For example] once there was a person called Nanda who harbored much desire for women. Even though he had committed wrongs, through practicing this power of renouncing evil, his faults were purified and he attained the state of an arhat.[200] [As already quoted:]

> Once someone who previously did not care
> later comes to learn to be heedful,
> he becomes beautified, like the moon breaking free from clouds,
> as was the case with Nanda, Aṅgulimāla, Ajātaśatru, and
> Udayana. SU 14

Fourth [of the four powers] is the *power of the support.* This comes from taking refuge and developing bodhicitta. Seeking shelter in the three most precious refuges will purify misdeeds, as it says in the *Story of the Sow*:

> Those who have taken refuge in the buddhas
> will not take birth in states of suffering.
> Having left their human bodies,
> they obtain celestial ones.[201]

The *Great [Passing into] Nirvana Sutra* says:

> One who has sought refuge in the Three Jewels
> will attain fearlessness.[202]

The development of bodhicitta will purify misdeeds. The *Marvelous Array Sutra* says:

> It will put an end to all nonvirtuous actions, like burying them for good.... It will burn up all evil, like the fire at the end of the eon.[203]

Guide to the Bodhisattva Way of Life also tells us:

> The support of someone strong and fearless can free us from fear.
> Likewise, if supported in this way we will be quickly liberated,
> even though we may have committed unbearable wrongs.
> How then could those who care not rely on such support? BCA 1:13

Thus the power of the support purifies faults. For example, the support of refuge could be compared, it has been stated, to that of a strong person helping weak followers. The support of bodhicitta development could be compared to the neutralization of a powerful poison by reciting the appropriate mantra.

There was once a prince called Ajātaśatru who had committed the great evil of patricide.[204] Nevertheless he was purified through the power of support and became a bodhisattva. [Thus, as quoted above:]

Once someone who previously did not care
later comes to learn to be heedful,
he becomes beautified, like the moon breaking free from clouds,
as was the case with Nanda, Aṅgulimāla, Ajātaśatru, and
Udayana. SU 14

Since each of the above four powers is capable of purifying misdeeds, there is no need even to mention how effective all four combined will be. In actual practice, those who do admit and repair their wrongs, in the ways explained above, experience signs of their purification in dreams. The *Dhāraṇī of Encouragement* explains:

> Dreams of the following are signs of breaking free from fault: vomiting bad food, or drinking milk or yogurt or the like; seeing the sun and the moon; flying in the sky; seeing a blazing fire; seeing buffalo; seeing a dark, powerful person, or an assembly of monks or nuns; seeing a milk-producing tree; seeing elephants or mighty bulls; sitting on a mountain, a lion throne, or a mansion; listening to Dharma teachings; and so forth.[205]

This concludes the explanation on shedding past wrongs.

The third [of the six parts of the preparation] is *rejoicing in virtue*. This is about the need to cultivate a joyous appreciation of all the virtuous actions of sentient beings throughout the three times, thinking:

> I delight in all the roots of virtue established by every one of the limitless, inconceivable enlightened beings who have appeared in the past, throughout the universe, from their first generating bodhicitta all the way through to their perfect awakening due to their amassing the two accumulations and purifying the two obscurations. I further delight in whatever roots of virtue have been produced subsequent to their enlightenment, from the time they turned the wheel of Dharma to bring to maturity those ready for instruction, until they manifested leaving the world of suffering. I also delight in the roots of virtue generated by their teachings between their parinirvāṇa and the eventual disappearance of their teaching, as well as in the virtue produced

> by whatever bodhisattvas have appeared in the interim before the manifestation of the following Buddha. I further delight in whatever roots of virtue have been produced by accomplished pratyekabuddhas and likewise in those of any śrāvakas who have appeared. Further, I delight in the roots of virtue generated by ordinary people.

By contemplating joyfully in the above way, cultivate appreciation. Likewise, nurture similar thoughts about virtuous actions being performed in the present moment and those that will be performed in the future. In each instance, the training is to cultivate joyous appreciation. As it is said:

> I delight in the enlightenment of all the buddhas,
> and in the levels of the conqueror's heirs as well. BCA 3:3

The fourth [of the six parts of the preparation] is *requesting that the wheel of Dharma be turned*. Even at this moment in all the worlds of the ten directions, there are many buddhas not teaching Dharma. Addressing them mentally, offer requests to them to teach the Dharma. Thus one reads:

> With hands joined, I beseech the buddhas
> throughout the directions:
> please light the torch of Dharma
> for all beings obscured in the darkness of suffering! BCA 3:5

The fifth [of the six parts of the preparation] is *supplicating the buddhas not to pass away from the suffering worlds*. At present there are buddhas in the worlds of the ten directions who are at the point of entering into ultimate nirvana in order to stimulate those who believe in permanence to abandon their misconceptions and to inspire to diligence those who are wasting their time. With these buddhas in mind, supplication is made to them not to pass beyond the suffering worlds:

> I pray with joined hands to those victors
> who are considering passing beyond to nirvana
> to remain for countless ages,
> so as not to leave all their beings in obscurity. BCA 3:6

The sixth [and last part of the preparation] is *dedicating the roots of virtue.* All these previous roots of virtue are dedicated to removing the sufferings of all beings, and as a cause for their achieving happiness:

> Having thus engaged in all such deeds,
> whatever virtues I may have gathered,
> May this help clear away the sufferings of all beings. BCA 3:7

This and what precedes it conclude the explanation of the preparatory stage of the bodhisattva vow ceremony.

[THE ACTUAL CEREMONY FOR GENERATING BODHICITTA]

The *actual ceremony* consists of uttering the pledge in words. As stated in the *Compendium of Trainings*, just as when Ārya Mañjuśrī was King Amba he took the prātimokṣa and bodhisattva vows together from Buddha Megharava, likewise we too should receive [the two] simultaneously. Then recite such as the following three times:

> For as long as this samsara
> without beginning endures,
> so long I will engage in limitless deeds
> to benefit all other beings.
>
> Before the Buddha, protector of the world,
> I generate the mind for supreme enlightenment.[206]

Alternatively, one could receive on the basis of a more consdensed formula, such as the following from the *Guide to the Bodhisattva Way of Life*:

> Just as the sugatas of the past
> cultivated their minds toward supreme enlightenment
> and worked stage by stage
> through the bodhisattva training,
> so also will I, in order to benefit sentient beings,
> cultivate my mind toward enlightenment,

and train stage by stage
in the relevant disciplines. BCA 3:22–23

This is repeated three times. Should someone wish to receive the bodhicitta and bodhisattva vows separately, the words relevant to whichever aspect is to be adopted should be recited. This concludes the actual ceremony.

[Conclusion of the ceremony]

As a **conclusion of the ceremony**, make offerings of thanksgiving to the most precious refuges and cultivate great joy and delight on the basis of contemplating the great purpose [of bringing about others' welfare]. So one reads:

The wise, having seized with a clear confidence
the mind for enlightenment, should,
to be victorious at the conclusion as well,
uplift their minds in this manner. BCA 3:24

This and more is said. This concludes the explanations on the preparation, actual ceremony, and conclusion for taking the bodhisattva commitment according to the tradition of Dharma Master Śāntideva.

Master Serlingpa's Tradition

According to this system of lineage, passed down from Ārya Maitreya to Dharma Master Asaṅga, there are two parts: generating the aspiring bodhicitta, and upholding the engaged bodhicitta vow. The first has three parts: the preparation, the actual ceremony, and its conclusion.

First, the *preparation* also has three parts: supplication, establishing the accumulations, and taking the special form of refuge.

For the first, *supplication*, the person wishing to dedicate him or herself to enlightenment should go to a properly qualified spiritual mentor and pay homage. That spiritual mentor too, having given some instruction, helps engender revulsion for samsara in the supplicant, compassion for sentient beings, aspiration for enlightenment, faith in the Three Jewels, and respect for one's gurus. Next, repeating after the preceptor, the student recites:

> Preceptor, pray heed me. Just as the tathāgatas, defeaters of the enemy, the utterly pure and perfectly enlightened ones, the blessed ones of the past, first raised an essential longing for the highest, utterly pure, and perfect enlightenment—as did the bodhisattvas who are now actually established in the bodhisattva levels—so also I, [such-and-such] by name, pray to you, the teacher, to awaken in me the essential force for unsurpassable, utterly pure, and perfect enlightenment.

Recite this three times.

For [the second,] *establishing the accumulations*, the supplicant first prostrates to the rare and precious refuges and to the preceptor. Then material offerings prepared for the occasion are offered, along with any amount of visualized and other offerings. It is taught that the novice vow is received from an abbot (*upādhyāya*) together with a preceptor (*ācārya*), that the full vow is received from the Sangha, and that the two types of bodhicitta are attained through the accumulation of merit.

It would be inappropriate for wealthy people to make meager offerings; they should offer on a grand scale. Extremely wealthy bodhisattvas of the past made such vast offerings. Some even, when they gave rise to bodhicitta, took their vow making offerings as extensive as ten million monastic residences (*vihāra*). The *Good Eon Sutra*[207] tells us:

> Sugata Yaśodatta first gave rise to bodhicitta
> when, as king of Jambudvīpa,
> he offered ten million monastic residences
> to Tathāgata Śaśiketu.[208]

However, it suffices for someone who is not rich to make only modest offerings. In the past, poor bodhisattvas made very simple gifts; some even gave rise to bodhicitta offering the light of a burning twist of straw.

> Sugata Arciṣmant first gave rise to bodhicitta
> when, as a poor city dweller,
> he offered grass "candles"
> to Tathāgata Anantaprabha.[209]

For one who possesses nothing at all, it suffices to make three prostrations. In the past there were certain bodhisattvas who had nothing and who awakened their bodhicitta joining their hands in homage three times:

> Tathāgata Guṇamālin first gave rise to bodhicitta
> when he joined his hands in homage
> and three times said "Praise to the Awakened One"
> to Tathāgata Vijṛmbhitagāmī.[210]

The third, *taking the special form of refuge*, is to be done as explained in the previous chapter.

For the *actual ceremony*, the preceptor should instruct the student as follows and help him contemplate thus:

> Wherever there is space, there are sentient beings. Wherever there are beings, there are afflictions. Wherever there are afflictions, there is harmful karma, and whenever there is harmful karma, there will be suffering. All those beings beset by suffering are actually our parents; all our parents have been exceedingly kind to us. All those former parents who were so kind in the past are presently plunged into this powerful ocean of samsara, enduring immeasurable sufferings. With no one to protect them and be their refuge, they undergo terrible hardships and great pain. Thinking, "Oh, if only they could find happiness; if only they could get free from suffering," rest your mind in loving kindness and compassion for a while.
>
> Now think, "At present, I have no power to help these beings. Therefore, to be able to come to their aid, I will achieve what is known as pure and perfect enlightenment—the ending of all that is wrong, the perfection of every quality, the power to accomplish the benefit of all beings, however many they may be." Rest your mind in these thoughts for a while.

Then, repeating after the preceptor, the supplicant should recite the following formula three times:

> All buddhas and bodhisattvas throughout the ten directions, pray heed me. I, [such-and-such] by name, do now—by the power of the roots of virtue that I gathered in former lives through the practice of generosity, moral discipline, and meditation, through the roots of virtue that I have encouraged others to establish, and through those that I have joyously appreciated—take the commitment to reach unsurpassable, pure, and perfect enlightenment, in the same way as in the past the tathāgatas, the victorious ones, the pure and perfect buddhas, the perfectly gifted and liberated victors first took the commitment to reach pure and perfect great enlightenment, and as did those bodhisattvas of the bodhisattva levels. Like them, I, [such-and-such] by name, will, from this moment until I reach the essence of enlightenment, awaken the force of unsurpassable, pure, and perfect, highest enlightenment in order to rescue beings who are to be carried over, liberate those who are not free, let release their breath those who have not let out their breath, and take completely beyond suffering those who have not yet completely gone beyond it.

Through repeating these words after the teacher, the vow is taken.

The meaning of these words is as follows: Those "who are to be carried over" are hell beings, hungry spirits, and animals, since they have yet to cross the ocean-like sufferings of samsara. "To rescue" them means to free them from the sufferings of the three lower states and establish them in the higher states so that they can continue in human or divine existences. "Those who are not free" are the humans and gods, since they are not yet free from the bondage of the afflictions, which are like shackles. "To liberate" means to help free them from the bondage of the afflictions by setting them on the path of liberation so that they can attain liberation. "Those who have not yet let out their breath" are the śrāvakas and the pratyekabuddhas, because they have not yet relaxed into the Mahayana path. "Those who have not yet gone completely beyond suffering" are the bodhisattvas, because they have yet to achieve the nirvana that is rooted in neither samsara nor peace. "In order to" is the commitment to achieve buddhahood in order to be able to accomplish all the above aims.

As for the *conclusion*, make the students generate great joy and delight on the basis of thinking that a tremendous and useful thing has just been achieved. The preceptor should also pronounce the precepts as well.

Someone who has thus developed the initial commitment of bodhicitta is called a *bodhisattva*, because they have the wish to achieve enlightenment for the sake of other sentient beings, because they focus on enlightenment as well as the sentient beings, and because they rmaintain their courage for the sake [of beings] and are endowed with courageous determination.

This concludes the traditional ceremony for giving rise to the aspiration for supreme enlightenment.

[Taking the vow of engaged bodhicitta]

Taking the vow of engaged bodhicitta too has three parts: preparation, actual ceremony, and conclusion.

First is the *preparation*. It is in ten parts, in which the preceptor: (1) [leads with the formal] supplication, (2) enquires about any general obstacles there may be to taking it, (3) explains the gravity of breaking the commitment, (4) [outlines] the harmful consequences of letting it degrade, (5) [outlines] the benefits of adopting it, (6) [helps the supplicant] establish the accumulations, (7) inquires about any specific obstacles, (8) encourages the supplicant, (9) inspires a special motivation in the supplicant, and (10) gives some summarized instruction.

Second, with respect to the *actual ceremony*, the student should generate the intention to take the vow. Then the preceptor says:

> Child of good family, known as [such-and-such], do you wish to receive from me, bodhisattva [such-and-such], the following commitments to follow whatever was the basis of training and moral discipline of all the bodhisattvas of the past, to follow whatever will be the basis of training and moral discipline of all the bodhisattvas of the future, and to follow whatever is the basis of training and moral discipline of all the bodhisattvas presently throughout the universe in the ten directions? Such moral discipline was what the bodhisattvas of the past trained in, is what the bodhisattvas of the future will train in, and remains what the bodhisattvas throughout the universe in the ten directions at present are training in. That basis of training and way of right

> action are all founded in the moral discipline of restraint, the moral discipline of accumulating virtue, and the moral discipline of working for the welfare of sentient beings. Do you wish to receive these from me?[211]

This is asked three times of the supplicant, who assents "Yes, I do" each time.

Third, the *conclusion* [of the ceremony] has six parts. (1) The supplicant requests the preceptor's kind attention, and the preceptor (2) gives an explanation of the benefits of gaining insight into pristine awareness, (3) explains the importance of not speaking about the vows to others casually for no reason, and (4) gives a summary instruction to help understand the precepts. Then the supplicant (5) makes offerings in recognition of the [preceptor's] kindness and (6) dedicates the roots of virtue.

This concludes the explanation of the tradition of the illustrious Serlingpa.

Eighth topic: The benefits of bodhicitta

The eighth point concerns the **benefits** of developing bodhicitta. These are of two types: enumerable and unenumerable.

First, the *enumerable benefits* are themselves of two types: those arising from aspiration bodhicitta and those arising from engaged bodhicitta. The first [*those arising from aspiration bodhicitta*] are eightfold: (1) you enter the Mahayana, (2) it serves as the basis for all the other aspects of bodhisattva training, (3) it helps you eradicate all evils, (4) it helps you plant the root of unsurpassable enlightenment, (5) it helps you gain unsurpassable merit, (6) all the buddhas are pleased, (7) all beings are benefitted, and (8) perfect buddhahood is swiftly attained.

The first of these points is explained as follows. People's conduct may be the very best possible, but if they have not given birth to bodhicitta, then they have not yet entered the Mahayana. Without entering the Mahayana, buddhahood cannot be attained. A person who has awakened the bodhisattva mind becomes a Mahayanist. Thus it says in *Bodhisattva Levels*:

> As soon as one has generated this mind, one has entered the Great Vehicle to unsurpassable enlightenment.[212]

The second point is explained as follows. If you do not have aspiration bodhicitta—the longing to achieve enlightenment—you cannot generate and sustain the bodhisattva's training consisting of the threefold moral discipline. However, if you do so aspire, you lay the very foundation for what is achieved by first adopting the threefold moral discipline and then training in it. *Bodhisattva Levels* says:

> Giving rise to this attitude is the basis for all the bodhisattvas' training.[213]

The third point is that virtue is the remedy for former wrongs. The best of all virtues is the bodhisattva mind. By bringing this remedy into play, all adverse factors will be annihilated. Thus one reads:

> Blazing like the fire at the age's end, instantly
> it will definitely burn away the great wrongs.[214] BCA 1:14AB

The fourth point is that when the moisture of loving kindness and compassion saturates the ground that is the mind of a being, into which the root—the mind set on enlightenment—has been well and firmly planted, then the branches full of leaves—the thirty-seven factors conducive to awakening—are developed. Once the fruit—perfect buddhahood—has ripened, great benefit and happiness will arise from it for all beings. Thus when the bodhisattva mind has arisen, the root of buddhahood is firmly planted. *Bodhisattva Levels* says:

> The awakening of the bodhisattva mind is the root of unsurpassable, pure, and perfect enlightenment.[215]

The fifth point is that immeasurable merit is obtained. The *Questions of the Layman Vīradatta Sutra* says:

> Whatever merit there is of bodhicitta,
> if it were to possess a form,
> would fill the whole expanse of space
> and extend well beyond its bounds.[216]

The sixth point is that it pleases all the buddhas. The same sutra says:

> Were one person to fill as many buddhafields
> as there are grains of sand on the banks of the Ganges
> with gems and most precious substances
> and offer them to all the buddhas,
> and were another person, through compassion,
> to join his hands and incline the mind to enlightenment,
> then it would be the latter who made the superior offering.
> For this has no limits.[217]

The seventh point is that it will benefit all beings. The *Marvelous Array Sutra* says:

> It is like a foundation because it brings benefit to all beings.[218]

The last of the eight points is that one will quickly become a genuinely perfect buddha. It says in *Bodhisattva Levels*:

> Once this mentality has arisen, one will dwell in neither of the two extremes but quickly achieve really perfect buddhahood.[219]

The enumerable benefits *arising through the engaged bodhisattva* are tenfold. These are the eight mentioned above along with (9) you derive constant benefit and (10) it accomplishes the welfare of others, in all kinds of ways.

The ninth point is that once this commitment to bodhisattva practice has been undertaken, unlike previously, the flow of merit will be uninterrupted in all circumstances, even when asleep, unconscious, not being especially conscientious, and so forth. *Guide to the Bodhisattva Way of Life* says:

> From the moment this mind is adopted,
> whether the person is asleep or remains idle,
> a multitude of merits equal to the expanse of space
> will occur with their force uninterrupted. BCA 1:19

The tenth benefit is that it will dispel the sufferings of beings, bring them happiness, and sever their afflictions. *Guide to the Bodhisattva Way of Life* says:

> To those who are deprived of happiness
> and who experience many sufferings,
> it brings the satisfaction of many forms of happiness,
> it eradicates sufferings,
> and, moreover, it dispels ignorance.
> Is there any virtue that can match this?
> Is there anywhere such a friend
> or merit in such measure? BCA 1:29–30

The *unenumerable benefits* consist of all the qualities that emerge between its [initial] adoption and [the attainment of final] enlightenment. They remain beyond calculation.

Ninth topic: The consequences of abandoning bodhicitta

The ninth point describes the **harmful consequences of abandoning bodhicitta**. This is a damaging thing, because those who abandon it will (1) be reborn in states of suffering, (2) impair their capacity to help others, and (3) delay considerably any achievement of the bodhisattva levels.

The first of these is that by not fulfilling the bodhisattva promise and abandoning the commitment to enlightenment, a person is effectively cheating all beings. Rebirth in states of suffering is the consequence of such deception. *Guide to the Bodhisattva Way of Life* says of this:

> Should it happen that, having made the pledge,
> I do not do the work that needs to be accomplished,
> what sort of a being will I become,
> after having thus deceived all those beings? BCA 4:4

The second point is that the capacity to help others is impaired:

> If such a thing should happen,
> the welfare of all beings is diminished. BCA 4:9

The third point is the delay in achieving the [sublime bodhisattva] levels. It says:

> Those who alternate between strong lapses
> and strong bodhicitta
> will remain in the round of samsara
> and experience serious delay in attaining the bodhisattva levels.
> BCA 4:11

Tenth topic: The causes for losing the cultivated bodhicitta

The tenth point concerns the **causes of losing the cultivated bodhicitta.** These are considered in two areas: the causes for losing the aspiration and the causes for losing the practice.

The aspiration vow will be lost by abandoning any sentient being from your intention, by adhering to the four dark actions, or by adopting an attitude incompatible with the aspiration. The practice vow will be lost according to *Bodhisattva Levels*, as follows:

> If you have committed the four great offences analogous to the grounds of defeat with great involvement—this is described as loss of [the vow]. It is further stated that committing them with a medium or a lesser involvement will damage it.[220]

In *Twenty Verses on the Vows* it states that the loss of aspiration bodhicitta also brings the loss of engaged bodhicitta. In *Establishing Summaries of the Levels of Yogic Practice*, it is stated that there are four causes for relinquishing the bodhisattva vow.[221] These are the two mentioned above [abandoning any sentient being from one's intention and indulging in the four dark actions] and third, renouncing the bodhisattva training, and fourth, giving rise to aberrant views. Master Śāntideva, too, says that engendering an incompatible mental attitude will break the vow.[222]

Eleventh topic: How, if lost, to restore the bodhisattva vow

As for **how, if lost, to restore the vow**, if it is the aspiration vow that has been broken, it can be restored by taking it again. In the loss of the practice vow by virtue of having lost the aspiration vow, then rectifying the aspiration bodhicitta brings about automatic restoration of the practice bodhicitta vow. If the practice vow has been broken due to some other cause, it will have to be taken again. If it is lost due to committing the four offenses analogous to the grounds of defeat with a medium or lesser involvement, this can be rectified through declaration and purification.[223] *Twenty Verses on the Bodhisattva Vows* says:

> One needs to retake the vow.
> [If committed] with middling pollutant, confess it to three [or more],
> and in the presence of one for the rest.
> For those with [lesser] afflictions or none, purify them in your own mind.[224]

This concludes the ninth chapter, discussing the proper adoption of bodhicitta, from this *Ornament of Precious Liberation, a Wish-Fulfilling Gem of Sublime Dharma*.

10. Precepts for Generating Aspiring Bodhicitta

Twelfth topic: Precepts related to generating bodhicitta

The precepts related to the generation of bodhicitta are twofold: (1) the precepts related to aspiration bodhicitta and (2) the precepts related to engaged bodhicitta. To present the first, the synopsis is the following:

> **The precepts of aspiration are summed up in five points: to never exclude any sentient being from your intentions, to remain mindful of the benefits of bodhicitta, to gather the two accumulations, to repeatedly train in bodhicitta, and to nurture the four bright modes of action while abandoning the four dark ones.**

Of these five points, the first consists of the means for not abandoning bodhicitta; the second the means for preventing bodhicitta from degrading; the third the means for strengthening bodhicitta; the fourth the means to increase bodhicitta; and the fifth consists of the means for not forgetting bodhicitta.

To explain the first, namely to **never exclude any sentient being from your intentions,** which constitutes the means of ensuring that your bodhicitta does not get lost, the *Questions of* [*Nāga King*] *Anavatapta Sutra* says:

> What one thing could bodhisattvas possess that would embrace fully every quality of the Enlightened One, endowed with the best of everything? It is the aspiration to never exclude any being from their intentions.[225]

To exclude beings from your intentions means, for example, no longer feeling any sympathy for a person who has treated you unfairly, thinking,

"Even if I could help you, I wouldn't; were I able to save you from harm, I wouldn't." If you think like this, you have excluded someone from your compassionate intentions.

Does "exclude beings from your intentions" mean all beings or even just one being? Except for śrāvakas and pratyekabuddhas,[226] no one excludes all beings from the mind—not even birds of prey or wolves [do this]. Thus someone who has mentally excluded just one being and not rectified that within one watch of the day [i.e., four hours] has lost bodhicitta. This means that those who exclude beings from their intentions while engaging in bodhisattva conduct yet still think of themselves as bodhisattvas are completely mistaken. That would be like clinging to your only child's belongings after having killed him.

Since it is quite possible to drop the bodhisattva attitude even toward those who have been helpful, the risk of losing it toward those who are harmful is indeed high. Therefore, paying special attention to practicing compassion toward the latter, you should try to help them and make them happy. This is the way of the sublime beings, for it is said:

> Even if your kindness is repaid with harm,
> cultivate compassion in return.
> The most excellent beings of the world
> respond to even the negative with goodness.[227]

To explain the second point, to train in **remaining mindful of the benefits of bodhicitta**, which constitutes the means of guarding against its degradation, there are statements such as the following from the *Lamp for the Path to Awakening*:

> Whatever benefits there be
> in developing the aspiration for enlightenment
> have been explained by Maitreya,
> through the *Marvelous Array* [*Sutra*], and in similar texts. BP 21

In that sutra, the benefits of bodhicitta are presented through two hundred and thirty similes, and it states that all of these benefits can be subsumed into four main categories.

The sutra states, "Child of good family! This bodhicitta is like the seed of all the buddhas' qualities. Because it dispels spiritual poverty, it is like the god of wealth."[228] This and other similes concern the *benefits for oneself*. Then it says, "Because it provides excellent protection for all beings, it is like a refuge," and "Because it sustains all beings, it is like the supporting earth."[229] This statement and others illustrate the *benefit for others*. Next, it says, "Because it defeats the enemy, the afflictions, it is like a spear. . . . Because it fells the mighty tree of suffering, it is like an axe."[230] These statements and others illustrate the *benefit it brings in cutting away wrong views*. Then it says, "Because it completely fulfills all intentions, it is like the enchanted vase. . . . Because it makes all wishes come true, it is like a wish-fulfilling gem."[231] These statements illustrate its *benefit in causing the accomplishment of everything that goes in the right direction*.

Through being mindful of the above benefits, you will come to greatly value the bodhisattva mind and appreciate its excellence. When this has been first achieved and then maintained through practice, it protects bodhicitta from degradation. Therefore always be mindful of bodhicitta's benefits, even should it be just for a short while in every watch of the day.

To explain the third point, training in **gathering the two accumulations**, which constitutes the means of strengthening bodhicitta, the *Lamp for the Path to Awakening*, for instance, states the following:

> The accumulations, consisting of virtue and pristine awareness,
> are the cause for perfect [enlightenment]. BP 34

Of these, the *accumulation of merit* consists of the skillful means aspect, comprising the ten activities pertaining to Dharma practice and the four means of gathering beings[232] and so on. The *accumulation of pristine awareness* consists of the profound wisdom aspect, such as the awareness of the total purity of the three spheres.

Thus it is through gathering the two accumulations that the force of bodhicitta arises within your mental continuum. Therefore always gather the two accumulations. Since even a simple recitation of a brief mantra once during each watch of the day can lead to completion of the two accumulations, even if it is only for a brief moment, you should gather the accumulations. *A Discussion of Accumulation* says of this:

> "What will I do today to gather
> the accumulations of merit or of wisdom?"
> "What will I do today to help sentient beings?"
> So a bodhisattva constantly contemplates.[233]

To explain the fourth point, **training repeatedly in bodhicitta**, which constitutes the means to increase bodhicitta, *Lamp for the Path to Awakening* says:

> Having given rise to bodhicitta as an aspiration,
> strive to increase it in every way. BP 18AB

This striving should be understood as applying to three areas of activity: (1) training in the attitude that gives rise to bodhicitta, (2) training in bodhicitta itself, and (3) training in the attitude related to bodhisattva conduct.

The attitude that gives rise to bodhicitta is to always be disposed to loving kindness and compassion toward sentient beings, or at least to engender such a thought once every watch of the day.

Training in bodhicitta itself is to nurture an intention longing to attain enlightenment so as to be able to benefit beings. This should be the subject of contemplation during the three periods of the day and the three periods of the night. Alternatively, the longer bodhisattva ritual can be performed; or else, at a minimum, the following prayer, [recommended by] the great Atiśa, can be recited once every watch of the day:

> I take refuge in the buddhas, the Dharma, and the supreme
> community
> until my attainment of enlightenment.
> Through engaging in generosity and so forth,
> may I achieve buddhahood for the benefit of all sentient beings.[234]

Training in the *attitude related to bodhisattva conduct* is twofold: developing the willingness to work for the benefit of others and developing the intention to purify the mind. The first of these means dedicating body, possessions, and whatever virtues have been established in the three times to the service of others and their happiness; it implies cultivating a willingness to give. Developing the intention to purify the mind involves constant examination of personal conduct as well as the elimination of afflictions and harmful actions.

To explain the fifth point, **abandoning the four dark actions and nurturing the four bright ones**, which constitutes the means for not forgetting bodhicitta, *Lamp for the Path to Awakening* says:

> To remember this in other lives as well,
> carefully observe the precepts thus explained. BP 18CD

Where are these precepts explained? The *Kāśyapa Chapter Sutra* states the following, with respect to the four dark actions, for instance:

> Kāśyapa! A bodhisattva possessing these four things will forget his bodhicitta. What are these four? They are . . .[235]

To summarize them, the four dark actions are: (1) to deceive a guru or person worthy of receiving offerings, (2) to cause others to regret actions that should not be regretted, (3) to speak improperly to a bodhisattva—that is, one who has taken the vow—and (4) to cheat or deeive any sentient being.

The four bright actions are also taught in that same sutra:

> Kāśyapa! Should a bodhisattva possess these four, then in all future lives bodhicitta will definitely manifest from birth onward. Without any interruption, that bodhicitta will never be forgotten until enlightenment is attained. What are these four? They are . . .[236]

To summarize the four, they are: (1) never knowingly to tell lies,[237] even should it cost your life; (2) to establish all beings in virtue and, further, to establish them in Mahayana virtue; (3) to consider a bodhisattva, meaning one who has taken the vow, as being the Teacher, the Enlightened One, and to proclaim that person's qualities in every quarter; and (4) to constantly abide within a noble disposition of mind, free of pretense and deceit toward any sentient being.

I will now explain the *first dark action* [and its opposite, bright action]. If, with an intention to deceive, you have actually been deceitful toward anyone "worthy of offerings"—meaning a guru, an abbot, a preceptor, or a person who is an object of your giving—the bodhisattva vow is broken, unless you do something to remedy the fault within a single watch of the day. It does not matter whether or not the person knew he [or she] was being deceived, whether or not the deception caused displeasure, whether it was a major or minor deception, or whether or not the deceit actually worked. Whatever the case, the vow is broken. The remedy to this is the *first bright action*, which is, in all circumstances, to avoid the intentional telling of untruths, even should that put your life at risk.

The *second dark action* occurs in relation to the virtuous actions of others.[238] It involves trying to make them feel remorseful by stirring up notions of regret [for the good they have done]. In the case of generosity, we could take the giver as an example. Although that person did a good deed, someone else may try to stir up regret by saying that in days to come the loss of resources caused by the generosity will leave the giver hungry and a beggar—and then what will he do? If this dark action is not remedied within a watch of the day, the bodhisattva vow has been broken, whether or not the person actually does regret the deed. The remedy for this is the *second bright action*: to establish all beings in virtue, and in particular in Mahayana virtue.

The *third dark action* occurs through anger or hatred and involves talking about the faults of someone who has taken the bodhisattva vow. They may be ordinary faults or Dharma failings, addressed directly to that person or indirectly, and it could be done in a pleasant or an unpleasant way. Whether or not the bodhisattva concerned is disturbed by what has been said, the bodhisattva vow is broken unless this is remedied within a watch of the day. The remedy is the *third bright action*: to conceive of anyone who has taken the bodhisattva vow just as you would conceive of a buddha and to let their qualities be known everywhere.

The *fourth dark action* entails intentionally trying to deceive anyone at all. Unless remedied within a watch of the day, this will break the bodhisattva vow, whether or not the person is aware of the deception and whether or not any actual harm is done. The remedy is the *fourth bright action*: to act always with the noblest intentions toward beings. This means intending to benefit them without self-interest.

This concludes the tenth chapter, on how to develop aspiration bodhicitta, of this *Ornament of Precious Liberation, a Wish-Fulfilling Gem of Sublime Dharma.*

11. Presentation of the Six Perfections

The precepts related to engaged bodhicitta are threefold: (1) higher training in moral discipline, (2) higher training in [applying] the mind [i.e., meditation], and (3) higher training in wisdom. In this respect, *Lamp for the Path to Awakening* says:

> Those who abide within the vow of engaged bodhicitta,
> having correctly trained in the three aspects of moral discipline,
> will greatly deepen their appreciation of those three trainings.
> BP 32A–C

The higher training in *moral discipline* consists of three: generosity, discipline, and forbearance; the higher training in *mind* consists of meditative concentration; and the higher training in *wisdom* consists of profound wisdom. As for diligence it serves as a complementary factor to all three [trainings]. The *Ornament of Mahayana Sutras* says:

> The Victorious One has most perfectly explained
> the six perfections in terms of the three trainings:
> the first three are the first training, the last two are the last two,
> while one [diligence] applies to all three. MSA 16:7

Thus the synopsis for this chapter is the following:

> **Training in engaged bodhicitta can be summarized as sixfold: generosity, moral discipline, forbearance, diligence, meditative concentration, and wisdom.**

In the *Questions of Subāhu Sutra*, too, it says:

> Subāhu! For a great bodhisattva to quickly achieve real and perfect enlightenment, the six perfections must be applied constantly and in all circumstances until their utter completion. What are those six? They are the perfection of generosity, the perfection of moral discipline, the perfection of forbearance, the perfection of diligence, the perfection of meditative concentration, and sixth, the perfection of wisdom.[239]

One should understand these six perfections in two ways: (1) through a summarized explanation or an overview, treating them as a group, and (2) through a detailed explanation of the individual perfections. First to present the summary, the synopsis is this:

> **The six perfections are summarized through six topics: their definite number, definite order, essential characteristics, etymology, subdivisions, and groupings.**

First, their **definite number** is six. In terms of higher states of rebirth and liberation, there are three conducive to higher rebirth and three conducive to liberation. Of the three that lead to higher states, the perfection of generosity nurtures material prosperity, the perfection of moral discipline nurtures a good physical existence, and the perfection of forbearance nurtures a favorable environment.[240] Of the three that lead to liberation, the perfection of diligence nurtures increase of qualities, the perfection of meditative concentration nurtures tranquility (*śamatha*), and the perfection of wisdom—the *prajñāpāramitā*—nurtures profound insight (*vipaśyanā*). The *Ornament of Mahayana Sutras* says:

> Higher states—the best possible prosperity, body, and retinue . . .
> MSA 17:2

Second, the perfections occur in a **definite order**. First, there is the *order in which they develop within the mental continuum of a person.* Generosity enables proper conduct without concern for material well-being. Possessing moral discipline, forbearance can be cultivated. Through forbearance, diligence is enabled. Through diligence, meditative concentration can be developed. The mind that rests skillfully in meditative concentration will know properly the true nature of phenomena, just as it is. Alternatively, the order of sequence could be considered in terms of the *gradual progression from lesser to higher*. The lesser are those explained first, and those founded in what is nobler are explained subsequently. Or the order of sequence relates to the *gradual progression from the grosser to the subtler*. That which is grosser is easier to engage in and is thus presented earlier, while those that are subtler, because of their being more difficult to engage in, are presented later. In this regard, the *Ornament of Mahayana Sutras* says:

> The latter arises on the basis of what comes before;
> and since some are inferior and others superior,
> some grosser and others subtler,
> they abide in their respective sequence. MSA 17:14

The third point concerns the four **essential characteristics** of bodhisattva generosity and the other perfections: (1) they diminish the strength of the unfavorable forces; (2) they enable the arising of pristine awareness, utterly free of concepts; (3) they bring perfect accomplishment of aspirations; and (4) they bring sentient beings to their full maturity in three ways [of the vehicles]. The *Ornament of Mahayana Sutras* says of this:

> Generosity curtails unfavorable forces,
> brings nonconceptual pristine awareness,
> perfectly fulfills all wishes,
> and brings beings to maturity in three ways. MSA 17:8

The fourth point relates to the **etymology** of the perfections. Since it clears away suffering, it is *generosity*;[241] since it is the attainment of coolness, it is *moral discipline*; since it copes with [what would cause] anger, it is *forbearance*, since it is application to that which is sublime, it is *diligence*; since it keeps the mind turned inward, it is *meditative concentration*; and since it causes awareness of that which is ultimate and meaningful, it is *wisdom*. Since all of them transport one from samsara to the far shore—namely, to nirvana—they are referred to as "what lead to the far shore" (*pāramitā*).[242] In this regard, the *Ornament of Mahayana Sutras* states:

> Since through them one eliminates poverty,
> obtains coolness, forbears wrath,
> connects with the supreme goal, retains the mind,
> and knows the ultimate, they are thus termed. MSA 17:15

The fifth point concerns the six **subdivisions** within each of the perfections—the generosity of generosity, the moral discipline of generosity, and so forth, thus giving rise to thirty-six subdivisions. The *Ornament of Clear Realization* says:

> The six perfections, generosity and so forth, each subdivide into
> six in terms of each other
> and as being an armor-like, complete means of attainment. AA 1:43

The sixth point examines their **groupings**. They fall into two groups based on the two accumulations. Generosity and moral discipline belong to the accumulation of merit. Wisdom belongs to the accumulation of pristine awareness. Forbearance, diligence, and meditative concentration belong to both. Thus the *Ornament of Mahayana Sutras* says:

> Generosity and moral discipline belong
> to the accumulation of merit, while wisdom belongs
> to the accumulation of pristine awareness,
> and the remaining three belong to both. MSA 19:39

This concludes the presentation of the six perfections, the eleventh chapter of the *Ornament of Precious Liberation, a Wish-Fulfilling Gem of Sublime Dharma.*

12. The Perfection of Generosity

Of the detailed explanation of the individual perfections, first, to explain the perfection of generosity, the synopsis is the following:

> **The perfection of generosity is summarized as sevenfold: reflections on the drawbacks of its absence and the benefits of its practice; its nature; its different aspects; the defining characteristics of each aspect; how it can be increased; how it can be made pure; and its fruits.**

The first point is reflections on **the drawbacks of its absence and the benefits of its practice.** A person lacking generosity will constantly suffer from poverty. Rebirth among hungry spirits is most likely, but should there be human rebirth, the person will be poverty-stricken. The *Verse Summary of the Perfection of Wisdom* says of this:

> The miserly will be reborn among hungry spirits.
> Even if reborn human, they will be poor. RS 31:11CD

Also, in the *Basis of Vinaya*, we find the following where a hungry spirit responds to the questions of Śroṇa:

> "We who are ridden with miserliness
> never practiced giving even the slightest.
> Thus we are condemned to this hungry spirit state."[243]

Furthermore, without generosity, a person can neither help others nor achieve buddhahood. So it is said:

> Those unaccustomed to giving are without wealth
> and have no power at all to gather beings to them,

so what need is there even to consider
their chances of reaching enlightenment?[244]

The opposite of this is that generous people will be happy due to having plentiful possessions throughout all their existences. The *Verse Summary of the Perfection of Wisdom* says:

> Bodhisattva generosity severs the possibilities of rebirth as a hungry spirit.
> It will abolish poverty and destroy all afflictions.
> Giving will bring limitless and tremendous wealth. RS 32:1A–C

The *Letter to a Friend* tells us:

> Practice generosity correctly;
> there is no better friend for the next life. SU 6CD

Further, in *Entering the Middle Way* it says:

> Everyone manifestly wishes for happiness;
> human happiness cannot be attained without resources;
> and because the Enlightened One knew that wealth comes through generosity,
> the Sage taught the practice of generosity first. MA 1:10

Generosity also brings the ability to help others. Those drawn to someone through generosity can then be established in sublime Dharma. So it is said:

> It is through generosity that suffering beings are brought to full maturity. RS 32:1D

Furthermore, being generous makes it easier to achieve enlightenment. The *Bodhisattva Collection* says:

> Enlightenment is not hard to find for those who have been generous.[245]

Also the *Clouds of Jewels Sutra* says:

> Generosity brings about the enlightenment of a bodhisattva.[246]

Further, we find a presentation of the drawbacks of a lack of generosity and the advantages of its practice interspersed in the *Questions of the Layman Ugra Sutra*:

> What I have given is mine; what I have hoarded is not mine. What has been given has purpose; what is hoarded is pointless. That which has been given does not require protection; what is hoarded does. What has been given brings no anxiety; whatever is hoarded is accompanied by worries. What has been given shows the way to buddhahood; what is hoarded shows the quick way to evil. Giving will bring great wealth, and hoarding will not. Giving will never know the end of wealth; hoarding will exhaust it.[247]

The second point is **its nature**. Generosity means to give completely, with an unattached mind. *Bodhisattva Levels* says:

> What is the essence of generosity? It is to give what is appropriate to be given on the basis of being motivated by mental states that arise together with nonattachment.[248]

The third point concerns **its different aspects**. There are three: giving material necessities, giving freedom from fear, and giving the Dharma. Of these, material generosity strengthens others' physical existence, giving freedom from fear strengthens the quality of others' lives, and giving the Dharma strengthens their minds. Furthermore, the first two kinds of generosity bring well-being to others in this life, whereas the gift of Dharma brings well-being for [both this and] future lives.

The fourth point develops **the essential characteristics of each aspect**. *Material generosity* is itself of two kinds, proper and improper, the former to be cultivated and the latter abandoned.

Improper material giving is discussed in terms of four aspects: improper motivation, inappropriate gifts, inappropriate receiver, and an improper way of giving.

An improper motivation can be either a distorted motivation or an inferior one. Giving out of distorted motivation is giving in order to harm others, to gain fame, or because of competition. A bodhisattva should renounce all three. *Bodhisattva Levels* says:

> Bodhisattvas should not give in order that others be killed, tied up, punished, imprisoned, or banished.[249]

and

> Bodhisattvas should not give in order to acquire fame or be praised.[250]

and

> Bodhisattvas should not give in order to compete with others.[251]

Giving through inferior motivation means practicing generosity through fear of poverty in future lives or through hoping for it to be the cause of future human or divine rebirth and future wealth. Bodhisattvas should not have these two types of motivation. It says:

> Bodhisattvas should not give through fear of poverty. Bodhisattvas should not give in order to gain the backing of Indra, a universal monarch, or Īśvara.[252]

Bodhisattva Levels discusses other kinds of improper giving as well. To summarize, inappropriate giving that needs to be abandoned involves giving of fire, poison, weapons, and the like, which can harm either their receiver or someone else.[253] Bodhisattvas should not respond to requests for snares, hunting devices, and so forth—in brief, for whatever may harm others. They should not give away their parents or use them as collateral. They should not give away a nonconsenting spouse or offspring. A person of much wealth should not give little. Communal wealth should not be misused as charity.

Abandoning inappropriate recipients refers to the following. Even though demons with harmful intentions may beg you for your body, you should give neither it nor parts of it to them. Neither should you give your body to those who are under the sway of demons or to those who are mad or temporarily deranged. Their need is not real: they are irresponsible, and their words are for the most part nonsense. It is not generosity to give food and drink to those who are well sated.

Abandoning an improper manner of giving means that it is not a correct generosity to give reluctantly, to be angry about the giving, or to give with a disturbed mind. One should not give to the deprived in a state of contempt or disrespect for them; neither should one dishearten, threaten, or deride the person begging.

As for the practice of *proper [material] giving*, [first] there are three points—the objects, the recipient, and the manner of giving. The first, in turn, is explained in terms of "inner" and "outer" objects. The inner ones are body-related. For example, the *Questions of Nārāyaṇa Sutra* says:

> If it is beneficial to give and if a person's attitude is pure, a hand can be given if a hand is required, a leg if a leg is required, an eye if an eye is required, flesh if that is what is needed, and blood if that is required.[254]

Those bodhisattvas on the beginner's stage, who have not yet realized the mental state of equalizing and exchanging of self and others, may give their body in its entirety, not through separating it into bits and pieces. The *Guide to the Bodhisattva Way of Life* says of this:

> Without a pure mind of compassion
> do not give away your body;
> that would be to give up the basis for achieving
> very great goals in this life and the next. BCA 3:87

The outer objects are food, drink, or whatever else nourishes, steeds, children, spouse, and so forth that have been acquired in a way that accords with Dharma. The *Questions of Nārāyaṇā Sutra* says:

> What are "outer objects"? It is the likes of wealth, grain, silver, gold, jewelry, ornaments, horses, elephants, sons, daughters.[255]

Lay bodhisattvas are permitted to give away whatever inner or outer gifts they possess. The *Ornament of Mahayana Sutras* says:

> There is nothing that a bodhisattva would not give to others,
> be it his body, wealth, and so on. MSA 9:16

Ordained bodhisattvas are allowed to give everything except their three Dharma robes. In *Guide to the Bodhisattva Way of Life*, we read:

> One should give everything except the three Dharma robes. BCA 5:85D

This is because giving away these three robes could undermine your work for the benefit of beings.

As for the recipient, there are four types: (1) those particularly designated by their qualities—gurus, the Three Jewels, and so forth; (2) those particularly designated by the benefit they have brought—father, mother, and so forth; (3) those particularly designated by their sufferings—the sick, the unprotected, and so forth; and (4) those particularly designated by the harm they have done—enemies and so forth. The *Guide to the Bodhisattva Way of Life* says:

> If one strives in the arenas of qualities, benefits, and suffering,
> great good will ensue. BCA 5:81CD

Concerning the way in which the gift is given, (1) there is the giving with the very best of intentions, and (2) the act of giving must be accomplished in the best way. The first consists of giving with a compassionate motivation to attain enlightenment and to benefit beings. As for the second, giving through the best possible action, it is said in *Bodhisattva Levels*:

> A bodhisattva should give joyfully, with respect, in person, at the right time, and without harming others.[256]

The first of these means to be joyful about giving during all three periods of the act—that is, to be glad about it before giving, to give with clear-minded joy, and to have no regrets once the giving has been done. "With respect" means with respect for the receiver. "In person" means not delegating the task to someone else. "At the right time" means when what is pledged has already been acquired. "Without harming others" means giving in a way that does not cause harm to your immediate circles or to their guardians. In this respect, you should not give something, even though it may be yours to give, if so doing brings tears [of sadness] to the eyes of those within your immediate circles who helped acquire it. Generosity should not be practiced by giving goods that have been embezzled, burgled, or misappropriated.

The *Compendium of Higher Knowledge* says:

> Give again and again, give without bias, and give in order to fulfill wishes most perfectly.[257]

In this quotation, "give again and again" is the particular quality of the donor, who should practice generosity repeatedly. "Give without bias" is the particular quality related to the receiver and means giving impartially. "Give in order to perfectly fulfill wishes" is related to the gift itself. It means giving what corresponds most closely to the expectations of the receiver.

This concludes the section on material generosity.

Giving freedom from fear refers to giving protection to those who are afraid of robbers, thieves, beasts of prey, illness, water, and so forth. *Bodhisattva Levels* says:

> The gift of fearlessness should be known as the provision of complete protection from lions, tigers, crocodiles, kings, robbers, water, and so forth.[258]

This concludes the teachings on supportive generosity.

Giving the Dharma is explained through four points: (1) the person being taught, (2) the motivation, (3) giving authentic Dharma, and (4) the actual presentation. The first of these means explaining the Buddhist teaching to those who wish to hear it and who have respect both for it and for the person expounding it.

As for motivation, wrong motivations are to be abandoned and only correct ones should be present. To give up wrong motivations means to teach Dharma without concern for honors, praise, or fame and to not have materialistic incentives. The *Verse Summary of the Perfection of Wisdom* says:

> Without material gain one teaches the Dharma to beings. RS 17:4B

In the *Kāśyapa Chapter Sutra* it says:

> The Buddha speaks highly of the gift of Dharma
> being given with a pure mind unconcerned with material gain.[259]

Having correct motivation means that compassion should be your motivation for teaching Dharma. The *Verse Summary of the Perfection of Wisdom* says:

> One gives the Dharma to the world in order to extinguish suffering. RS 26:2

Giving authentic Dharma means teaching unerringly the unmistaken meaning of the sutras and other texts. *Bodhisattva Levels* says:

> Giving the Dharma means to teach the unerring Dharma, to teach the appropriate Dharma, and to make sure that the fundamental points of training are well understood.[260]

As for the actual manner in which the Dharma is taught, when someone requests Dharma instruction, it is not fitting to explain things there and then. The *Candraprabha Sutra* says:

> Should someone request you
> for a gift of the Dharma,
> you should first utter the words
> "I have not studied it extensively."

and

> Do not teach straightaway;
> examine the suitability.
> However, if you know the person to be a worthy vessel,
> then teach the Dharma even without being requested.[261]

When teaching the Dharma, it should be in a clean and pleasant place. The *Lotus Sutra* says:

> In a clean and pleasant place,
> arrange well a wide seat [for teaching].[262]

In such a place, you should sit on a teaching throne and then expound [the Dharma]. It says:

> Well seated on an elevated Dharma seat
> that is beautifully arranged with various pieces of cloth . . .[263]

The teacher should bathe, be properly dressed and tidy, and explain the Dharma in an appropriate demeanor. The *Questions of Sāgaramati Sutra* says:

> One who teaches Dharma should be tidy and behave in a proper fashion. He should have bathed and be nicely attired.[264]

When everyone has assembled and taken their seats and the person teaching is on the Dharma seat, the latter should recite the following mantra that overcomes the power of harmful influences (*māra*), so that their hindering power cannot obstruct the teaching. The *Questions of Sāgaramati Sutra* says:

> It is this: *Tatyathā śame śamevati śametaśatruṁ aṁkure maṁkure mārajite karoṭe keyūre tejovati oloyani viśuddha nirmale malāpanaye khukhure khakha grasane omukhi paraṁukhi amukhi śamitvani sarvagraha bhandhanāne nigrihitva sarvapārapravādina vimukta mārapāśa sthāpitva buddhamudra anuṅgarirva sarva mare pucari tapari śuddhe vigacchantu sarvamāra karmaṇi*
>
> Sāgaramati! If someone recites the words of this mantra beforehand, no demons or negative forces within a radius of a hundred leagues will be able to come and harm the teaching. Even were they to manage to come, they would be unable to create

> an obstacle. Thereafter, the Dharma words should be explained clearly, articulately, and in just the right amount.[265]

This concludes the explanation of Dharma generosity.

The fifth point is **how generosity can be increased**. There are ways of transforming even a small amount of the above three types of generosity into something much greater. In the *Bodhisattva Collection* it says:

> Śāriputra! Skillful bodhisattvas transform a little generosity into a lot. The power of pristine awareness elevates it, the power of wisdom expands it, and the power of dedication makes it immeasurable.[266]

"The power of pristine awareness elevates it" signifies awareness of the utter purity of the three spheres [of the act of giving]. "The power of wisdom expands it" means that deep understanding is applied in order to give rise to a vast amount of merit, as follows. At the outset, whatever is given is done so in order to establish all beings in the state of buddhahood. During the giving there is no attachment to the gift itself. At the conclusion there is no expectation of good future-life consequences from giving. The *Verse Summary of the Perfection of Wisdom* says:

> Not making their giving something substantially existent
> and never practicing generosity in anticipation of its full karmic rewards—
> such is the way the wise and skillful practice generosity;
> so a little gift becomes much, to an inestimable extent. RS 31:14

"The power of dedication makes it immeasurable" means dedicating such generosity to the ultimate enlightenment of every sentient being. *Bodhisattva Levels* says:

> Do not be generous with a view to the specific results of that act of generosity. Dedicate all generosity to the ultimate, perfectly pure, and complete enlightenment of each and every sentient being.[267]

Dedication not only increases [the results] but makes them inexhaustible. The *Akṣayamati Sutra* says:

> Noble son of Śāradvati! Should a drop of water be put in the ocean, it will not be consumed until the end of the eon. Likewise the roots of virtue dedicated to enlightenment will never become exhausted or in the least diminished until the very heart of enlightenment is reached.[268]

The sixth point concerns **how generosity can be made pure**. To quote the *Compendium of Trainings*:

> Applying emptiness with compassion as its essence,
> virtue will be made pure.[269]

When the above-mentioned forms of generosity are supported by realization of emptiness, they will not become a cause for samsara. When they are supported by compassion, they will not become a cause for [attaining] the Hinayana. In such a way, generosity is made pure because it becomes a cause solely for attaining the nonabiding nirvana. In the *Questions of Ratnacūḍa Sutra*, it is taught that generosity is marked with four seals of emptiness. It says:

> Practice generosity by applying four seals to it. What are these four? To apply the seal of emptiness of the inner, one's body; to apply the seal of emptiness of the outer, the gift; to apply the seal of emptiness to the mind, the subject; and to apply the seal of the emptiness to the reality, enlightenment. Having applied those four seals, one engages in the act of giving.[270]

"Being supported by compassion" means to engage in giving because one is unable to tolerate the suffering of other beings in general or more specific kinds.

The seventh point concerns the **fruits of generosity**, which should be understood in both temporary and ultimate terms. Ultimately, generosity brings total enlightenment. *Bodhisattva Levels* says:

> When bodhisattvas totally complete the perfection of generosity, they truly become perfect buddhas who have reached peerless, manifest, and perfect enlightenment.[271]

The temporary results are that material giving brings the most perfect wealth even if one does not desire it. Furthermore, having attracted others through giving one can connect them with the supreme attainment as well. The *Verse Summary of the Perfection of Wisdom* says:

> Bodhisattva generosity destroys the route to rebirth as a hungry spirit.
> It suppresses poverty and also cuts through affliction.
> While practicing, they will enjoy vast and limitless wealth.
> Through giving they will bring suffering beings to greater maturity. RS 32:1

Bodhisattva Levels says:

> Gifts of food will bring strength,
> gifts of clothes will bring a good complexion,
> gifts of steeds will provide the basis for happiness,
> and offering oil lamps will bring good eyesight.[272]

Giving freedom from fear brings immunity from harm by negative forces and obstacles. The *Precious Garland* says:

> By giving freedom from fear to the fearful,
> you will not be harmed by any negative force
> and will become supreme among the mighty. RA 3:91

By giving the gift of Dharma, someone will soon meet the buddhas, be close to them, and attain everything wished for. The *Precious Garland* says:

> Through giving the Dharma to those who listen,
> you eliminate their obscurations,
> and by being a companion of the buddhas,
> you will swiftly attain what is longed for. RA 3:89

This concludes the twelfth chapter, presenting the perfection of generosity, in this *Ornament of Precious Liberation, a Wish-Fulfilling Gem of Sublime Dharma*.

13. The Perfection of Moral Discipline

To present the perfection of moral discipline, the synopsis is:

> **The perfection of moral discipline is summarized as sevenfold: reflections on the drawbacks of its absence and the benefits of its practice; its nature; its different aspects; the essential characteristics of each aspect; how it can be increased; how it can be made pure; and its fruits.**

The first point concerns reflections on **the drawbacks of its absence and the benefits of its practice.** Someone possessing the quality of generosity but lacking moral discipline will be unable to obtain the very best physical human or divine existence. In *Entering the Middle Way* it says:

> A person who breaks his limbs of moral discipline
> may obtain wealth through generosity but will fall into lower realms. MA 2:4AB

Further, one who lacks moral discipline will not encounter the Buddhadharma. The *Sutra on Moral Discipline* says:

> Just as the blind cannot see form,
> so those without moral discipline will not see the Dharma.[273]

Nor will those without moral discipline become free from existence within the three realms of samsara. That same sutra says:

> How can the legless walk along a path?
> Likewise those without moral discipline cannot become liberated.[274]

Those lacking moral discipline also cannot attain enlightenment because their path to buddhahood is incomplete. In contrast, someone having the qualities of moral discipline will attain the very best physical existence. The *Verse Summary of the Perfection of Wisdom* says:

> Moral discipline eliminates the very nature of [what causes rebirth in] various animal forms and the eight unfavorable rebirths.
> Through it, a rebirth with freedoms is always encountered. RS 32:2

Further, if you possess moral discipline, you lay the very foundation of all that is excellent and joyous. The *Letter to a Friend* says:

> Moral discipline is taught as being the very foundation and basis for every quality,
> just as the earth is the basis for all animate and inanimate life. SU 7

Also, possessing moral discipline is like owning a fertile field from which crop after crop of good qualities can be harvested. Therefore it says in *Entering the Middle Way*:

> Because good qualities develop specifically on the field of moral discipline, the fruition draws nearer, inevitably. MA 2:6

Further, someone with moral discipline will find that it opens many doors of meditative absorption. Thus the *Candraprabha Sutra* says:

> The rapid attainment of meditative absorption free of afflictions
> is a benefit arising from very pure moral discipline.[275]

Also, if you have moral discipline, whatever prayers are made will be fulfilled. Thus the *Meeting of Father and Son Sutra* says:

> It is through properly maintained moral discipline
> that every prayer made comes true.[276]

Moreover, if you possess moral discipline, you will attain enlightenment more easily. The same sutra says:

> Since purity of discipline brings so many benefits,
> it will not be difficult to achieve enlightenment.[277]

Thus there are the above and other benefits. The *Sutra on Moral Discipline* says, among other things:

> Those with moral discipline encounter the coming of the buddhas;
> those with moral discipline are the finest of all ornaments;
> those with moral discipline are the source of every joy;
> those with moral discipline are praised by all.[278]

The second, **the nature** of moral discipline is that it is characterized by four qualities. For example, *Bodhisattva Levels* states:

> The essential nature of moral discipline should be known as having four qualities. What are these four? (1) It has been adopted from another, most properly and purely; (2) the intention is extremely pure in every respect; (3) it is rectified if it deteriorates, and (4) to prevent its deterioration, it is respected and ever borne in mind.[279]

The four qualities mentioned above can be summed up as covering two main areas: the correct adoption of moral discipline, which relates to the first, and its proper maintenance—the latter three.

The third, in terms of **its different aspects**, moral discipline is threefold: (1) the moral discipline of restraint [vows], (2) the moral discipline of amassing virtues, and (3) the moral discipline of working for the welfare of others. The first pertains to stabilizing the mind, the second brings the elements within the person's mental continuum to maturity, and the third causes other beings to achieve full maturity.

The fourth, to explain the **essential characteristics of each aspect**, first, the *moral discipline of restraint* consists of both what is common and what is uncommon. The *common vows* refer to the seven classes of prātimokṣa vows. *Bodhisattva Levels* says:

> Right bodhisattva conduct related to abandoning wrong activity refers to the seven categories of prātimokṣa of those who have

> most properly adopted the precepts: those with the moral discipline of a monk, nun, novice monk, trainee nun, novice nun, ordained layman, and ordained laywoman. These should be understood as applying to those who have fully renounced and to laypersons, as appropriate.[280]

All of these represent turning away from harming others as well as from the bases of such harm. Within this, the prātimokṣa vows on their own turn away [harm] for one's own sake, while bodhisattvas refrain from harm out of concern for the welfare of others. The *Questions of Nārāyaṇa Sutra* says that:

> Moral discipline is not to be observed in order to gain royal status, nor for the sake of higher rebirth, nor to become like Indra or Brahma, nor for the sake of possessions, nor for the sake of physical well-being, and so on. Likewise moral discipline is not to be observed through fear of the horrors of rebirth in hell, fear of rebirth in animal states, or fear of the terrifying worlds of the Lord of Death. Not for those sorts of things but through considering it as the way to enlightenment is moral discipline observed—and so that every being can be drawn closer to what is beneficial and joyous.[281]

As for the *uncommon vows*, those in the tradition coming through Master Śāntideva follow the *Ākāśagarbha Sutra*. In this view, there are five root downfalls specific to monarchs, five specific to ministers, and eight specific to Dharma novices. Altogether these make eighteen in number, but in substance there are fourteen root infractions that need to be relinquished. So it is understood. Thus it says:

> 1. To steal what belongs to the Three Jewels—this is held to be a downfall and a state of defeat.
> 2. To make others abandon the Dharma; this and the above were declared by the Sage.
> 3. To take away the robes of a fully ordained monk, to have him beaten or imprisoned, or to oblige him to give up his commitments, even if he has broken vows.

4. To commit one of the five heinous acts.
5. To adhere to aberrant philosophy.
6. To destroy towns and the like.

These were taught by the Buddha as root downfalls.[282]

1. To speak about emptiness to those inadequately prepared.
2. To turn those who have entered the way to buddhahood away from perfect enlightenment.
3. To practice Mahayana yet totally abandon prātimokṣa ethics.
4. To believe that the Śrāvaka Vehicle cannot eliminate desire and so forth and to cause others to so believe.
5. To extol one's own qualities in pursuit of wealth, respect, or praise, and to denigrate others.
6. To lie about attainment, such as saying, "I have realization of profound emptiness."[283]
7. To have promised to do something virtuous and then go back on the promise, or to make offerings to the Three Jewels and then take them back.
8. To abandon tranquility and immersion in the highest reality in favor of ritual recitations.

> These then are the root downfalls
> and a prime cause of the great hells.[284]

Lord Serlingpa [Dharmakīrti], following [Asaṅga's] *Bodhisattva Levels*, states the need to train in relinquishing four offenses analogous to the grounds of defeat and forty secondary faults.

The four actions analogous to the grounds of defeat are described as the following in *Twenty Verses on the Bodhisattva Vow*, which is an abridgement of *Bodhisattva Levels*:

> Praising oneself and denigrating others, seeking honor and respect;
> out of avarice not giving wealth or Dharma to those who are suffering and helpless;
> inflicting vengeance, even though someone may have apologized;
> abandoning authentic Mahayana and teaching a [mere] semblance of Dharma.[285]

As for the forty-six faults, the same text says the following, for example:

> Not making offerings to the Three Jewels three times daily,
> being carried away by desires . . .[286]

The second, *moral discipline of amassing virtues*, is as follows. Once the bodhisattva right conduct based on vows is properly taken and practiced, it is the basis on which every possible and appropriate virtue of body and speech must be built, so that there is progress toward great enlightenment. These are many. They are known collectively as "the moral discipline of amassing virtues." What are they? In *Bodhisattva Levels* it says:

> The following is to be understood as being the bodhisattva's moral discipline of amassing what is virtuous. Relying on and abiding within the bodhisattva's moral discipline, it is to enthusiastically apply yourself to study, contemplation, and meditation and to maintain solitude. It is to respect gurus and to serve them, and to serve and care for the sick. It is to give properly and proclaim good qualities, to appreciate the attributes of others and to be patient with those who are scornful. It is to dedicate virtue to enlightenment and make earnest prayers to that end; to make offerings to the Three Jewels and strive to be diligent; to be ever caring and careful, to be mindful of the training and through awareness to keep to it; to guard the doors of the senses and to know how much to consume; to not sleep in the first and last parts of the night but to persevere in joining the mind with what is wholesome; to rely on holy individuals and Dharma masters and to examine delusions, admit them, and get rid of them. These sorts of qualities need to be practiced, nurtured, and thoroughly increased.[287]

The third, *the moral discipline of working for the welfare of others*, can be known in brief in terms of eleven. What are they? *Bodhisattva Levels* states:

> To support those doing worthwhile activities; to remove the suffering of beings in torment; to teach those without skill how to

> deal with things intelligently; to recognize others' kindness and to render benefit in return; to protect beings from dangers; to alleviate the distress of those who are suffering; to provide those deprived of resources with provisions; to skillfully assemble a Dharma following; to engage them in accordance with their mentalities; to make them happy through the very finest of qualities; to tame [the wrathful] with firmness; and to inspire awe through extraordinary abilities and longing [for the good and wholesome].[288]

Furthermore, both to instill confidence in others and to prevent their own conduct from degrading, bodhisattvas should get rid of impure physical, verbal, and mental behavior and only resort to what is pure. Concerning *impure physical behavior*, avoid unnecessary wild behavior—running, jumping, and so forth. Purity means you remain relaxed and smooth, with a kind expression on your face. It says:

> Having thus become self-controlled,
> always have a smiling face.
> Completely rid yourself of that constant frown and those dark looks,
> and become a friend to beings and treat them sincerely. BCA 5:71

How should you look at others? It says:

> When looking at others,
> look at them in a pleasant, kind way,
> knowing that it is through them
> that you will become a buddha. BCA 5:80

As to how to sit it says:

> Do not sit with legs outstretched
> or fidget with the hands. BCA 5:92CD

On how to eat it says:

When eating, do not overfill your mouth
or chew noisily, with the mouth agape. BCA 5:92AB

As to how to move around:

Do not be noisy and hasty
when, for example, getting up from a seat,
and do not slam doors.
Take pleasure in being unobtrusive. BCA 5:72

And on how to sleep it says:

Oriented in whichever direction you prefer,
assume the posture the Protector took for nirvana. BCA 5:96

With regard to *impure speech*, you should give up excessive or harsh speech. The shortcomings of *excessive speech* are explained below in the *Clouds of Jewels Sutra*:

The childish completely undermine the sublime Dharma.
Taking away the mind's flexibility and making it rough,
taking one far from tranquility and profound insight—
such are the flaws of delighting in excessive speech.

One will have little respect for Dharma masters.
People come to enjoy corrupt speech, becoming absorbed
in what is of meager value, and wisdom deteriorates—
such are the flaws of delighting in excessive speech.[289]

About the faults of *harsh speech* it says in the *Candraprabha Sutra*:

Even if you may see another's error,
do not broadcast it;
for whatever kinds of acts you engage in,
you yourself will obtain the commensurate results.[290]

In the *Sutra Teaching the Nonorigination of All Things* it says of this, among other things:

> If you describe the lapses of a bodhisattva, enlightenment recedes into the distance. If you talk through jealousy, enlightenment recedes far into the distance.[291]

Therefore excessive and harsh speech are to be given up.

How then should you speak? As stated in the following:

> When speaking, say something that is purposeful,
> clear in meaning and appealing,
> free from greed and aversion,
> smooth, and in just the right amount. BCA 5:79

The *impurity of mental engagement* refers to faults such as clinging to material gifts and honors as well as being attached to sleep and mental dullness. The fault of craving for material gain and honor is explained in the *Sutra Encouraging Nobler Intention*:

> Maitreya! A bodhisattva should examine how gaining material gifts and being honored in such a way gives rise to desire and attachment. He should know how gaining material gifts and being honored give rise to anger and aversion. He should know how material gifts and honors give rise to confused ignorance. He should know how material gifts and honors give rise to underhandedness. He should consider how none of the buddhas ever encouraged material gifts or receiving honors, and he should examine how material gifts and honors steal the roots of virtue. He should consider how material gifts and honors are like a prostitute trying to seduce a potential client.[292]

This and more is said. Even if material things are gained, the thirst for them is never sated. The *Meeting of Father and Son Sutra* says:

> Just as water imagined in a dream
> does not quench thirst even when drunk,

> likewise the objects of sensory pleasures
> even when acquired do not satisfy.[293]

Having considered in this manner, reduce your desires and be content with what you have.

Of the fault of enjoying sleep, it is said:

> Those who are addicted to sleep and inertia
> will suffer considerable degradation in their understanding.
> Their mental capacity will deteriorate, too.
> Whatever arises from pristine awareness will be constantly impaired.[294]

and

> Those who are addicted to sleep and inertia
> will disintegrate through ignorance, lassitude, and laziness.
> Such people become prey to nonhuman forces
> and may be harmed by them when meditating alone in the forests.[295]

Therefore the above forms of impure mental conduct should be abandoned.

Pure mental engagement is abiding with faith and the other qualities mentioned above.

The fifth, **how the power of moral discipline can be increased**, refers to enhancing [moral discipline] by means of the three factors already referred to earlier—these being (1) pristine awareness, (2) wisdom, and (3) dedication.[296]

The sixth, **making one's moral discipline pure**, refers to it being sustained by emptiness and compassion, as mentioned earlier.

Seventh, the **fruits of moral discipline**, should be understood as twofold—its temporary and ultimate results. Its ultimate fruit is the attainment of unsurpassed enlightenment. *Bodhisattva Levels* says:

> A bodhisattva who has completely perfected moral discipline genuinely becomes a perfect buddha, with peerless, true, and perfect enlightenment.[297]

The temporary results, whether sought or not, are to obtain greatest happiness and well-being within the samsaric world. The *Bodhisattva Collection* says:

> Śāriputra! There will not be even a single one of the most wonderful splendors known to gods and humans that a bodhisattva who keeps such completely immaculate conduct will not be able to experience.[298]

There may be these worldly delights and joys, yet the bodhisattva will not be dazzled by them and will enter the path to enlightenment. In the *Questions of Nārāyaṇa Sutra* it says:

> A bodhisattva endowed with such amassed moral discipline will not become corrupted in any way, even by the possessions of a universal monarch. That bodhisattva will still exercise mindful care and will still long for enlightenment. That bodhisattva will not take a detour even though he becomes Indra. Then, too, the bodhisattva will exercise mindful care and long for enlightenment.[299]

Furthermore, those who are endowed with moral discipline will receive offerings from and be cared for by humans and nonhumans alike. It says in the same sutra:

> The gods always respect those who keep the amassed virtues of moral discipline; the nāgas will constantly express their appreciation of them; the yakṣas will ever praise them; the gandharvas will constantly make offerings to them; brahmans, princes, merchants, and landowners will supplicate them; the buddhas will constantly embrace them with their compassion; and they will gain power over worlds and the divine forces present therein.[300]

This concludes the thirteenth chapter, discussing the perfection of moral discipline, in this *Ornament of Precious Liberation, a Wish-Fulfilling Gem of Sublime Dharma*.

14. The Perfection of Forbearance

The synopsis for the perfection of forbearance is:

> **The perfection of forbearance is summarized as sevenfold: reflections on the drawbacks of its absence and the benefits of its practice; its nature; its different aspects; the essential characteristics of each aspect; how it can be increased; how it can be made pure; and its fruits.**

The first reflects on **the drawbacks of its absence and the benefits of practicing it.** If someone possesses generosity and moral discipline yet lacks forbearance, anger can still arise. Once anger has arisen, all the virtue created up to that time—through generosity, moral discipline, and so on—can be consumed right there and then. Thus it says in the *Bodhisattva Collection*:

> This thing we call anger can overpower the roots of virtue established over a hundred thousand eons.[301]

Guide to the Bodhisattva Way of Life also says:

> Whatever excellent deeds—
> generosity, making offerings to the buddhas, and so forth—
> one may have gathered over a thousand eons
> may be destroyed by one burst of anger. BCA 6:1

Furthermore, anger that has found a niche inside someone lacking forbearance is like the festering wound of a poisoned arrow. The mind thus afflicted knows no joy, no peace, and in the end the person cannot even find rest in sleep. Thus it is said:

> In the grip of anger's affliction
> the mind cannot experience peace;
> it cannot find joy or well-being,
> and thus a person cannot sleep and becomes unstable. BCA 6:3

and

> In brief, through their anger,
> those in good circumstances find no joy. BCA 6:5CD

The anger dwelling within someone lacking forbearance will also show on the outside as a violent demeanor. Through this, friends, relatives, and employees all become fed up with the angry person; even gifts of money or valuables cannot persuade them to put up with his or her presence any longer. Thus it says:

> Friends and loved ones grow wary;
> even if lured through giving, they are not loyal.
> BCA 6:5AB

Furthermore, those lacking forbearance lay themselves open to harmful forces (*māra*), which then create obstacles for them. Therefore the *Bodhisattva Collection* says:

> A mind under the influence of anger is prey to harmful forces
> and encounters obstacles.[302]

Moreover, if you lack forbearance, you will not get the benefit of having all six perfections, the combination of which forms the path to buddhahood. Thus you will not attain enlightenment. Therefore the *Verse Summary of the Perfection of Wisdom* says:

> Where there is anger and no forbearance, how can there be
> enlightenment? RS 24:4C

In contrast, if you possess forbearance, it stands supreme among all the roots of virtue. Therefore it is said:

There is no evil comparable to anger
and there is no fortitude like forbearance.
Therefore cultivate forbearance most earnestly
by every means available. BCA 6:2

Besides this, if you are endowed with forbearance, all sorts of happiness and well-being are found in everyday circumstances. Therefore it is said:

Whoever, through self-control, overcomes anger
will be happy in this and other lives. BCA 6:6CD

Furthermore, if you possess forbearance, you will attain the unsurpassed enlightenment. Thus it says in the *Meeting of Father and Son Sutra*:

Knowing "Anger is not the way of the buddhas"
and cultivating loving kindness in all circumstances,
enlightenment will arise.[303]

The second, **the nature of forbearance**, consists of being unperturbed by anything.[304] *Bodhisattva Levels* says:

To have no regard for material gains and to dwell solely in compassion, upset by nothing: understand this, in brief, to constitute the essence of the bodhisattva's forbearance.[305]

The third, to classify **its different aspects**, forbearance is threefold: (1) forbearance when confronted with harmful beings, (2) forbearance as voluntary acceptance of suffering, and (3) forbearance as confidence born of definite contemplation of the Dharma. Of these, the first is to be forbearing through analyzing the nature of the beings who cause harm, the second is to be forbearing through analyzing the essential nature of suffering itself, and the third is to be forbearing through a discerning analysis of the correct nature of phenomena. The first two aspects cultivate forbearance in terms of [contemplating] the relative, the third in terms of the ultimate.

Fourth is to explain **the essential characteristics of each aspect**. Of these, the first refers to being patient on your part when confronted with situations where someone does something undesirable—such as strike, insult, show hostility, or defame you or your loved ones—or obstructs you from obtaining what you want. What does it mean to be forbearing in such circumstances? Forbearance means remaining unperturbed, not retaliating in kind, or not holding on to the event in one's mind.

According to Master Śāntideva's teachings, we are taught to cultivate forbearance on the basis of considering: (1) the fact that the other person, the aggressor, has no control, (2) the fault due to your own karma, (3) the fault of your physical existence, (4) the fault of your mind, (5) how there is no difference of fault, (6) the practical utility, (7) the enormous kindness, (8) that the buddhas will be delighted, and (9) the tremendous benefits.

For the first, *the fact that the aggressor has no control*, reflect, "Those who do me harm have lost control of themselves through anger, as did Devadatta toward the Buddha. Anger is such that people lose all restraint when something they do not like occurs. Since they are not in control of their acts, it is inappropriate to retaliate." Therefore it says:

> All beings are thus under some influence and are,
> by that very fact, not in control of themselves.
> Knowing this, someone will not become angry
> toward concrete realities that are but mental projections. BCA 6:31

Considering *the fault of your own karma* means to reflect, "The harm that I am experiencing now is a hurt arising through something quite similar that I did in a previous existence. Therefore it is not fitting to retaliate against someone else for the mistakes of my own bad karma." Hence it is said:

> Since I harmed sentient beings
> in former times in just this sort of way,
> it is fitting that this harm should come
> to me now for my aggression. BCA 6:42

Considering *the fault of your physical existence* means reflecting, "If I did not have this body, then the others' weapons and so forth would have nothing to harm. The actual hurt occurs through the presence of this body, and from that point of view it is not right to retaliate." Thus:

His weapon and my body
are both causes for this suffering.
He brought the weapon and I my body,
so who should I be angry at? BCA 6:43

Considering *the fault of mind* involves reflecting, "This mind of mine did not take on a really good body—one that could not be harmed by others. By having taken a lesser and vulnerable body, it is afflicted by harms. Therefore, since it is my own mind that caused such a body to be mine, it is not right to retaliate against someone else." Thus it says:

A human body is like a sore:
it cannot bear to be touched.
As it was I, craving blindly, who took it on,
with whom should I get angry for the harms it encounters?
BCA 6:44

Considering *how there is no difference of fault* means to reflect:

Some, through ignorance, make harm;
others, through ignorance, get angry at them.
Who among them is faultless?
Who is at fault? BCA 6:67

As this is the case, you should avoid the faults and practice forbearance instead.

Considering the *practical utility* means that to develop forbearance you need to have a source of harm. Through cultivating forbearance, wrongdoings are purified and the accumulations are perfected. Through perfecting the accumulations, there will be enlightenment. Therefore, having harm is incredibly useful, and so you should practice forbearance:

In dependence on them, many wrongs
are purified because of my forbearance. BCA 6:48

Considering the *enormous kindness* means to recognize that without the perfection of forbearance, enlightenment will not be achieved, and to cultivate forbearance, the presence of perpetrators of harm is indispensable. Therefore this person, the agent of harm, is a most kind Dharma support. Hence you should be forbearing toward him. It says:

> I should be joyful about my enemy
> because he supports my bodhicitta practice.
>
> By achieving forbearance through them,
> both of us will receive its results;
> since he is the cause of my forbearance,
> he deserves its results first. BCA 6:107CD–108

Considering that *the buddhas will be delighted*:

> Furthermore, the buddhas are the most steadfast of friends
> and benefit us immeasurably.
> What way is there to repay their kindness
> other than by respecting beings? BCA 6:119

Considering the *tremendous benefit*:

> These who show respect in many ways
> thereby cross excellently to the other shore. BCA 6:112CD

Bodhisattva Levels teaches us to cultivate forbearance on the basis of developing five recognitions. It says:

> Recognize the perpetrator of the harm as someone dear to your heart, as a mere phenomenal reality, as impermanent, as suffering, and as someone to be utterly cared for.[306]

Recognizing the harmer as someone dear to your heart means that these beings who are at present causing harm were not like this in former lives. Then they were parents, relatives, or teachers, and there is not one of them who was not at one time your mother. In that sense they have been helpful and beneficial to a degree that no one could ever calculate, and hence it is not right to retaliate against the sort of trouble they are making at present. Forbearance can be found through relating to the situation in these terms.

Recognizing the harmer as a mere phenomenal reality means that the harm that is taking place is dependent on conditions. As such, it is no more than mere notions, mere phenomena. There is not even the slightest trace of an instigator, a life, or a sentient being who is being abusive or who can strike you, defame you, or obstruct your activities. Practice forbearance through notions like these.

Recognizing the harmer as impermanent means to contemplate thus. Sentient beings are impermanent; they are mortal, and the greatest harm that can befall them is to lose their lives. Thus you can practice forbearance by contemplating that there is no need to kill them since they will die anyway, due to the very nature of their existence.

Recognizing the harmer's suffering: Every sentient being is afflicted by the three types of suffering. Think that you should be removing sufferings and not creating further ones. This is practicing forbearance by seeing suffering.

Recognizing the harmer as someone to be utterly cared for means thinking, "Since I have taken the bodhisattva vow, I should be working for the welfare of all sentient beings." Bearing this in mind, hold every sentient being very dear to your heart, with a fondness like you have for your own spouse. Give rise to forbearance by seeing that it is not fitting to retaliate for trivial harms done by someone treasured so dearly.

The second [aspect of forbearance], *forbearance as voluntary acceptance of suffering*, means accepting joyfully and without regret all the sufferings involved in achieving highest enlightenment. It says in *Bodhisattva Levels*:

> It is to accept the eight sorts of suffering, such as those due to one's dwelling and so forth.[307]

The main points here are to accept the sufferings encountered in one's efforts to acquire Dharma robes, alms, and so forth following becoming a renunciate, the sufferings faced in one's efforts in making offerings to and respectfully serving the most precious refuges and gurus, in studying the Dharma, in explaining it, in reciting texts, in meditating, in striving in yoga during the first and last parts of the night instead of sleeping, in working for the welfare of others in the eleven ways mentioned above, and so forth, and to do so without being discouraged by such factors as physical hardship, exhaustion, heat, cold, hunger, thirst, or mental anxiety. An analogy of such voluntary acceptance is to be found in the way someone is glad to receive a painful treatment—such as blood-letting or moxibustion—in order to be cured of a serious illness. *Guide to the Bodhisattva Way of Life* says of this:

> The suffering of my achieving
> enlightenment is limited.
> It is like the suffering inflicted on the body by surgery
> to rid it of an unbearably painful internal ailment. BCA 7:22

Someone who accepts the suffering involved in Dharma development and who manages to swing the battle with samsara and defeat the enemy—the afflictions—is a truly great hero. There are some people renowned in the world as heroes, but there is really no comparison, because they only defeat ordinary enemies, who by their very mortal nature will be slaughtered by death anyway. What they achieve is like striking a corpse with a weapon. The *Guide to the Bodhisattva Way of Life* says:

> By slaughtering reservations about any sort of suffering,
> you defeat the enemies—anger, hatred, and so on.
> Someone who achieves that victory is a real hero;
> the rest is akin to slaying a corpse. BCA 6:20

The third [aspect], *forbearance as confidence born of definite contemplation of the Dharma*, is explained in *Bodhisattva Levels* in terms of "confidence with respect to eight factors, such as the qualities of the Three Jewels."[308] It also relates to the forbearance born [of contemplating] the meaning of suchness—that is, the emptiness of the two types of self-entity.

The fifth, **how forbearance can be increased**, refers to it being enhanced by means of pristine awareness, wisdom, and dedication. This is as already explained earlier [in the context of the perfection of generosity].

The sixth, **how it can be made pure**, refers to forbearance being supported by emptiness and compassion, as explained earlier.

The seventh, **the fruits of forbearance**, should be understood as twofold—temporary and ultimate fruits. The ultimate fruit is to attain unsurpassed enlightenment. *Bodhisattva Levels* says:

> Vast and immeasurable forbearance will result in great enlightenment. Relying on this, bodhisattvas will become purely, most excellently, and perfectly enlightened.[309]

In the meantime the temporary fruits, even though not intentionally sought, are to attain, in every future existence, a beautiful form, good health, fame and acclaim, a long life, and the attributes of a universal monarch. Thus *Guide to the Bodhisattva Way of Life* says:

> While in samsara, through forbearance
> one obtains beauty and so forth and will live long,
> with absence of illness and with fame;
> one will attain the delights of a universal monarch. BCA 6:134

This concludes the fourteenth chapter, on the perfection of forbearance, in this *Ornament of Precious Liberation, a Wish-Fulfilling Gem of Sublime Dharma*.

15. The Perfection of Diligence

The synopsis for the perfection of diligence is:

> **The perfection of diligence is summarized as sevenfold: reflections on the drawbacks of its absence and the benefits of its practice; its nature; its different aspects; the essential characteristics of each aspect; how it can be increased; how it can be made pure; and its fruits.**

To explain the first, reflection on **the drawbacks of its absence and the benefits of its practice.** Even though possessing the qualities of generosity and so forth, a person devoid of diligence will waste their time. When time is wasted, virtue is not accomplished, there is no ability to benefit others, and enlightenment is not attained. Therefore the *Questions of Sāgaramati Sutra* says:

> A person who wastes their time is without generosity, moral discipline, forbearance, meditative concentration, and wisdom. A person who wastes their time performs no actions to benefit others. For a person who wastes their time, enlightenment is far, exceedingly far.[310]

Possession of diligence—the opposite of wasting time—prevents all the bright qualities from becoming tainted and fosters their increase. The *Verse Summary of the Perfection of Wisdom* says:

> Through diligence the bright qualities will not become tainted,
> and the buddhas' treasure of infinite pristine awareness will be
> found. RS 32:3AB

Furthermore, someone endowed with diligence will be able to get across the mountain that is [the ego view of the] perishable composite.[311] Thus the *Ornament of Mahayana Sutras* says:

> Through diligence, someone goes beyond the perishable composite and is liberated. MSA 17:67C

Moreover, if someone possesses diligence, the attainment of enlightenment will be rapid. Therefore the *Ornament of Mahayana Sutras* says:

> Through diligence one will become supremely enlightened as a buddha.[312]

The *Questions of Sāgaramati Sutra* also says:

> Ultimate, totally pure, and perfect enlightenment is not difficult for those who practice diligence. Why is this? Sāgaramati! Whoever has diligence has enlightenment.[313]

The *Questions of Pūrṇa Sutra* says in a similar vein:

> It will not be difficult for enlightenment to come
> to one who constantly exerts diligence.[314]

The second, the **nature** of diligence, is to delight in virtue. Thus the *Compendium of Higher Knowledge* says:

> What is diligence? It is the antidote to wasting time, for it makes one's mind to take genuine delight in virtue.[315]

The *Commentary on the Ornament of Mahayana Sutras* also says:

> "To take utter delight in virtue" presents its essential nature.[316]

When it refers to "the antidote to wasting time," wasting time, its opposite, is threefold: (1) wasting time as idleness, (2) wasting time as underestimating potential, and (3) wasting time in the form of lowly pursuits.

Wasting time as idleness means being attached to the pleasures of letting the mind drift: through sleep, idling in bed, and lounging around. These are to be given up. Why give them up? Because there is no time for such things in this life. It is said:

> Monks! Your cognition will dim, your life will be cut off, and your life drive will be lost. Even the Teacher's doctrine will disappear for certain. Why would you not practice with diligence and unflinching discipline?[317]

Guide to the Bodhisattva Way of Life says too:

> While death is swiftly encroaching,
> I must gather the accumulations. BCA 7:7AB

Someone may think that it will be all right to gather the accumulations [of virtue and wisdom] at the time of death, but when that time comes, there will be no freedom to establish anything. As it says:

> At death, even if you were to stop wasting time,
> what is the point, for it is too late! BCA 7:7CD

You may feel falsely confident, thinking that somehow death will not happen before you have completed your [accumulation of] virtue. That is an unreliable notion. As is said:

> It is wrong to feel so confident.
> My death will not wait for me to finish the things I have to do.
> As far as this ephemeral life is concerned,
> it matters not whether I am sick or healthy. BCA 2:33

This being the case, you might ask, "How then do I eliminate wasting time through idleness?" You should relinquish it as you would react to a snake that had slithered onto your lap or if your hair were on fire. Thus *Guide to the Bodhisattva Way of Life* says:

> Just as you would hurriedly jump up
> if a snake came onto your lap,

so when sleep and idleness come along,
swiftly counteract them! BCA 7:72

And *Letter to a Friend* says:

If your hair or clothes suddenly catch fire,
you do everything possible to put out the blaze:
strive just as much to extinguish future uncontrolled rebirth.
Nothing else is as important as that. SU 104

Wasting time as underestimating potential refers to a defeatist attitude whereby you feel, "How could a lowly person like me ever achieve enlightenment, even were I to make great efforts?" Such discouragement is unnecessary. In fact, the waste of potential caused by such an attitude needs to annihilated. Those who wonder why such discouragement is unnecessary [should take heart from the scripture] that says:

If they develop the power of diligence,
even bees, flies, mosquitoes,
or any insect whatsoever
will achieve enlightenment, so hard to attain!

That being the case, how could one like me—
born human and knowing what is beneficial and what is harmful—
not achieve enlightenment,
provided I do not abandon the bodhisattva conduct? BCA 7:18–19

Wasting time through lowly pursuits means involvement in nonvirtuous activities such as overcoming enemies, amassing possessions, and the like. As those are very real causes of suffering, they are to be abandoned.

Third, the **different aspects** of diligence. Diligence is threefold: armor-like diligence, applied diligence, and insatiable diligence. The first is the most excellent attitude. The second is the most excellent activity. The third is what carries the first two through to their conclusion.

The fourth point develops the **essential characteristics of each aspect.** [First,] you wear the *armor*[*-like diligence*] of the attitude, "From this moment onward and until every sentient being has been established in highest enlightenment, I will never lay aside diligence in virtue." It is said in the *Bodhisattva Collection*:

> Śāriputra! Wear this as inconceivable armor: until the furthermost end of samsara, whatever it may be, and never relax your diligence dedicated to enlightenment.[318]

The *Sutra Teaching the Wearing of Armor* also says:

> Bodhisattvas should wear such armor
> in order to gather beings to them.
> Since the number of beings is incalculable,
> the time for wearing of the armor should likewise be limitless.[319]

The *Akṣayamati Sutra* also says:

> The bodhisattva does not seek enlightenment on the basis of calculating the eons in terms of "I shall wear armor for this many eons and not for this many eons" but puts on armor for an inconceivable length of time.[320]

Bodhisattva Levels says:

> "If, to liberate one single being from suffering, I must abide in hell for a thousand eons, this fills me with joy. It does not matter how much or how little time it takes or how much or how little suffering it involves." Such an attitude is the bodhisattva's armor-like diligence.[321]

[Second,] *applied diligence* has three aspects: (1) diligence in getting rid of affliction, (2) diligence in accomplishing virtue, and (3) diligence in working for the welfare of others.

[1] For the first, [*diligence in getting rid of affliction,*] it is the afflictions—desire and so forth, as well as the actions they motivate—that are the root of suffering. Therefore, to put a stop to its arising, a correspondingly prolonged action that is both specific and global is needed. *Guide to the Bodhisattva Way of Life* says:

> Amid the hordes of the amassed afflictions,
> keep your stance firm in a thousand ways;
> like a lion among foxes,
> do not let the hosts of the afflictions injure you. BCA 7:60

Is there in fact some example of the vigilance and discipline that are needed? It is said:

> One observing the discipline should be as vigilant
> as a terrified person carrying a pot full of mustard oil
> while being held at sword-point,
> threatened with death should a drop be spilled. BCA 7:71

[2] *Diligence in accomplishing virtue* involves striving hard in the practice of the six perfections, without any regard for life or physical well-being. How to strive? By means of five aspects of diligence: continuous diligence, enthusiastic diligence, unshakable diligence, diligence as remaining undeterred, and humble diligence.

Continuous diligence means working uninterruptedly. Of this the *Clouds of Jewels Sutra* says:

> Since bodhisattvas apply diligence to every aspect of their daily lives, nothing can make them regret their acts of body or mind. Such application is known as "a bodhisattva's continuous diligence."[322]

Enthusiastic diligence means acting joyfully, appreciatively, and rapidly. As it is said:

> Since this task must be completed,
> plunge into it
> like an elephant scorched by the midday sun
> plunges into a pool. BCA 7:66

Unshakable diligence means not being distracted from the task by impediments due to thoughts, afflictions, or sufferings.

Diligence as remaining undeterred means not being deterred by witnessing others' violence, brutishness, aggressiveness, degenerate views, or the like, as is mentioned in the *Vajra Victory Banner Sutra*.[323]

Humble diligence means practicing the above forms of diligence without a haughty mind.

[3] *Diligence in accomplishing the welfare of others* is to make effort in the eleven fields, such as supporting activities that are unsupported and so forth.

[Third,] *insatiable diligence* is striving after virtue in a way that knows no satisfaction until enlightenment is reached. As it is said:

> If you cannot get enough of sense pleasures,
> which are like honey on a razor's edge,
> how could you ever be satisfied by whatever peaceful,
> happy results ripen from virtue? BCA 7:65

The fifth point concerns **how diligence can be increased.** It is increased by the three powers taught above: pristine awareness, deep understanding, and dedication, as explained before.

The sixth point is **how it can be made pure.** This is accomplished through the two supports—emptiness and compassion—mentioned above.

The seventh point, the **fruits of diligence** is to be understood as twofold: immediate and ultimate fruits. The ultimate fruit is to attain unsurpassed enlightenment. *Bodhisattva Levels* says:

> Through perfectly completing the perfection of diligence, bodhisattvas truly became perfect buddhas, are truly becoming perfect buddhas, and will truly become perfect buddhas with highest, utterly pure, and perfect enlightenment.[324]

The temporary fruit consists of achieving the highest happiness for as long as one remains in samsara. Thus the *Ornament of Mahayana Sutras* says:

> Through diligence, the pleasures of existence are achieved. MSA 17:67A

This concludes the fifteenth chapter, on the perfection of diligence, in this *Ornament of Precious Liberation, a Wish-Fulfilling Gem of Sublime Dharma.*

16. The Perfection of Meditative Concentration

The synopsis for the perfection of meditative concentration is:

> **The perfection of meditative concentration is summarized as sevenfold: reflections on the drawbacks of its absence and the benefits of its practice; its nature; its different aspects; the essential characteristics of each aspect; how it can be increased; how it can be made pure; and its fruits.**

The first of these, [namely, the **drawbacks of its absence and the benefits of its practice,**] is as follows. Someone possessing the qualities of generosity and so forth but lacking meditative concentration can be overpowered by distractions and so will be wounded by the sharp fangs of the afflictions. Thus *Guide to the Bodhisattva Way of Life* says:

> Humans whose minds are very distracted
> live between the fangs of the afflictions. BCA 8:1

Furthermore, without meditative concentration, the clear cognitions[325] will not arise, and without them you will not be fully equipped to benefit others. *Lamp for the Path to Awakening* says:

> Without the achievement of tranquility,
> the clear cognitions will not emerge. BP 38
> And without the force of the clear cognitions,
> others' welfare will not be achieved. BP 35

Moreover, if you lack meditative concentration, wisdom will not arise, and if wisdom has not arisen, enlightenment will not be attained. Thus the *Letter to a Friend* says:

> There is no wisdom where there is no meditative concentration.
> SU 107

In contrast, if you are endowed with meditative concentration, you will abandon craving for lesser things, clairvoyance will emerge, and many doors of meditative absorption (*samādhi*) will be opened within you. Thus the *Verse Summary of the Perfection of Wisdom* says:

> Through meditative concentration, craving for lowly sensual pleasures are rejected,
> and one truly attains intelligence, the clear cognitions, and meditative absorption. RS 32:3CD

Furthermore, if you are endowed with meditative concentration, wisdom will develop, and this will cause every affliction to be overcome. Thus *Guide to the Bodhisattva Way of Life* says:

> Understanding that the afflictions are totally vanquished
> by profound insight (*vipaśyanā*) conjoined with tranquility . . .
> BCA 8:4

Moreover, if you are endowed with meditative concentration, you will have insight into the perfect truth and therefore generate compassion for sentient beings. Thus *Perfectly Gathering the Qualities* [*of Avalokiteśvara*] says:

> Through settling the mind in meditative equipoise, there will be insight into the ultimate just as it is. Through insight into the ultimate just as it is, bodhisattvas will enter into a state of great compassion for sentient beings.[326]

Further, through being endowed with meditative concentration, you will establish disciples in enlightenment. Thus the *Ornament of Mahayana Sutras* says:

> It is through meditative concentration itself that all individuals become established in the three types of enlightenment.[327]
> MSA 17:40C

The second, the **nature** of meditative concentration, is this: It is characterized by tranquility wherein the mind rests within, focused on virtue. Therefore, in the section dealing with the nature of meditative concentration of the *Bodhisattva Levels*, it says:

> It is a one-pointed mind, abiding in virtue.[328]

This kind of meditative concentration is attained through eliminating its opposing force, namely, powerful distractions. Hence the first priority is to overcome distraction. This involves seclusion, inasmuch as the body needs to be secluded from worldly pursuits and the mind needs to be secluded from its habitual thought processes. Thus *Guide to the Bodhisattva Way of Life* says:

> With body and mind secluded,
> distracted thoughts will not arise. BCA 8:2AB

Of these two, *secluding the body from worldly pursuits* will be explained through six points: (1) the nature of distractive activities, (2) the cause of distractive activities, and (3) harmfulness of distractive activities, (4) the nature of seclusion, (5) the cause of seclusion, and (6) the benefits of seclusion.

(1) The *nature of distractive activities* is to be in a state of distraction due to involvement with children, spouse, acquaintances, or possessions.

(2) The *cause of distractive activities* is attachment, meaning attachment to people, such as spouse, household, and the like; attachment to material things, such as food, clothing, and the like; and attachment to reputation and respect, such as others' praise and so on. Being attached to such things, it becomes impossible to shake free from worldly busyness. Thus it is said:

> Because of attachment and craving for material possessions,
> the world is not relinquished. BCA 8:3AB

(3) The *harmfulness of distractive activities* should be known in terms of both the general and the specific. The general harm caused by distractive activities is explained in the *Sutra Encouraging Nobler Intention*:

> Maitreya! The twenty shortcomings of distractive activities are these. What are they? There is no restraint of body, there is no restraint of speech, there is no restaint of the mind, the afflictions are strong, one is polluted by mundane talk, one will be vulnerable to negative influences, one will be given over to heedlessness, one will fail to attain tranquility and insight.[329]

With respect to the specific harms of distractive activities, through attachment to people you will not attain enlightenment. The *Candraprabha Sutra* says:

> Indulging in desires thoroughly,
> you become attached to children and spouse
> and rely on the pitiable home [life],
> thereby never attaining unsurpassed enlightenment.[330]

Guide to the Bodhisattva Way of Life also says of this:

> Through attachment to those beings,
> the highest purpose is completely blotted out. BCA 8:8AB

[The meditator] should therefore get rid of attachment to those people. As it is said:

> Neither do they benefit you
> nor do you benefit them,
> so steer well clear of the immature! BCA 8:14CD–15A

On the benefits of casting off these attachments the *Candraprabha Sutra* says:

> Perfect enlightenment is not hard to find
> for those who, having rid themselves of clinging
> to spouse and offspring and fearing domestic life,
> have genuinely shaken free from it.[331]

The harm caused by attachment to material possessions and to reputation is twofold: one cannot sustain them permanently, and they give rise to suffering. It says of the first in *Guide to the Bodhisattva Way of Life*:

> What has become of those who have amassed
> wealth and fame is quite unknown. 8:20CD

Of the second it says:

> Whatever you are attached to
> will come back a thousandfold as suffering. 8:18CD

(4) The *nature of seclusion* consists in being free from distracting pursuits.

(5) The *cause of seclusion* is to abide in solitude in an isolated place. An isolated place would be the likes of charnal grounds, forests, caves, meadows, and so forth. To qualify as an isolated place, it should be out of earshot of worldly habitations, meaning a distance of some five hundred bow-spans. It says in the *Treasury of Higher Knowledge*:

> A place is considered secluded when it is out of earshot,
> which means five hundred bow-spans away [from dwellings]. AK 3:87

(6) The *benefits of seclusion* is as follows. When someone has abandoned distractive activities and gone to stay in seclusion, for the sake of both enlightenment and other sentient beings, the *benefits* are manifold: it is the best way to serve and respect enlightened beings; the mind will emerge from its samsara, there will be freedom from the eight worldly concerns, and afflictions will not increase; and meditative absorption swiftly develops. These will be explained point by point.

As for the first point, [seclusion being the best way to serve the buddhas:] When, through bodhicitta, just seven paces are taken toward a hermitage with the intention of staying in retreat to benefit beings, it is far more pleasing to the totally pure and perfect buddhas than offering them food, drink, flowers, and so on. Thus the *Candraprabha Sutra* says:

> Food, drink, and robes,
> flowers, incense, and garlands are

not what best serve and honor the Victor, the finest being of all.
Whoever, longing for enlightenment and saddened with
the evils of conditioned life, takes seven paces toward a place of
retreat
with the intention of staying there to benefit beings
his merit is far greater than those who make such offerings.[332]

The same sutra explains how the mind will shake free from samsara and from the eight worldly concerns and how afflictions will not be fostered:

Likewise you will definitively transcend [life's] artifices,
you will be without the slightest longing for worldly things,
and things that are tainted will not be fostered.[333]

It also tells how what is needed more than all else—meditative absorption—will swiftly develop. The same sutra states:

Leave enjoyment of towns and village
and ever resort to solitude and the forests.
Like a rhinoceros, always remain single-pointed,
and before long the best meditative absorptions will be attained.[334]

This concludes the explanation of the need for physical seclusion, away from distractive activities.

To *seclude your mind from habitual thought processes*, you should abide in quiet retreats. While staying in retreat, contemplate, "Why exactly did I come to this hermitage? I came to this secluded place in fear and in terror of the places of distraction, such as towns and cities. Fleeing them, I came to retreat." What was so frightening there? The *Questions of the Layman Ugra Sutra* says:

I am afraid and terrified of the distractive activities; I am afraid and terrified of material possessions and honors; I am afraid and terrified of corrupting friends; I am afraid and terrified of those who teach bad ways; I am afraid and terrified of the dangers of desire, anger, and delusion; I am afraid and terrified of the māra of the aggregates, the māra of afflictions, the māra of death,

> and the māra of seductive pleasure; I am afraid and terrified of the three rebirths—animals, hungry spirits, and hell beings. Through such fear and terror I have come to the wilderness.[335]

Being afraid and terrified in the manner described above, think, "Here, in this place of solitude, what are my body, speech, and mind doing right now?"

Contemplate, "If while in retreat my body is killing, stealing, or the like, then there is no difference between myself and beasts of prey, hunters, thieves, and robbers. Is this really accomplishing my initial purpose in coming here?" In this way counter these behaviors.

Examining your speech, contemplate, "If while in retreat I chatter, slander, misuse speech, and so forth, then there is no difference between myself and peacocks, parrots, songbirds, larks, and the like. Is this really accomplishing my initial purpose in coming here?" In this way, counteract these [inappropriate speech activities].

Examine your mind and contemplate, "If while here in retreat I have unwholesome thoughts of desire, anger, and jealousy, then I am no different from wild animals, baboons, monkeys, wild bears, northern bears, and the like.[336] Is this really accomplishing my initial purpose in coming here?" In this way, counteract these [inappropriate mental activities].

This concludes the explanation of secluding the mind from unwholesome thoughts.

When body and mind are both secluded, distractions will no longer arise, and once free of distraction, one can enter into meditative concentration. For that, the mind needs to be cultivated. First there should be some reflection with a view to establishing which affliction is the greatest, and then follow this by cultivating its counterforce. As the remedy for desire, meditate on what is unpleasant; as the remedy for anger, meditate on loving kindness; as the remedy for ignorance, meditate on dependent origination; as the remedy for jealousy, meditate on the equality of self and others; as the remedy for pride, meditate on exchanging of self and others; and if all the afflictions are equal in their coarseness, or in the case of excessive thought processes, as the remedy, meditate on your breathing.

(1) If *desire is your predominant affliction*, the remedy is to meditate on the unpleasant as follows. First contemplate your body as being composed of thirty-six impure substances—flesh, blood, skin, bones, marrow, serum,

bile, phlegm, mucus, saliva, urine, and so forth. Then go to a charnel ground and observe the corpses that were placed there—fresh ones, two-day-old ones, three-day-old ones, four-day-old ones, and five-day-old ones. Observe their decay, their complete transformation, and how they become black and eaten by small worms. Then reflect, "My own body is also of that nature, a similar phenomenon, and I have not yet transcended such a condition." When observing corpses brought to the charnel ground, skeletons with little flesh left, those where there is just the muscle structure as interwoven fibers, those broken down into many pieces, or skeletons of those dead for many years, of which the bones are shell- or pigeon-colored, meditate as above, thinking, "My own body is also of that nature, a similar phenomenon, and I have not yet transcended such a condition."

(2) If *anger is predominant* in you, its remedy is to meditate on loving kindness as follows. In general there are three aspects of loving kindness, as mentioned in an earlier chapter.[337] The aspect developed in this context is loving kindness focused on sentient beings. First consider someone naturally dear to you and start thinking about making that person happy and well cared for. This should generate corresponding feelings of loving kindness [in you for that person]. That feeling of love is then extended toward others with whom you are familiar. It is next expanded to embrace ordinary people, then to people within your vicinity, then to those living in your town, and finally to include everyone living in all ten directions.

(3) If *ignorance is predominant* in you, its remedy is to meditate on dependent origination as follows. It says in the *Rice Shoot Sutra*:

> Monks! Whoever understands this rice shoot understands dependent origination. Whoever understands dependent origination understands the nature of phenomena. Whoever understands phenomena understands buddhahood.[338]

There are two ways of presenting dependent origination: the dependent origination of the forward order pertaining to origination of samsara, and the dependent origination of the reverse order pertaining to nirvana.

The first, in turn, is twofold: the dependent origination of inner phenomena and the dependent origination of outer phenomena.[339] This former is discussed in terms of two aspects—the dependent origination of inner phenomena in terms of their causes and the dependent origination of inner phenomena in terms of their conditions. With respect to the first [the Buddha stated]:

> "Monks! Because this exists, this will come to be. This having arisen, this arises. That is how it is. Conditioned by ignorance, there will be formations"[340] and so forth, up to "birth, and through that condition there will be aging and death, sorrow and lamentations, pain, mental stress, and disturbances. That is how this great cluster of nothing but misery is produced."[341]

This [quote] relates to the desire realm in terms of dimension of existence and to a womb birth in terms of mode of birth.[342]

Here, first what is referred to as *ignorance*, which is confused about the nature of what is to be known, arises. Stirred by this, one comes to form the contaminated actions, such as those that are virtuous and nonvirtuous. This is what is referred to as "Conditioned by ignorance, *formations* come to be." The mind that is imbued by the seed of that karma is what is being referred to in the phrase "Conditioned by karma, *consciousness* comes to be." Due to the power of karma, one's mind becomes distorted and joins up with the procreative elements in the mother's womb to become the various stages of embryo and then fetus. This is what is referred to as "Conditioned by consciousness, *name and form* come to be." Through the development of this name and form, the various sense faculties—of sight, smell, and so forth—become complete. This is what is known as "Conditioned by name and form, the *six sense bases* come to be." When these various sense faculties, such as sight and so on, meet up with their corresponding objective fields through the appropriate consciousness, the meeting of the three causes an actual experience of the object. This is known as "Conditioned by the six sense bases, *contact* comes to be." Just as the contact arises, feeling, in the sense of a pleasant, unpleasant, or indifferent experience arises. This is known as "Conditioned by contact, *feeling* comes to be." Taking pleasure in that feeling, craving and intensely craving for it, is known as "Conditioned by feeling, *craving* comes to be." On the basis of such clinging, and with the thought "May I never be separated from this," attachment in the form of not wanting to let go and in the form of longing for it arise. This is known as "Conditioned by craving, *grasping* comes to be." Due to this striving, actions are performed—physically, verbally, or mentally—that give rise to rebirth. This is known as "Conditioned by grasping, *becoming* comes to be." Whatever existence composed of the five aggregates is generated by those actions is known as "Conditioned by becoming, *birth* comes to be." Through having been born, the development and maturity of the aggregates is aging and their destruction is death. Thus, "Conditioned by birth, there will be *aging and death*."

At death, when you manifestly grasp on to things due to ignorance and are thoroughly assailed within by forces such as attachment, this is *sorrow*. *Lamentations* are the verbal outcry emerging from such sorrow. *Pain* means the unpleasant sensations experienced by the five groups of consciousness. *Mental distress* is the pain in the mind resulting from various sorts of mental activity. The various other forms of distress are the *disturbances*—a term relating to the secondary afflictions.

The above factors of dependent origination should be understood as falling into three distinct groups: ignorance, craving, and grasping are *afflictions*; formations and becoming are *karma*; and the other seven factors—consciousness and so forth—are *suffering*. The *Verses on the Essence of Dependent Origination* says:

> The twelve specific links
> should be understood in terms of three groups.
> These links of dependent origination taught by the Sage
> are encompassed by three categories:
> affliction, karma, and suffering.
> The first, eighth, and ninth are afflictions,
> the second and tenth are karma,
> while the remaining seven are suffering.[343]

Furthermore, to illustrate them by means of analogy, ignorance is like the one who sows a seed, karma is like the field, consciousness like the seed itself, craving is like moisture, name and form like a shoot, and the remaining links are like the branches and leaves [of the plant].

Now if ignorance did not occur, formations too would not manifest. Likewise, if birth did not happen, then aging and death could not occur. However, it is because of the presence of ignorance that formations and so forth do actually come into being. Therefore, because of the existence of birth, aging and death will actually happen. In these processes, however, it is not the case that ignorance consciously thinks, "I will make formations truly manifest," nor do the formations have the thought, "We were made to be manifested by, and created by, ignorance." Likewise birth does not think, "I will make aging and death truly happen," nor do aging and death consider themselves actually brought into being by birth.

Nevertheless, it is through the existence of ignorance that formations and so forth do become manifest realities and will occur, and it is likewise through the existence of birth that aging and death are made manifest and will happen. This is how to view inner dependent origination in terms of its causes.

The dependent origination of inner phenomena is connected also with *conditions*. This is because they are comprised of the six elements—earth, water, fire, wind, space, and consciousness. Here, the "earth element" is the body's firmness and its actual material existence; the "water element" is what holds the body together; the "fire element" transmutes food, drink, and so forth; the "wind element" moves the breath in and out; the "space element" refers to the inner cavities of the body; the "consciousness element" is comprised of the five sense consciousnesses and the tainted[344] mental consciousness. Without these conditions, a body cannot come into being; furthermore, the presence of all six inner elements is universal and hence comprises everything. It is due to them that the body will have its actual manifest existence.

In these [processes], the six elements do not think, "I will establish the body's firmness," and so on, and neither does the body think, "I am generated by these specific conditions." Nevertheless, it is through these specific conditions that the body occurs in all the ways it does.

In how many lives do these twelve links of dependent origination complete their cycle? In this respect, the *Ten Levels Sutra* says:

> Formations due to the condition of ignorance applies to what happened in past lives. The [links] from consciousness up to feelings apply to the present life. Craving through to becoming apply to the next life. Everything else emerges inexorably from that.[345]

Dependent origination as the reverse order that pertains to nirvana refers to the following. Through realizing the true nature (*dharmatā*) of all phenomena to be emptiness, ignorance ceases, and through its cessation, [all the other links] through to aging and death will come to cease in their due order. As is said:

> By stopping ignorance, karmic formation is stopped . . . [up to] by stopping birth, aging and death, and sorrow and lamentations, pain, mental stress, and disturbances are stopped. That is how this great cluster of nothing but misery will cease.[346]

(4) If *jealousy is predominant* in you, meditate on the equality of yourself and others as a remedy as follows. Just as you wish happiness for yourself, so do other beings wish happiness for themselves. Just as you do not want suffering yourself, neither do other beings want to suffer. Thinking in such a way, cultivate the same care for others as you have for yourself. *Guide to the Bodhisattva Way of Life* says:

> From the very outset make efforts
> to meditate on the equality of self and others.
> Protect all beings as you protect yourself,
> since all are equal in wanting happiness and not suffering. BCA 8:90

(5) If *pride is predominant* in you, the remedy is to meditate on substituting self for others as follows. Immature beings suffer in a samsara that they themselves have created through a motivation of caring for self alone. Buddhas, motivated by their care for others and acting solely for the welfare of others, have attained enlightenment. Thus it says:

> Immature beings act out of self-interest.
> Sages act for the good of others.
> Consider the difference between these two! BCA 8:130B–D

Therefore cast off self-grasping by understanding self-cherishing to be a fault. Treat others as yourself by understanding cherishing others to be a positive quality. The *Guide to the Bodhisattva Way of Life* says:

> Through understanding ego to be faulty
> and others to be an ocean of qualities,

> cultivate a rejection of self-grasping
> and a commitment toward others. BCA 8:113

(6) If *all the afflictions are equally present* in you or if there is excessive discursive thought, the remedy is to train in breath-based meditations as follows. These are the six [main] aspects of practice, such as counting the breaths, following after them, and so on, presented in the *Treasury of Higher Knowledge*:

> There are held to be six:
> counting, following, resting,
> thinking, transformation,
> and utterly purifying them. AK 6:12

The practices whereby these afflictions are neither eliminated, indulged in, or transmuted, such as according to the way of secret mantra or of the tradition and instructions of Marpa and his spiritual heirs, are to be learned orally [from a qualified guru]. You should understand the Innate Union [of Mahāmudrā][347] and the Six Practices of Nāropa.[348]

All the above represent the various stages of mental training that lead to [the practice of] meditative concentration.

The third point concerns the **different aspects of meditative concentration itself.** There are three: (1) meditative concentration that procures tangible well-being, (2) meditative concentration that gives rise to good qualities, and (3) meditative concentration that accomplishes the welfare of others. The first of these makes one's mind a suitable vessel, the second produces enlightened qualities in someone who is already a fit vessel, and the third works for the benefit of beings.

The fourth point concerns the **essential characteristics of each aspect.** *Meditative concentration that procures tangible well-being* is described in *Bodhisattva Levels*:

> This is the meditative concentration of bodhisattvas. It is free of all discursive thought. It gives rise to excellent mastery of mind and body. It is supremely peaceful in the very best way. It is without arrogance, it does not get involved with experiencing the taste of meditation, and it is free from any [clinging to] signs.

> Such is what should be understood by "well-being during this life."[349]

In the above: "Free of all discursive thought" means that it remains fully concentrated without any interference due to the discursive intellect producing ideas of existence, nonexistence, and so on. "It gives rise to excellent mastery of mind and body" means the destruction of every bad condition that body or mind might adopt. "Supremely peaceful in the very best way" means that it enters such a condition naturally. "Without arrogance" refers to an absence of the affliction of [false] views. "Does not get involved with experiencing the taste of meditation" refers to an absence of the affliction of craving. "Free from any [clinging to] signs" means free from experiencing sense objects such as form and so on [as though they were independent entities].

In terms of the gateway to all [higher qualities], there are four meditative concentrations (*dhyāna*): the first dhyāna, the second dhyāna, the third dhyāna, and the fourth dhyāna. Of these, the first dhyāna is accompanied by investigation and sustained analysis, the second dhyāna is accompanied by bliss, the third dhyāna is accompanied by joy, and the fourth dhyāna is accompanied by equanimity.

Meditative concentration that produces good qualities is of two kinds: the exceptional and the common. The first refers to the various meditative absorptions encompassed within the ten powers, which are immeasurable and inconceivable. Since śrāvakas and pratyekabuddhas are not even aware of the names of such meditative attainments, what need is there to speak of their ever actually engaging in them?

The common ones refer to the likes of the "complete liberations," "surpassings," "gateways of exhaustion," "excellent specific intelligences," and so forth, which are common to both the Mahayana and the śrāvakayāna. It is on the level of their names they share commonality; in actual fact, however, they are not identical at all.

As for *meditative concentration that accomplishes the welfare of others*, whichever meditative concentration is resorted to, there can be countless physical emanations. These meditative concentrations operate for the benefit of beings in eleven ways, such as supporting beings according to their needs and so forth.

You might ask, "Since there are tranquility and insight, which are well known, what is tranquility and what is insight?" *Tranquility* refers to placing one's mind within the mind on the basis of perfect meditative absorption. *Insight* refers to what follows on from this, an excellent discerning awareness of phenomena that understands what is and what is not to be done. The *Ornament of Mahayana Sutras* says:

> Through abiding in the most excellent,
> mind is made to rest within mind,
> and there is supreme discernment of things.
> These are tranquility and insight. MSA 19:67

Tranquility is the meditative concentration itself, and insight is the wisdom aspect.

The fifth point is **how the power of meditative concentration can be increased.** It is increased by the three powers described above: pristine awareness, wisdom, and dedication. This is as explained before.

The sixth point, **how it can be made pure,** refers to meditative concentration being supported by emptiness and compassion, just as described above.

The seventh point, the **fruits of meditative concentration**, should be understood as twofold—its temporary and ultimate results. Its ultimate result is to attain unsurpassed enlightenment. *Bodhisattva Levels* says:

> Through taking the perfection of meditative concentration to its utter completion, bodhisattvas truly became perfect buddhas, are truly becoming perfect buddhas, and will truly become perfect buddhas—with highest, utterly pure, and perfect enlightenment.[350]

In the meanwhile, one will obtain the existence of birth as a god free of desire. Master Nāgārjuna says:

> Due to the four meditative concentrations,
> through which sensory experience, physical bliss, mental joy,
> and suffering are completely shed,

you attain a state similar to that of the gods
in the Brahma, Luminous, Complete Virtue, and Great Result
heavens. SU 41

This concludes the sixteenth chapter, on the perfection of meditative concentration, in this *Ornament of Precious Liberation, a Wish-Fulfilling Gem of Sublime Dharma.*

17. The Perfection of Wisdom

For the perfection of wisdom, the following is the synopsis:

> **The perfection of wisdom is summarized as sevenfold: reflections on the drawbacks of its absence and the benefits of its practice; its nature; its different aspects; the essential characteristics of each aspect; that which is to be understood; how to cultivate it; and its fruits.**

The first point is to reflect on **the drawbacks of its absence and the benefits of its practice.** A bodhisattva may abide within the perfections from generosity through to meditative concentration, yet will never attain the state of omniscience if the perfection of wisdom is lacking. Why is this so? The [first five perfections] are like a group of blind people without a guide and hence unable to journey to the city they wish to visit. Thus the *Verse Summary of the Perfection of Wisdom* says:

> Without a guide, how could even a trillion blind people
> who are unfamiliar with the road ever find the city gate?
> Without wisdom, the five perfections are sightless;
> without a guide, one cannot reach enlightenment. RS 7:1

In contrast, when they possess wisdom, all the wholesome aspects of virtue—generosity and so on—are transformed into the path to buddhahood, and the state of omniscience will be attained, like a throng of blind people being led by their guide to the city. Thus *Entering the Middle Way* says:

> Just as a whole group of blind people is easily led
> to the place of their choice by one sighted person,

so are the sightless qualities
led to the Conqueror's state by wisdom. MA 6:2

The *Verse Summary of the Perfection of Wisdom* says:

Every aspect of the three realms will be completely transcended
by thoroughly understanding the nature of phenomena through wisdom. RS 32:4AB

This being so, some may wonder, "Wisdom alone might suffice, and what need is there for the skillful means—generosity and so forth?" This is not the case. *Lamp for the Path to Awakening* says:

Wisdom lacking skillful means
and skillful means lacking wisdom
are both bondage, it has been taught.
Therefore do not abandon this combination. BP 43

Exactly what bondage occurs if either wisdom or skillful means are practiced on their own? A bodhisattva who resorts to wisdom without skillful means will fall into the partial nirvana considered to be peace by the śrāvakas and become utterly bound, never reaching nonabiding nirvana. According to the viewpoint that upholds the ultimacy of the three vehicles, it is maintained that one remains stuck in that [nirvana] state permanently. However, according to the theory of a single vehicle, it is maintained that one will remain in that state for eighty thousand major eons.

With wisdom lacking skillful means, one is tied to nirvana. With skillful means lacking wisdom, one is tied to samsara. Therefore the two must be combined.[351]

It also says in the *Teachings of Vimalakīrti Sutra*:

What is bondage for bodhisattvas and what is their liberation? Their bondage is wisdom not supported by skillful means whereas their liberation is wisdom supported by skillful means.[352]

Hence to practice either skillful means or wisdom on its own is to engage in the work of Māra. The *Questions of Nāga King Anavatapta Sutra* says:

> The works of Māra are two: skillful means without wisdom and wisdom without skillful means. Those should be recognized as the work of Māra and rejected.[353]

Further, to give an analogy, just as someone wishing to reach the town of his choice needs a combination of eyes to survey the way and legs to cover the distance, so those going to the city of nonabiding nirvana need the union of the eyes of wisdom and the legs of skillful means. The *Gayāśīrṣa Hill Sutra* says:

> In brief, Mahayana is twofold: means and wisdom.[354]

Wisdom will not arise of its own accord. For example, while a small amount of wood may be ignited but never becomes a powerful, enduring blaze, a great quantity of extremely dry branches stacked together can be ignited to make a mighty, long-lasting blaze that is inextinguishable. Similarly, if only a small amount of wholesome action has been established, great wisdom will not arise, but when vast amounts of the great merits of generosity, moral discipline, and so forth have been established, a great wisdom will emerge, and this will burn away all the obscurations. Therefore it is for the sake of wisdom alone that one must resort to generosity and so forth. The *Guide to the Bodhisattva Way of Life* says:

> The Victor has taught that all these factors
> are for the sake of wisdom. BCA 9:1AB

The second point, the **nature** of wisdom, consists of an accurate, discerning appreciation of phenomena. Thus the *Compendium of Higher Knowledge* says:

> What is wisdom? It is an accurate, discerning appreciation of phenomena.[355]

The third point concerns **its different aspects.** The commentary to the *Ornament of Mahayana Sutras* speaks of three types of wisdom: mundane wisdom, lesser supramundane wisdom, and greater supramundane wisdom.

The fourth point explains the **essential characteristics of each aspect.** *Mundane wisdom* is the wisdom emerging from the four domains of knowledge: the sciences of healing, logic and epistemology, linguistics, and creative skill.[356] *Lesser supramundane wisdom* is the wisdom that arises through the study, contemplation, and meditation of the śrāvakas and pratyekabuddhas. It is to realize the self-perpetuating aggregates to be impure, ridden with suffering, impermanent, and devoid of any entity. *Greater supramundane wisdom* is the wisdom that arises from Mahayana study, contemplation, and meditation. It is the awareness that each and every phenomenon is, by its very nature, empty, unborn, without foundation, and without root. Thus it says in the *Perfection of Wisdom in Seven Hundred Lines*:

> To understand that every phenomenon has no existence as something arisen—that is the perfection of wisdom.[357]

The *Verse Summary of the Perfection of Wisdom* also says:

> To understand every phenomenon to be without inherent existence
> is to engage in the practice of excellent perfection of wisdom.
> RS 1:28CD

Lamp for the Path to Awakening says:

> It is clearly stated that wisdom is
> to understand emptiness, the essential nature,
> through perceiving the aggregates,
> the sense bases, and elements to be devoid of arising. BP 47

The fifth point concerns **that which is to be understood.** Of the three types of wisdom mentioned above, it is the third type—greater supramundane wisdom—that one needs to understand. I shall present this by means of six topics:

A. Refutation of belief in substantial reality
B. Refutation of belief in unreality
C. The mistake of belief in nonexistence
D. The mistake of both beliefs
E. The path to liberation
F. The nature of liberation—nirvana

A. Refutation of belief in substantial reality

In his *Lamp for the Path to Awakening*, Atiśa presents this on the basis of analysis through the major reasoning. He says:

> It is illogical for something existing to arise;
> for nonexistents also, they are like sky flowers. BP 48

As he explains in the teachings on the gradual path, all substantial realities, or beliefs in substantiality, are included within the two kinds of self-entity, and both those entities are by their very nature emptiness. What, then, are the two kinds of self-entity? They are known as the *self of persons* and the *self of phenomena*. What is the self-entity of persons?[358] There are many views on this. In fact, what is referred to as a "person" is the continuum of aggregates accompanied by awareness; it is that which does all sorts of things, always thinking this and that, moving and hopping about. About this the *Sutra of Fragments* says:

> The continuum is termed "person";
> it is this that constantly moves about and scatters.

Believing such a person to be an eternal and unitary entity, and grasping on to it and being attached to it, is called the "selfhood of person" or of mind. Through the notion of selfhood, afflictions will be generated; through the afflictions, karma will be generated; and through karma, suffering will be generated. Thus the root of all sufferings and faults is the self or mind. Therefore the *Thorough Exposition of Valid Cognition* says:

> When "I" exists, "other" is known.
> Through the I-and-other pair comes

clinging and aversion.
Through the complex interaction of these arises all harm. PV 2:221

What is the self-entity of phenomena? Here, *phenomena* refers to the outer perceived world and the inner perceiving mind. Why are those two aspects called *phenomena* (*dharma*)? Because they possess their own defining characteristics.[359] Thus the *Sutra of Fragments* says:

> That which holds defining characteristics is called *dharma*.

Thus holding the two—the objective perceived world and the subjective perceiving world—to possess substantial reality and clinging to them is called *self of phenomena.*

(1) To present how these two types of self-entity are empty by nature, first there is the *refutation of the self of persons*. Master Nāgārjuna says in his *Precious Garland*:

> The notions "I" and "mine"
> deviate from what is ultimately true. RA 1:28AB

This means that, from the point of view of ultimate reality, those aspects of self-entity do not exist. If such a self existed as an ultimate reality, it should equally be there when ultimate truth is "seen"; yet when a mind with insight into the truth sees the essential nature, there is no such self. Therefore it does not have any true existence. The *Precious Garland* says:

> For when the ultimately pure is fully recognized
> just as it is, these two will not arise. RA 1:28CD

In that text, "the ultimately pure is fully recognized just as it is" refers to insight into the truth. "These two will not arise" means that there will be no grasping at "I" or "mine."

[a] Were a mind or self to truly exist, it could be examined as originating from itself, from something else, or through the three phases of time.

It does not arise from itself because [as far as the process of origination is concerned] its production must have either already happened or have not yet happened. If it does not yet exist, it cannot possibly serve as a cause [for its own production,] and if it does already exist, it cannot possibly become [its own] result. Thus something producing itself is a contradiction.

It does not arise from others because they are substances [other than itself]. Why can they not be causes? A "cause" only exists with respect to a result, and as long as there is no result, there is no cause. As long as there is no cause, no result can manifest either. This is similar to the previous argument.[360]

It does not arise from both [self and others] of the above since both concepts are faulty, as explained above.

It does not arise from the three phases of time: It is not a product of the past because the past, like a seed gone rotten, no longer has any power. It is not produced by the future—that would be like the child of a barren woman. It is not a product of the present because it is illogical that it could be both creation and creator [in the same instant]. Thus the *Precious Garland* says:

> As it is not being obtained from itself,
> something other, a combination, or the three times,
> belief in a self will be consumed. RA I:37A–C

"Not being obtained from" means not generated by.

[b] Alternatively, one should understand it in the following manner. Examine whether or not this "self" exists in the body, in the mind, or in a name.

The nature of *the body* is that of the four elements: the body's solidity is the earth element, its fluids are the water element, its warmth is the fire element, and its breathing and movement constitute the wind element. The four elements possess neither self nor mind, just as the four outer elements—earth, water, and so on—are without mind or self.

Does the self exist in *the mind*, then? Mind has no existence whatsoever, for neither you nor anyone else has ever seen it. If mind has no actual existence, then self as mind can have no actual existence either.

Does self or own mind exist in *the name*? A name is merely something given arbitrarily; it has no substantial existence and bears no relation to a self.

Thus the three reasons presented above demonstrate that the self or mind of persons has no true existence.

(2) Second there is the *refutation of the self of phenomena*. This is in two

parts, demonstrating the nonexistence of the objective perceived world and the nonexistence of the subjective perceiving mind.

[a] As for the first, [the *nonexistence of the objective perceived world,*] some believe in the substantial existence of the objective perceived world. Vaibhāṣikas, for example, hold there to be minute particles of matter that exist substantially; they are round and partless. The aggregation of these particles constitutes objects such as material form and so forth. As the particles agglomerate, there are interstices between them. They presently appear as something homogeneous, just as a yak's tail or a pasture of grass does. The minute particles do not drift apart because the karma of beings causes them to bond as they do. Sautrāntikas hold that when such partless particles conglomerate, they are without interstices yet do not actually touch. These are the views of those [two main Hinayana traditions,] but neither is really the case.

Were such a particle to be unitary, then would it not have sides? If so, would it not have relative east, west, north, south, top, and bottom areas? This makes six sides and destroys the contention of it being unitary. If it had no spatial dimension, all matter would be, by nature, a sole atom. This is obviously not the case either. The *Twenty Stanzas* says:

> If the six are applied to what is one,
> the ultimate particle has six different parts.
> If those six are one,
> then substance is only one particle.[361]

Are particles multiple? If one partless particle could be proved to exist, it would be reasonable to propose that many of them could conglomerate to make multiple entities, but since the existence of a partless unit cannot be proved, multiples of them cannot be proved to exist either. As a consequence, since particles have no substantial existence, an outer substantial reality composed of particles of such a nature cannot exist either.

You may wonder, "What is actually manifesting right now?" It is an image in the mind that appears to the mind as being an outer world. This occurs through delusion. If you ask, "How can we know that is so?" the answer is that it can be known through scriptural authority, reason, and examples:

The *scriptural authority* can be found in the *Flower Ornament Sutra*, where it says:

> Children of good family! This world of the three realms is mind only.[362]

Also in the *Sutra on Going to Laṅka*, where it says:

> Mind agitated by its imprints
> will manifest thoroughly as objective realities.[363]
> There are no objective realities but mind alone;
> the perception of external reality is erroneous.[364]

[Refutation of external reality through] *reason* can be presented in the form of the syllogism: "Those things that appear as external" is the logical subject; "they are illusory manifestations of mind" is the proposition; "because that which has no true existence is being perceived" is the reason. (For instance, human horns or a visualized tree.)[365]

Such manifestations (the subject) are also simply illusory projections of the mind (the proposition) because they do not appear as what they really are—changing appearances brought about by certain causes and conditions, or appearances that can transmute and disappear through the power of imagination and familiarization, the way things manifest being different according to the projections of each of the six types of sentient being (the reason). *Examples* of such a process would be dreams, magical illusions, and the like.

Thus the above presents how the external perceived world is devoid of [substantial] existence.

[b] The second point [is the *nonexistence of a perceiving mind*]. Some—pratyekabuddhas and Cittamātrins—consider the subjective, perceiving mind really to exist, as something apperceptive and self-illuminating. They hold such a view, but it is inaccurate for three reasons:

1. Mind does not exist when examined in terms of moments of time.
2. Mind does not exist because no one has ever witnessed it.
3. Mind does not exist because there is no objective reality.

(1) Concerning the first of these, [nonexistence *in terms of moments of time*]: "Is the apperceptive, self-illuminating mind that you postulate present in one instant or several? Were it truly to exist in each instant, would that instant have past, present, and future?[366] If it were so, this would refute its existence as a unique existing unit of mind. If it were not so, [the idea of sequences of] many instants becomes absurd." Thus the *Precious Garland* says:

> One must examine the instant: just as it has an end,
> it must also have a middle and a beginning.
> Since an instant is thus threefold,
> the world cannot exist as an instant. RA 1:69

Without the existence of the threefold division of time, the [true existence of the] instant is refuted by its being insubstantial. Through the instant being unproven, the existence of mind [composed of such instants] is also unproven.

Does mind exist as multiple instants? Were one instant to be proven, it would be reasonable to postulate an accumulation of many instants, but since the existence of one instant is not proven, the idea of mind as multiple instants is not demonstrated either.

(2) Now for the second point, the nonexistence of the perceiving mind *because it has never been witnessed*. Seek out the location of "mind"—in the body, outside it, or between the two; seek it high and low. Examine most thoroughly to determine whether it has any form or color whatsoever. Seek until there is a sense of conviction, whatever it may be. Search for it according to the master's instructions—such as how to vary the object of inspection. When, no matter how you seek, mind is never seen, never encountered, and no substantial characteristic such as color or something visible is to be found, it is not the case that mind exists but you have not yet been able to find it or witness it. If it cannot be seen, no matter where it is sought, it is because the investigator is the investigated and the seeker is beyond the scope of his or her own intellect—beyond the scope of words, thoughts, ideas, or expression. That is why in the *Kāśyapa Chapter Sutra* it says:

> Kāśyapa! Mind is found neither within, without, nor in between. Kāśyapa! Mind cannot be investigated, cannot be shown, can-

> not be used as a basis, cannot appear, cannot be known, and has no abiding. Kāśyapa! Mind has never, is never, and will never be seen, even by any of the buddhas.[367]

In the *Sutra That Perfectly Seizes Sublime Dharma* it says:

> Therefore, by coming to understand perfectly
> the various degrees to which
> mind is a contrivance, a fake,
> one will no longer perceive it as an essence.
> Devoid of any essence,
> phenomena are without any real existence.
> All phenomena are imputed;
> I have taught their nature to be such.
> Outshining the two extremes,
> the wise practice the middle way;
> this emptiness of essential reality,
> this is the path to enlightenment;
> I too have taught this path.[368]

The *Unwavering Suchness Sutra* says:

> Every phenomenon is, by its very nature, unborn, essentially nonabiding, free from the extremes of acting and action, and beyond the scope of thought and nonthought.[369]

Since no one has ever witnessed mind, it is pointless to speak of it in terms of apperception and self-illumination. As *Guide to the Bodhisattva Way of Life* states:

> Since none has ever seen it at any time,
> to ask whether it is self-illuminating
> is as meaningless as discussing
> the elegance of a barren woman's child. BCA 9:22

Tilopa said:

Marvel! This is the self-cognizing pristine awareness;
it is beyond speech and is not the domain of the intellect.[370]

(3) The third point—the nonexistence of the perceiving mind *because no objective reality exists*—is explained as follows. Since, as was demonstrated above, visual forms and so forth—the outer objective reality—have no substantial existence, the inner mind that perceives them cannot have substantial existence either. In the *Sutra on the Indivisibility of the Dharmadhātu* it says:

> Investigate whether this thing you call "mind" is blue, yellow, red, white, maroon, or transparent; whether it is pure or impure, "permanent" or "impermanent," and whether or not it is endowed with form. Mind has no physical form; it cannot be shown. It does not manifest, it is intangible, it does not cognize, it resides neither inside, outside, nor anywhere in between. Thus it is utterly pure, totally nonexistent. There is nothing of it to liberate; it is the very nature of the dharmadhātu.[371]

Furthermore, *Guide to the Bodhisattva Way of Life* says:

When there is nothing to be known,
what is the point of speaking of knowing? BCA 9:60CD

and

It is certain, therefore, that without the presence
of something knowable, there can be no knowledge. BCA 9:61CD

Through the above points, it has been demonstrated that the perceiving mind, a subjective mind, has no ultimate existence. This concludes the section discussing the belief in substantial reality.

B. Refutation of Belief in Unreality

If the two types of self-entity have no authentic existence as real things, could they be nonexistent, unreal? In fact, they do not even exist as unrealities. Why? Were one or the other to have had true existence in the first place, as something real, and then to have ceased existing, a "nonexistence" would be feasible. However, since neither the two kinds of self-entity nor mind ever had substantial existence in the first place, they cannot be classed in either of these extreme definitions of existing or nonexisting. Saraha said:

> To believe in reality is to be like cattle.
> But to believe in unreality is even more stupid![372]

The *Sutra on Going to Laṅka* says:

> Externals are neither existent nor nonexistent.
> Mind cannot be truly apprehended either.
> The characteristic of the unborn is
> to be utterly other than all these views.[373]

The *Precious Garland* says:

> When no substantial reality can be found,
> how can there be unrealities? RA 1:98CD

C. The mistake of belief in nonexistence

If belief in existence is the root of samsara, will those who hold a view of nonexistence become liberated from samsara? In fact, this mistake is even worse than the one explained above. As [already mentioned,] Saraha said:

> To believe in reality is to be like cattle.
> But to believe in unreality is even more stupid![374]

It also says in the Heap of Jewels [in the *Kāśyapa Chapter Sutra*]:

> Kāśyapa, the view of personality—even if it is as big as Mount Meru—is relatively easy [to abandon], but not so for a decidedly arrogant view of emptiness.

And furthermore:

> Flawed views concerning emptiness will be
> the downfall of those of little wisdom.[375]

In the *Fundamental Verses on the Middle Way* it says:

> Those who believe in emptiness
> are said to be incurable. MMK 13:8CD

Why are they incurable? Take the example of a strong purgative: if both the constipation and the medicine are eliminated, the patient will recover. If the blockage is removed but the patient fails to cleanse the purgative itself from his system, he may not recover and may even die. Likewise, belief in substantial reality is eliminated by cultivating the notion of emptiness, but if the person clings to emptiness and makes it a "view," the "master of emptiness" will annihilate himself and be on his way to the lower states. The *Precious Garland* says:

> A realist goes to the higher states;
> a nihilist to the lower ones. RA 1:57AB

Thus the latter mistake is worse than the former.

D. The mistake of both beliefs

In fact, belief in existence and belief in nonexistence are both mistakes because they are beliefs that have fallen into the two extremes of eternalism and nihilism. The *Fundamental Verses on the Middle Way* says:

> "Exists" is the view of eternalism,
> and "does not exist" is the view of nihilism. MMK 15:10AB

To fall into the extremes of eternalism or nihilism is confused ignorance, and while there is such confused ignorance there will be no liberation from samsara. The *Precious Garland* says:

To believe that this mirage-like world
either "exists" or "does not exist"
is confused ignorance.
With [such] confusion, there is no liberation. RA 1:56

E. The path to liberation

"Well, then, what does bring liberation?" It is a middle way that does not abide in extremes and that leads to liberation. As the *Precious Garland* says:

> Those who fully understand the truth just as it is (that each and every phenomenon is and always has been nonproduced)
> and do not depend on the two (eternalism and nihilism) will become liberated (from samsara). RA 1:57CD

Thus someone who does not resort to them (the extremes of eternalism and nihilism) is liberated, so it is taught. The *Fundamental Verses on the Middle Way*, too, says:

> Therefore the wise should not dwell
> on existence or nonexistence. MMK 15:10CD

What is the "Middle Way" that abolishes the two extremes? The Heap of Jewels [in the *Three Vows Chapter*] answers:

> Kāśyapa! What is the correct way for bodhisattvas to approach phenomena? It is this. It is the middle way; the correct, discerning appreciation of phenomena. Kāśyapa! What is this middle way that is a proper, discerning appreciation of phenomena? Kāśyapa! "Permanence" makes one extreme. "Impermanence" makes a second extreme. Whatever lies between these two extremes cannot be analyzed, cannot be shown, is not apparent, and is totally unknowable. Kāśyapa! This is the "middle way that is a correct, discerning appreciation of phenomena." Kāśyapa! "Self" is one extreme. "Selfless" is a second extreme ... [etc.]. Kāśyapa! "Samsara" is one extreme. This nirvana is a

> second extreme. Whatever lies between these two extremes cannot be analyzed, cannot be shown, is not apparent, and is totally unknowable. This is the "middle way that is a correct, discerning appreciation of phenomena."[376]

Also, Master Śāntideva has taught:

> Neither inside nor outside,
> nor elsewhere can the mind be found. BCA 9:102CD
>
> It is not a combination [with the body],
> and neither is it something other.
> It is not the slightest thing.
> The very nature of sentient beings is nirvana. BCA 103B–D

Therefore, even though someone may practice this middle way that does not consider things in terms of the two extremes, the middle itself is never something that can be examined. It abides beyond the intellect, free from understanding that believes sense data to be this or that. Atiśa has said:

> Likewise, the past mind has ceased and is destroyed. The future mind is not born and has not yet occurred. The present mind is exceedingly hard to investigate, is colorless, without form, and, like space, without concrete existence.[377]

The *Ornament of Clear Realization* also says:

> Not in the extremes of this shore or that
> nor abiding between the two.
> And since it perceives all times to be the same,
> it is held to be the perfection of wisdom. AA 3:1

F. The nature of liberation—nirvana

If all the phenomena of samsara have no true existence, either as things substantial or insubstantial, then is "nirvana" something that has substantial or insubstantial reality? Some philosophers do consider nirvana actually to have some concrete existence. However, this is not correct, as the *Precious Garland* explains:

> Since nirvana is not even unreal,
> how could it be substantially real? RA 1:42AB

Were nirvana something substantial, it would have to be a composite thing, and whatever is composite will eventually disintegrate. Hence the *Fundamental Verses on the Middle Way* states, among other things:

> Were nirvana to be substantially real,
> it would be a composite thing. MMK 25:5AB

It is also not the case that it is something unreal. The same work says:

> There is no unreality in it. MMK 25:7D

Well then, what is it? Nirvana is "the exhaustion of all of the grasping at substantial reality and unreality. It is beyond the scope of the intellect and is beyond words." The *Precious Garland*:

> The cessation of all notions of substantial reality
> or unreality: that is "nirvana." RA 1:42CD

It also says in *Guide to the Bodhisattva Way of Life*:

> Whenever substantial reality or unreality
> no longer dwell before the mind,
> since there will be no other alternative way,
> free of objectification, one will be utterly at peace. BCA 9:34

The *Questions of Brahma Viśesacinti Sutra* says:

> *Total nirvana* is the complete pacification of every distinctive characteristic and freedom from any sort of fluctuation.[378]

The *Lotus Sutra* says:

> Kāśyapa! To comprehend the utter equality of all phenomena, this is nirvana.

Therefore, other than being the pacification of all mental activity, nirvana does not exist in terms of any phenomena, as something that arises or ceases, or as something to be eliminated or attained. The *Fundamental Verses on the Middle Way* states:

> No abandoning, no acquiring,
> no nihilism, no eternalism,
> no cessation, no arising:
> this is nirvana. MMK 25:3

Since nirvana is without any arising, cessation, relinquishment, or attainment whatsoever, there is nothing in relation to nirvana that is, on your part, constructed, fabricated, or modified. Therefore the *Precious Space Sutra* says:

> Nothing to remove from this;
> not the slightest thing thereon to add.
> Perfectly viewing the perfect truth,
> when perfectly seen, total freedom.[379]

Therefore, although the terms "what is to be known is one's own mind" or "what is to be known is wisdom (*prajñā*)" and so forth are employed in the context of analytical investigation, in actual fact, wisdom or mind remain beyond cognition or verbal expression. As the *Sutra Requested by Suvikrāntavikrami* says:

> As the perfection of wisdom cannot be expressed through anything phenomenal, it transcends all words.[380]

Furthermore, in *Rāhula's Praises to the Mother* it says:

> I prostrate to the mother of all the Victors of the three
> times:

the perfection of wisdom inexpressible in word or thought;
unborn, unceasing, the very essence of space;
the field of experience of discerning, self-knowing pristine awareness.[381]

With this, the explanation of what is known as wisdom is completed.

Now, I will explain the sixth point, **how to cultivate deep wisdom.**

"If all phenomena are emptiness," someone may wonder, "is it really necessary to cultivate this awareness?" Indeed it is necessary. For instance, even though silver ore has the very nature of silver, the silver itself will not be apparent until the ore has been smelted and worked on. Likewise all things have always been by their very nature emptiness, beyond every form of conceptual elaboration, yet nevertheless there is a need to develop awareness of it because beings experience it in various material ways and undergo various sufferings. Therefore, having become aware of what was explained above, cultivating this awareness has four elements:

A. The preliminary practices
B. The meditation session [practice]
C. The post-meditation [practices]
D. The signs of having cultivated

(A) The first, the *preliminary practices*, involves bringing your mind to a natural settled state.[382] How does one achieve this? By following what it says in the *Perfection of Wisdom in Seven Hundred Lines*:

> Sons and daughters of this noble line should seek the path of solitude! They should delight in the absence of distractive activities. They should sit cross-legged, not bringing to their attention any extraneous signs.[383]

You should do these as found in the Mahāmudrā preparatory practices.[384]

(B) Next, the method for the *actual meditation session [practice]*, is to follow the Mahāmudrā system of instruction, letting the mind settle free from any effort to posit, negate, affirm, or reject. Tilopa says:

Not dwelling on, not intending, not analyzing,
not meditating, not rationalizing,
leave mind to itself.[385]

Also, about letting the mind rest:

Listen, child! Whatever mental activity occurs,
within this there is no one bound, no one free.
Therefore, O joy, shedding your fatigue,
rest naturally, without contrivance or distraction.[386]

Nāgārjuna has also said:

A mind that has stably relaxed within itself,
like an elephant that has been trained,
has stopped running to and fro, and remains naturally at ease.
Thus have I realized, and hence what need have I of teachings?[387]

And the same said:

Don't adopt an attitude or think in any way whatsoever.
Don't interfere or contrive but leave mind loose in its natural state.
The uncontrived is the unborn, true nature.
This is of the trail set by all the victors of the three times.[388]

The Lord of Hermits [i.e., the Indian mahasiddha Śavaripa] has also said:

Do not see fault anywhere.
Practice that which is nothing whatsoever.
Do not foster longing for signs of progress and the like.
Although it is taught that there is nothing whatsoever to meditate on,
do not fall under the sway of inactivity and indifference.
In all circumstances, practice with mindfulness.[389]

In the *Achievement of the Very Point of Meditation* it says:

> When meditating, do not meditate on anything whatsoever.
> To call it "meditation" is simply to use a convention.[390]

As Saraha said:

> If there is involvement with anything, let it go;
> once realization has occurred, everything is that;
> apart from this, no one will ever know anything else.[391]

In the words of Atiśa:

> This is suchness, profound and free of elaboration.
> Luminous and unconditioned,
> unborn and unceasing,
> it is primordially pure.
>
> It is the natural nirvana of dharmadhātu,
> without middle or end;
> behold it with the fine eye of mind free of concept
> and without the distortions of sluggishness or agitation.[392]

and

> Place your mind free of conceptual elaboration
> in the ultimate expanse free of conceptual elaboration.[393]

Placing the mind in the way described above is to employ an unerring method for cultivating the perfection of profound wisdom. The *Perfection of Wisdom in Seven Hundred Lines* says:

> Not to engage in, hold on to, or reject anything—that is to meditate on the perfection of wisdom. Not dwelling on anything is to meditate on the perfection of wisdom. Not to think about anything and not to focus on anything whatsoever is to meditate on the perfection of wisdom.[394]

The *Perfection of Wisdom in Eight Thousand Lines* says:

> To cultivate the perfection of wisdom is to cultivate no thing whatsoever.[395]

and

> To cultivate the perfection of wisdom is to cultivate space.[396]

How can one "cultivate space"? The same sutra tells us:

> The perfection of wisdom has even more of a nonconceptual nature than space.[397]

The *Verse Summary of the Perfection of Wisdom* also says:

> The practice of the perfection of wisdom
> is not to be thinking either *absence of arising* or *arising*. RS I:26CD

In the words of the great master Vāgīśvarakīrti:

> Do not think about the thinkable.
> Do not think about the unthinkable either.
> By thinking about neither the thinkable nor the unthinkable,
> emptiness will be seen.[398]

How does someone "see emptiness"? As it says in the *Perfectly Gathering the Qualities [of Avalokiteśvara] Sutra*:

> To see emptiness is not to see [anything] at all.

and

> Blessed One! Not to see any thing is to see excellently.

and

> Without seeing any thing whatsoever, the one and only nature is seen.[399]

The *Shorter Text on Middle Way Truths* also says:

It says in some exceedingly profound discourses
that not-seeing is to see that [truth].[400]

The *Verse Summary of the Perfection of Wisdom* also remarks:

People talk of seeing space.
Think about it and consider how they see space.
The Tathāgatha taught that this is how to see phenomena. RS 12:9A–C

(C) The third point concerns the [*post-meditation* or] *between-sessions phase*. While viewing everything that occurs in between meditation sessions as illusory, every wholesome merit possible should be established, through the practice of generosity and so forth. As the *Verse Summary of the Perfection of Wisdom* says:

Whoever understands the five aggregates to be like an illusion
but does not make the aggregates and the illusion as separate things
and is free of the notion of multiplicity but experiences peace,
that is to practice the excellent perfection of wisdom. RS 1:14

The *King of Meditation Sutra* says:

Although magicians conjure up forms—
making horses, elephants, carts, and all sorts of things—
they know that nothing of what appears is actually there.
Recognize all phenomena to be likewise.[401]

It is said in the *Suchness of Conduct*:

The mind is attentive to not conceptualizing,
yet the amassing of merit never ceases.[402]

Through such familiarity, the meditation and post-meditation phases will become indistinguishable and one will become free of conceitedness. Thus it says:

He will have no conceit, thinking "I am in meditative equipoise"
or "I am arising from the equipoise."
Why? Because there is awareness of the very nature of things.
RS 1:11CD

To be immersed, even for a short moment, in the perfection of wisdom—the ultimate, emptiness—constitutes an incomparably greater virtue than to spend eons receiving Dharma teachings, reciting scriptures, or planting roots of virtue in the form of generosity and similar wholesome actions. The *Sutra Teaching Suchness* states:

> Śāriputra! Someone practicing meditative absorption on suchness for even the duration of a finger snap has an increase of merit far greater than those of another studying [the Dharma] for as much as an eon. Śāriputra! For this reason you should earnestly instruct others to practice meditative absorption on suchness. Śāriputra! All the bodhisattvas who have been predicted as being future buddhas also abide solely in that meditative absorption.[403]

It is also stated in the *Sutra on the Full Development of Great Realization*:

> It is more meaningful to practice meditative concentration for a session
> than to give life for beings of the three dimensions.[404]

In the *Great Uṣṇīṣa Sutra* it states:

> It is of greater merit to cultivate the true meaning of things for a day than to study and reflect for many cosmic eons. Why is this so? Because it takes one far away from the road of births and deaths.[405]

In the *Sutra on Excellently Nurturing Faith* [*in the Mahayana*] it says:

> There is greater merit in a yogi's session of emptiness meditation than there would be if all beings in the three dimensions spent their whole lives using their possessions to accumulate virtue.[406]

It is taught that if your mind is not dwelling on the key points of emptiness, then other virtues cannot deliver you to liberation. The *Sutra Teaching the Nonorigination of All Things*:

> Someone may observe moral discipline for a long time and practice meditative concentration for millions of eons, but without realization of this highest truth, those things cannot bring liberation, according to this teaching. Whoever understands this "nothing whatsoever" will never cling to anything whatsoever.[407]

In the *Ten Wheels of Kṣitigarbha Sutra* it states:

> It is through cultivating absorption doubts will be cut.
> Other than that, nothing can.
> Hence the cultivation of absorption is supreme,
> and the wise practice it diligently.[408]

Furthermore:

> The positive result of meditating for a day far exceeds that of writing out, reading, studying, reciting, or explaining the teachings for eons.[409]

Once you become endowed with the key point of emptiness, as described above, there is nothing at all that is not encompassed within it.

This constitutes taking refuge as well. For example, the *Questions of Nāga King Anavatapta Sutra* states:

> Bodhisattvas recognize all phenomena to be without a self-entity, without a sentient nature, without life, and without personhood. To see quite correctly in the way the tathāgatas see—not as forms, not as names, and not as specific phenomena—is to have taken refuge in the Buddha with a mind unpolluted by material consideration.
>
> The essence of the tathāgatas is the ultimate expanse; that which is ultimate expanse is referred to as that which pervades every thing. Thus, seeing it as the domain of all phenomena is to

> take refuge in the Dharma with a mind unpolluted by material consideration.
>
> Whoever is familiar with the ultimate expanse as being unconditioned and with the fact that the śrāvakayāna is founded in what is unconditioned, and who also understands the nonduality of the conditioned and the unconditioned, takes refuge in the Sangha with a mind unpolluted by material consideration.[410]

This constitutes the generation of bodhicitta as well. For example, the *Sutra of Great Bodhicitta*[411] says:

> Kāśyapa! Every phenomenon is, like space, without specific characteristics and is primordial lucid clarity and utter purity. That is "to give rise to bodhicitta."

The creation stage of deity meditation and mantra recitation are all complete within this as well. In the *Hevajra Tantra* it says:

> No meditation, no meditator,
> no deities and no mantra either;
> within the nature free of conceptual elaboration,
> the deities and mantras are truly present:
> Vairocana, Akṣobhya, Amoghasiddhi,
> Ratnasambhava, Amitābha, and Vajrasattva.[412]

The *Union with All the Buddhas Tantra* says:

> From a cast image and the like
> a true union (*yoga*) will not emerge,
> whereas the yogi who strives excellently
> in bodhicitta will actually become the deity.[413]

The *Vajra Peak Tantra* says:

> The intrinsic characteristic of every mantra
> is said to be the mind of all the buddhas;
> it is a means to cultivate the essence of Dharma.

> To be perfectly endowed with the ultimate expanse
> is said to be the intrinsic characteristic of mantras.[414]

It also comprises fire offerings. As the *King of Secret Nectar Tantra* says:

> What are fire offerings for?
> They are made to bestow the highest accomplishments
> and to overcome conceptualization.
> Burning wood and so forth is not a fire offering.[415]

The path in terms of the six perfections is also complete in it. The *Diamond Meditative Absorption Scripture* says:

> If unwavered from emptiness, the six perfections are embodied.[416]

According to the *Questions of Brahma Viśesacinti Sutra*:

> To be without intention is generosity. Not to dwell on the separatedness of things is moral discipline. Not to make differentiations is forbearance. Absence of adoption and rejection is diligence. Nonattachment is meditative concentration. Nonthought is wisdom.[417]

The *Ten Wheels of Kṣitigarbha Sutra* also states:

> The meditation of the wise and skillful on the teaching of
> emptiness
> does not resort to or dwell on anything of the world.
> It abides nowhere in any existence,
> and as such is the observance of pure moral discipline.[418]

It is said in the same sutra:

> All phenomena are of one taste,
> being equally empty and without any characteristics.
> The mind that does not dwell on or become attached
> to anything

is [practicing] forbearance, and through this, benefit will
increase greatly.[419]

The wise who practice diligence
have cast far away every attachment.
The mind that neither dwells on nor clings to anything
whatsoever
should be known as a "field of finest virtue."[420]

To practice meditative concentration
in order to bring happiness and well-being to all sentient beings
is something that removes a great burden.
To thus clear away every polluting affliction
is the defining characteristic of the truly wise.[421]

It also constitutes making prostrations. The *Precious Space Sutra* says:

Like water poured into water
and like butter poured into butter,
such is the pristine awareness
intelligent of itself, by itself.
Such excellent seeing
is prostration made to it.[422]

It also represents the making of offerings. The *Meeting of Father and Son Sutra* says:

To resort to the Dharma of emptiness
and aspire to that which is the domain of experience of the
buddhas—
such is to make offerings to the enlightened teacher,
and such offerings are unsurpassable.[423]

Also, in the *King of Secret Nectar Tantra* it says:

Meaningful offerings are pleasing,
but not so offerings of incense and the like.

By making the mind perfectly workable,
the great and pleasing offering is made.[424]

Furthermore, if you possess this perfection of wisdom, this constitutes the purification of past errors as well. In the *Sutra on Totally Purifying Karma* it says:

You who are desirous of atonement!
Sit straight and behold the perfect truth.
Perfectly beholding the perfect truth
is the most excellent form of repentence.[425]

It also comprises the observance of moral commitments. As is said in the *Questions of the Devaputra Susthitamati Sutra*:

When there is no longer the conceitedness of *vow* or *no-vow*, there is the moral discipline of nirvana; that is the purest moral discipline.[426]

The *Ten Wheels [of Kṣitigarbha] Sutra* also says:

Someone may be considered to be a layperson, living at home with head and beard unshaven. He may not wear monk's robes and may not even have taken [the precepts] of moral discipline. But if he is endowed with the suchness of the noble ones, that person is a true monk in the ultimate sense.[427]

Furthermore, it also comprises all three stages of wisdom—of study, of contemplation, and of meditation. As is said in the *Tantra of Supreme Nonabiding*:

If one has eaten the food of the uncontrived naturalness,
it fulfills all the philosophical tenets, whatever they may be.
The immature, lacking realization, rely on terminology.
Everything is but a characteristic of one's own mind.[428]

Saraha said, moreover:

> It is to read, it is to seize the meaning, and it is to meditate.
> It is also to assimilate the meaning of the treatises.
> There is no view capable of demonstrating it.[429]

It also comprises making torma offerings and similar Dharma activities. The *King of Secret Nectar Tantra* says:

> When someone has encountered the nature of mind,
> all different types of activity
> and deed are contained therein:
> offerings, *torma*, and so forth.[430]

Well, if meditation on this essence or the nature of mind comprises all those things, what was the reason for teaching so many graduated techniques? These evolved to guide those less-gifted beings who are still confused about the nature of things. The *Sutra Adorning the Brilliance of Pristine Awareness* says:

> Explanations of causes, conditions, and interdependence,
> as well as the teaching of the graduated path,
> were given as skillful means for the confused.
> As for this spontaneous Dharma,
> what graduated training could there be?[431]

In the *Tantra of the Arising of the Supremely Blissful* it says:

> Thus is attained an eternally liberated status—
> a status comparable to the vastness of space.[432]

In the *Precious Space Sutra* it is said:

> Before dwelling in the ocean of the ultimate expanse, the stages and levels are held to be different. Once the ocean of the ultimate expanse has been entered, there is not even the slightest traversing of stages and levels.[433]

Illustrious Atiśa has said:

> When a mind is firmly settled in the one,
> do not strive in physical and verbal virtues.[434]

(D) The *six signs of having cultivated wisdom* are: you become more heedful with respect to virtue, your afflictions decrease, compassion arises for sentient beings, you apply yourself earnestly to practice, you reject all forms of distraction, and you are no longer attached to or craving the things of this life. Therefore it is said in the *Precious Garland*:

> Through familiarity with emptiness,
> heedfulness with regard to virtue is attained. RA 3:88

The seventh point explains the **fruits of the perfection of wisdom.** These should be understood as being twofold: the ultimate result and the temporary consequences. The ultimate result is to attain enlightenment. Thus the *Perfection of Wisdom in Seven Hundred Lines* teaches:

> Mañjuśrī! Through practicing the perfection of wisdom, bodhisattva mahāsattvas will rapidly and genuinely become perfectly enlightened in peerless, unsurpassable perfect buddhahood.[435]

In the meantime, every good and excellent thing will occur. As it is said in the *Verse Summary of the Perfection of Wisdom*:

> Whatever delightful, happy things are encountered
> by bodhisattvas, śrāvakas, pratyekabuddhas, gods, or any being,
> all derive from the supreme perfection of wisdom. RS 28:4A–C

This concludes the seventeenth chapter, concerning the perfection of wisdom, in this *Ornament of Precious Liberation, a Wish-Fulfilling Gem of Sublime Dharma.*

18. The Presentation of the [Five] Paths

Having first given rise to the intention to achieve supreme enlightenment and having earnestly engaged in the training presented earlier, a person will traverse the paths and levels of the bodhisattva in their respective sequence. To present the path, the following:

> **The paths are totally encompassed within these five: the path of accumulation, the path of application, the path of seeing, the path of cultivation, and the path of complete accomplishment.**

According to the treatise *Lamp for the Path to Awakening,* these five paths are taught as follows. The first, the path of accumulation, lays the foundation through cultivating the Dharma instructions suited to those of initial and middling capacities. These are followed by development of the two aspects of bodhicitta—aspiration and engagement—and the amassing of the two accumulations. The text then teaches how the path of application occurs, "through an understanding acquired progressively through the subphases of heat and so forth."[436] The paths of seeing, cultivation, and complete accomplishment are taught through "the Joyous and so on are attained" BP 59.

First is the **path of accumulation.** It represents all the efforts that those endowed with the Mahayana potential will have to make in the practice of virtue, from the moment they first set their mind on supreme enlightenment and receive some advice and instruction from a teacher until such time as the attainment of the pristine awareness of the heat subphase [of the path of application]. This phase of the path is itself subdivided into four, according to whether it is informed by understanding, aspiration, longing for the sublime, or actual attainment.

Why is it called the *path of accumulation*? It is so called because of its activities, which serve to gather and establish the accumulations of virtue and so forth in order to make a person a vessel suitable for realizations such as those of heat and so forth to arise. They are also referred to as "roots of virtue conducive to liberation." During that particular period, one cultivates twelve—that is, three sets of four—[of the thirty-seven] factors conducive to awakening. They are: (1–4) the four foundations of mindfulness, (5–8) the four perfect endeavors, and (9–12) the four bases of superpowers.

Of these, the *four foundations of mindfulness*, which constitute the lower stage of the path of accumulation, involve developing: (1) mindfulness of body, (2) mindfulness of feelings, (3) mindfulness of mind, and (4) mindfulness of phenomena.

The *four perfect endeavors*, which constitute the middle stage of the path of accumulation, are: (1) relinquishing the existing evils and nonvirtues, (2) not giving rise to evils and nonvirtues currently absent, (3) giving rise to virtuous remedies not yet present, and (4) increasing virtues already developed.

The *four bases of superpowers*, which constitute the upper stage of the path of accumulation, are: (1) meditative absorption through aspiration, (2) meditative absorption through diligence, (3) meditative absorption through intention, and (4) meditative absorption through analysis. These above are encompassed within the path of accumulation.

The second is the **path of application.** This follows on from the proper completion of the path of accumulation. It is the birth of "the four subphases of definite breakthrough in understanding" conducive to realization of the four noble truths. The four subphases are called: heat, the peak, fearless acceptance, and the highest worldly realization.

Why is it called the *path of application*? Here "application" refers to connecting with a direct realization of truth. During the subphases of heat and the peak, *five faculties* are employed: faith, diligence, mindfulness, concentration, and wisdom. In the subphases of fearless acceptance and highest worldly realization, these become *five powers*: faith, diligence, mindfulness, meditative absorption, and wisdom.

The third is the **path of seeing.** This follows on from the highest wordly realization subphase. It is the combination of tranquility and insight focused on the four truths of the noble ones. In relation to [the first truth, that of] suffering, there are [aspects of insight known as]: (1) receptivity to knowledge of the nature of suffering, (2) knowledge of the nature of suffering, (3) receptivity to subsequent knowledge of the nature of suffering,

(4) subsequent knowledge of the nature of suffering. There are four such aspects for each of the four noble truths. The insight embodies these sixteen instants of receptivity and knowledge.

Why are those referred to as the *path of seeing*? Because at that stage authentic insight into the [four] truths of the noble ones is gained for the first time. During that stage, a person is endowed with the *seven aspects of enlightenment*: (1) right mindfulness, an aspect of enlightenment, (2) right discernment, (3) right diligence, (4) right joy, (5) right mastery, (6) right meditation, and (7) right equanimity, an aspect of enlightenment.

The fourth is the **path of cultivation**. It is what follows the path of seeing. It has two aspects: the mundane path and the supramundane path.

The mundane path of cultivation comprises the first, second, third, and fourth worldly meditative concentrations (*dhyāna*) and the [four formless meditative attainments in the form of] the spheres of (1) limitless space, (2) limitless consciousness, (3) nothing whatsoever, and (4) neither cognition nor absence of cognition. There are three purposes in cultivating these: (a) to overwhelm the afflictions that are to be removed at the level of the path of cultivation, (b) to enable achievement of exceptional qualities such as the four immeasurables, and (c) to provide a basis for the supramundane path of cultivation.

The supramundane path of cultivation consists of tranquility and insight—along with their accompanying qualities—focused on the two aspects of pristine awareness. Now, of the sixteen facets of insight—the two facets of receptivity and two facets of knowledge corresponding to each of the four noble truths—gained during the path of seeing, the eight receptivities are proper to the path of seeing, and the insight gained is all that is needed to complete them. The eight facets of knowledge, however, require ongoing familiarization, and this is what is being developed through the path of cultivation. It is achieved through continued familiarity with tranquility and insight on the basis of the four meditative concentrations and the first three of the four formless meditative attainments. Cultivating the realization of suchness belongs to the aspect [of the path] known as *knowledge of phenomena*, whereas cultivating the realization of pristine awareness belongs to the aspect known as *subsequent knowledge*.

As [for the final formless meditative attainment], the sphere of neither cognition nor absence of cognition remains entirely as a mundane sphere, for its awareness lacks clarity.

Why are the above called the *path of cultivation*? Because in it, the person cultivates familiarity with the realizations gained on the path of seeing. During this stage the meditator is endowed with the eightfold path of the noble ones: right view, right thought, right speech, right action, right livelihood, right effort, right mindfulness, and right meditation.

The fifth is the **path of complete accomplishment**. This occurs subsequent to the diamond-like meditative absorption, and it consists of the knowledge of cessation and that of nonarising. *Diamond-like meditative absorption* refers to the final stage of elimination on the path of cultivation and thus is encompassed within the preparatory and uninterrupted stages of the path of cultivation. Since this particular meditative absorption is unimpeded, durable, stable, of a single taste, and pervasive, it is called "diamond-like." It is *unimpeded* because no worldly activity can be a cause which might unsettle it. It is *durable* because none of the obscurations can damage it. It is *stable* because no thought can trouble it. It is of a *single taste* because it has one flavor. It is *pervasive* because it is focused on the ultimate nature common to each and every thing that is knowable.

Subsequent to the diamond-like meditative absorption, there is the *knowledge of cessation* of generation. This is pristine awareness focused on the four noble truths in terms of the exhaustion of all causes [of suffering]. There is also *knowledge of nonarising*. This pristine awareness is also focused on the four noble truths, but here in terms of the resultant sufferings themselves having been eliminated. In other words, pristine awareness related to the exhaustion of causes and the nonarising of results is the knowledge of cessation and nonarising.

Why are those referred to as the path of complete accomplishment? Because training has been completed, and it is the stage where the journey to the citadel of enlightenment has reached its end. At that stage there are *ten qualities of no-more training*.[437] They are [the eight qualities of the eightfold path—namely,] right view through to right meditation of no-more training, plus total liberation and perfect pristine awareness of no-more training. These ten factors, in which there is no more training to be performed, form five uncontaminated aggregates. Right speech, right action, and right livelihood of no-more training constitute the *moral discipline aggregate*; right mindfulness and right meditation of no-more training constitute the *meditative absorption aggregate*; right view, right thinking, and right effort of no-more training constitute the *wisdom aggregate*; total, utter liberation of no-more training constitutes the *total liberation aggregate*; and right pristine awareness of no-more training constitutes the *aggregate of seeing the pristine awareness of total liberation*.

This concludes the eighteenth chapter, concerning the presentation of the paths, in this *Ornament of Precious Liberation, a Wish-Fulfilling Gem of Sublime Dharma*.

19. The Presentation of the Levels

Do those five paths have various levels? Yes. The synopsis is:

> **The levels are thirteen: the beginner's level, the level of practice through aspiration, the ten bodhisattva levels, and the level of buddhahood.**

With respect to these levels *Lamp for the Path to Awakening* states:

> . . . the Joyous and so on are attained. BP 59C

Here, "the Joyous" is the name of the first bodhisattva level, and the words "and so on" include the two levels below it and the ten above it.

The first point concerns the **beginner's level.** This applies to the stage when the person is on the path of accumulation. It is so called because it brings that which is immature to maturity.

The second point concerns the **level of practice by means of aspiration.** This corresponds to the period of the path of application. It is so called because its activity aspires singly to the meaning of emptiness. During this phase the following are crushed so as never to reoccur: (1) factors incompatible with the perfections—avarice and so forth, (2) afflictions that will be eliminated through the path of seeing, and (3) the conceptual projections of the cognitive obscuration.

The third point concerns the **ten bodhisattva levels.** These are the levels from the Joyous through to the Cloud of Dharma. The *Ten Levels Sutra* says:

> O child of good family! These ten are the bodhisattva levels: the bodhisattva level of the Joyous . . .[438]

The Joyous—the first of the ten levels—corresponds to the path of seeing, in which emptiness is directly realized. The second through tenth levels are the path of cultivation. During these, insight into the suchness realized during the first level is cultivated.

These ten bodhisattva levels should be understood both in general and specifically. First, the *general points* concerning the ten bodhisattva levels are three: (1) their nature, (2) the etymology of *level*, and (3) the reason for a tenfold division.

As for the *nature* of the levels, they consist of the relevant presence in the continuum of the mind of both the wisdom directly realizing the absence of self-entity in phenomena and the accompanying meditative absorption that nurtures it.

Concerning their *etymology*: they are called *levels*, or *grounds*, because they each serve as bases for all the qualities associated with them as well as with the states they represent. Furthermore, each one serves as the foundation that gives rise to the subsequent level. The following are analogies for the etymology of the term *level*. It is called *level* (or *ground*) because all [higher qualities] reside within that pristine awareness and partake in it just as, for example, [all the cattle] reside within and use the cattle yard. Also, it is called the *level* (or *ground*) because [all higher qualities] traverse that pristine awareness just as [horses run on] the running tracks. Lastly, they are like fields, since they are the foundations on which grow all the qualities proper to pristine awareness.

The *reason for a tenfold division* is their specific particularities of complete nurturing.

Second, the *specific points* about each bodhisattva level will be presented through nine particularities for each level: (1) name, (2) etymology, (3) thorough training, (4) practice, (5) purity, (6) realization, (7) things abandoned, (8) state of birth, and (9) ability.

The First Bodhisattva Level

Its **specific name** is the Joyous.

Its **specific etymology**: Those who have achieved this level feel immense joy because enlightenment is close at hand and benefit for sentient beings is now really being accomplished: hence its name, the Joyous. Thus it says in the *Ornament of Mahayana Sutras*:

On seeing that enlightenment is close
and that the good of beings is accomplished,
the most supreme joy will arise.
For that reason it is called the Joyous. MSA 21:32

The **specific thorough training**: This level is achieved through mastery of ten qualities, such as having intentions that are never deceitful, no matter what domain of action or thought [the bodhisattva] is engaged in. Thus the *Ornament of Clear Realization* says:

Through ten aspects of thorough trainings,[439]
the first level will be attained. AA 1:49

The **specific practice**: Although bodhisattvas at this level practice all ten perfections, it is said that they place particular emphasis on practicing the perfection of generosity because of their wish to bring contentment to all beings. Thus the *Ten Levels Sutra* says:

> From the outset of the first level, among all ten perfections, the perfection of generosity is emphasized, although this does not mean that the others are neglected.[440]

The **specific purity**: As is said in the *Ten Levels Sutra*:

> On the first level, the Joyous, there is vast vision. Through the power of prayers, many buddhas are seen, many hundreds of buddhas, many thousands of buddhas . . . [etc.;] many hundreds of millions of buddhas manifest. On seeing them, you make offerings with a great and noble intention and express great respect . . . [etc.;] you also make offerings to their Sangha. You dedicate all those roots of virtue to unsurpassable enlightenment. You receive teachings from these buddhas, take them to heart, and remember them. These teachings are practiced earnestly, and beings are brought to maturity through the four means of attraction.[441]

In such a way, and for many eons, (1) they make offerings to the buddhas,

Dharma, and Sangha and are cared for by them; (2) they bring beings to spiritual maturity; and (3) they dedicate virtue to highest enlightenment.[442] Thus, through these three causes, all their roots of virtue are made very great and very pure. It says:

> For instance, the degree of refinement and purity of gold, and its ability to lend itself to any desired use, will depend on the amount of work the goldsmith has put into its smelting. Like this, the roots of virtue of bodhisattvas on the first level are perfectly refined, completely pure, and fit for any use.[443]

The **specific realization**: In general, realization is one and the same during meditative equipoise throughout the ten levels. The differences are in respect to the phases subsequent to the equipoise periods, and it is this aspect that will be considered relevant to each level. On this first level, the expanse of suchness is [realized as being] all-pervading, and this provides full realization of the sameness of self and others. Therefore the *Clear Differentiation of the Middle and Extremes* (MV 2:16a) speaks of the "all-pervading truth."

The **specific things abandoned**: In terms of the afflictions obscuration, all the eighty-two afflictions[444] to be overcome through the path of seeing have been eliminated. Of the three types of knowledge obscurations, the ones comparable to a rough outer skin are eliminated. Five types of fear or anxiety are absent. These are described in the *Ten Levels Sutra*:

> What are the five fears present until the level of the Joyous is attained? They are fear of not gaining a livelihood, fear of not having a good reputation, fear of death, fear of the lower states of existence, and anxiety about being stuck among many worldly people. At that level these are all annihilated.[445]

The **specific state of birth**: Bodhisattvas on this level are mostly reborn as universal monarchs in Jambudvīpa. There they remove the pollution of beings' avarice. The *Precious Garland* says:

> As a full consequence of this,
> they become a mighty ruler of Jambudvīpa. RA 5:42

Although this is the special particularity of birth mentioned, through their pure intention to benefit others, they can manifest themselves anywhere and in any way needed to train beings, as was well taught in the Jātaka stories.

Their **specific ability**: On this point it says:

> Bodhisattvas at this level of the Joyous exert themselves diligently through aspiration. The most advanced can, within an instant, a short moment, just a fraction of time: (1) enter into a hundredfold meditative absorptions and experience their stable fruition, (2) see a hundred buddhas, (3) most properly be aware of those buddhas' blessings, (4) make a hundred world systems tremble, (5) visit a hundred buddhafields, (6) illuminate a hundred world systems, (7) bring a hundred sentient beings to full maturity, (8) live for a hundred eons, (9) be excellently aware of the past and future up to a hundred eons past or future, (10) open a hundred doors of Dharma, (11) manifest a hundred emanations anywhere, and (12) constantly manifest each of these physical forms as being accompanied by a hundred other bodhisattvas.[446]

The Second Bodhisattva Level

Its **specific name** is the Stainless.

Its **specific etymology**: This level is known as the Stainless because it is unstained by violations of moral discipline:

> Being free from stains due to violations of proper conduct,
> it is known as the Stainless. MSA 21:33AB

Its **specific thorough training**: This level is attained through eight kinds of mastery, such as those of moral discipline, actions, and so forth:

> Moral discipline, the accomplishment of action, forbearance,
> supreme joy, great compassionate love, and so forth. AA 1:52

Its **specific practice**: Although bodhisattvas at this level practice all ten perfections, they are said to place particular emphasis on practicing the perfection of moral discipline.

Its **specific purity**: As previously explained, three causes make the roots of virtue created by these bodhisattvas very powerful and very pure:

> To give an example, fine gold re-treated and re-smelted by a goldsmith will be rid of all impurities, even more so than before. Likewise, the roots of virtue of the bodhisattvas on the second level are also purer, more refined, and more workable than before.[447]

The **specific realization**: On this level, the ultimate expanse is understood as being the highest and most significant thing. They think, "I will strive at all times and in all ways in the training through which it is really and totally achieved." Thus it is said: "Highest thing . . ." (MV 2:16a).

The **specific things abandoned** for this second level, and on through to the tenth level: As far as the afflictions are concerned, only the seeds of the sixteen afflictions that need to be eliminated by the path of cultivation have not been removed. Although they remain present, their manifest levels have been overcome. As for the knowledge obscurations, the inner layer, like the flesh of a fruit, is eliminated.

The **specific state of birth**: Many of the bodhisattvas on this level become universal monarchs holding sway over the four-world system. There they turn beings away from the ten vices and establish them in the ten virtues. Thus:

> Through the full maturation of this,
> they become universal monarchs
> who benefit beings through possessing
> the seven precious and illustrious attributes. RA 5:44

The **specific ability** is that, in one instant, a short moment, a fraction of time, they can enter into a thousand meditative absorptions and so forth.[448]

The Third Bodhisattva Level

Its **specific name** is the Shining.

The **specific etymology**: It is known as the Shining because in that state the light of Dharma and of meditative absorption is very clear. Furthermore, it illuminates others with the great light of Dharma. Thus it is said:

> It is the Shining
> because it makes the great radiance of Dharma. MSA 21:33CD

The **specific thorough training**: This level is achieved through having developed five things, such as an insatiable appetite for studying [Dharma]. As is taught:

> Insatiable with respect to Dharma study,
> they impart teachings without material concern. AA 1:53

The **specific practice**: Although bodhisattvas at this level practice all ten perfections, they are said to place particular emphasis on practicing the perfection of forbearance.

The **specific purity**: As explained above, three causes make the roots of virtue of these bodhisattvas very great and very pure:

> To give an example, if very fine gold is hand-polished by a skilled goldsmith, the defects and impurities are removed, yet this does not reduce the original weight of the gold itself. Likewise, the roots of virtue, established in the three periods of time by these bodhisattvas, remain undiminished and become very pure, very refined, and fit for any use.[449]

The **specific realization**: Bodhisattvas on this level understand the teachings of Dharma to be supreme among the favorable conditions conducive to [realizing] the ultimate expanse. To study just one verse of teaching, they would pass through a fire pit as large as a billionfold world system. Therefore:

> the supreme of meanings, which is conducive . . . MV 2:16B

The **specific things abandoned**: See the second level, above.

The **specific state of birth**: Most bodhisattvas on this level take rebirth as Indra, king of the gods. They are skilled in counteracting desires and attachments related to the desire realm:

> They become skillful great masters of the gods,
> who counteract attachment of the desire realm. RA 5:46CD

The **specific ability**: In an instant, a short moment of time, a small fraction of time, they can enter a hundred thousand meditative absorptions and so forth.

The Fourth Bodhisattva Level

Its **specific name** is the Blazing.

The **specific etymology**: It is called the Blazing because the brilliance of pristine awareness, endowed with the qualities favorable to enlightenment, blazes everywhere, having consumed the two obscurations. Thus:

> It is like a light since it thoroughly consumes
> the factors incompatible with enlightenment.
> Thus endowed, this level is Blazing,
> because the two have been consumed. MSA 21:34

The **specific thorough training**: This level is achieved through ten factors, such as remaining in solitude and so forth. Therefore:

> Remaining in forests, with little desire, easily contented,
> pure in behavior, observing vows . . . AA 1:53

The **specific practice**: Although bodhisattvas on this level practice all the ten perfections in general, it is said that they place particular emphasis on that of diligence.

The **specific purity**: As explained above, three causes make the roots of virtue of these bodhisattvas extremely great and pure:

> To give an example, fine gold fashioned into a piece of jewelry by a skilled goldsmith cannot be surpassed by pieces of gold as yet unworked. In a similar way, the roots of virtue of bodhisattvas

> on this level are not outshone by those of bodhisattvas on lower levels.[450]

The **specific realization**: Bodhisattvas on this level have truly realized that there is nothing whatsoever to really cling to. Thus all craving, even for Dharma, is quenched:

> The fact that there is nothing to really cling to and . . . MV 2:16C

The **specific things abandoned**: See the second level, above.

The **specific state of birth**: Most bodhisattvas on this level take birth as a king of gods in the Free from Conflict Heaven. They are skilled in dispelling mistaken philosophies based on the view that the perishable composite is permanent. Thus:

> They become divine monarchs
> in the Free from Conflict Heaven
> and are skilled in totally defeating views
> of the perishable composite where these are predominant. RA 5:48

The **specific ability**: In one moment, a short instant, a fraction of time, they can enter a billion meditative absorptions and so forth.

The Fifth Bodhisattva Level

Its **specific name** is Difficult to Master.

The **specific etymology**: On this level the bodhisattva strives to help beings to greater maturity, and in doing so they remain unassailed by the afflictions despite the repeated negative behavior of sentient beings. It is known as Difficult to Master because both [helping and not reacting] are hard to master. Thus:

> Since they accomplish the good of beings
> and guard their own minds,
> it is a difficult training for the bodhisattvas;
> therefore it is known as Difficult to Master. MSA 21:35

The **specific thorough training**: This level is achieved through the elimination of ten factors, such as association with worldly people for purposes of gain and so forth. For instance:

> To hanker after acquaintances, a dwelling,
> places brimming with distraction, and so forth . . . AA 1:56

The **specific practice**: Although bodhisattvas on this level practice all ten perfections in general, it is said that they place particular emphasis on that of meditative absorption.

The **specific purity**: As previously explained, three causes make the roots of virtue of these bodhisattvas particularly great and pure:

> To give an example, fine gold, first polished by a skilled goldsmith and then set with amber stones, will be incomparably beautiful; it cannot be outshone by other pieces made of [worked] gold alone. It is likewise for the roots of virtue of bodhisattvas on this fifth level. They are tested by the combination of wisdom and skillful means. They could never be outshone by the roots of virtue of bodhisattvas on lower levels.[451]

The **specific realization** is that bodhisattvas on this level realize the non-differentiation of [mind] streams. They are aware of ten sorts of sameness. Thus, "Undifferentiated streams and . . ."[452]

The **specific things abandoned**: See the second level.

The **specific state of birth**: Most bodhisattvas on this level take birth as divine monarchs in Tuṣita Heaven. They are skilled in refuting the views of those holding distorted religious beliefs. Therefore:

> As a full consequence of that
> they become monarchs of the Tuṣita gods
> and are skilled in refuting the foundations
> of the afflictions and distorted beliefs of all tīrthikas. RA 5:50

The **specific ability**: In one instant, a short moment, a small fraction of time, they can enter ten billion meditative absorptions and so forth.

The Sixth Bodhisattva Level

Its **specific name** is the Manifested.

The **specific etymology**: On account of the perfection of wisdom, there is no dwelling in [notions of] nirvana or samsara. Thus samsara and nirvana manifest as purity.[453] Hence the name of this level, the Manifested:

> Through the perfection of wisdom,
> since both samsara and nirvana
> have become manifest,
> it is called the Manifested. MSA 21:36

The **specific thorough training**: This level is achieved through twelve factors of training. These are learning how to accomplish totally and perfectly six things, such as generosity and so forth, and learning how to eliminate six things, such as longing for the śrāvaka or pratyekabuddha [states] and the like. Therefore:

> Through the utter perfection of generosity,
> moral discipline, forbearance, diligence,
> meditative concentration, and wisdom,
> there is awareness and so forth. AA 1:57

The **specific practice**: Although bodhisattvas on this level practice all ten perfections in general, it is said that they place particular emphasis on that of the perfection of deep wisdom.

The **specific purity**: As explained previously, three causes make the roots of virtue of bodhisattvas on this level extremely pure and powerful:

> To give an example, when a skilled goldsmith decorates fine gold with lapis lazuli, it becomes peerless and cannot be surpassed by other works of gold. Likewise, the roots of virtue of sixth-level bodhisattvas, assured by wisdom and skillful means, are both total purity and lucid clarity; they cannot be outshone by those of bodhisattvas dwelling on lower levels.[454]

The **specific realization**: On this level the bodhisattva realizes the nonexistence of both the afflictions and their purification. These bodhisattvas are aware that there are really no such things as affliction or purity, even though those things may arise through the play of dependent origination. Thus it is said: "... the meaning of no affliction and no purity" (MV 2:17a).

The **specific things abandoned**: See the second level.

The **specific state of birth**: Most bodhisattvas on this level take birth as a divine monarch among the Delighting in Manifesting gods. They are skilled in overcoming beings' vanity:

> Through this full consequence,
> they become kings of the Delighting in Manifesting gods.
> Unsurpassed by the śrāvakas,
> they eliminate vainglory. RA 5:52

The **specific ability** is that in one instant, a short moment, a small fraction of time, they can enter a trillion meditative absorptions and so forth.

The Seventh Bodhisattva Level

Its **specific name** is the Far-Reaching.

The **specific etymology**: This level is known as the Far-Reaching because it connects with the "one and only path" and one has come to the far end of activity:

> It is known as the Far-Reaching level because it connects with the sole path. MSA 21:37AB

The **specific thorough training**: This level is achieved through eliminating twenty factors, such as grasping at self, and through cultivating the opposite qualities, such as the three gates of total liberation and so forth. Therefore: "Grasping at self and persons ..." (AA 1:59A) and "Awareness of the three gates of total liberation ..." (AA 1:62A).

The **specific practice**: Although bodhisattvas on this level practice all ten perfections in general, it is said that they place particular emphasis on that of skillful means.

The **specific purity**: As explained previously, three causes make the roots of virtue of bodhisattvas on this level extremely pure and powerful:

> To give an example, when a skilled goldsmith decorates finest gold with all sorts of precious gems, it becomes most beautiful and cannot be excelled by other pieces of jewelry in this world. Likewise the roots of virtue of seventh-level bodhisattvas are extraordinarily great and pure; they cannot be excelled by those of śrāvakas, pratyekabuddha, or bodhisattvas established on lower levels.[455]

The **specific realization**: On this level the truth of the absence of differentiation is realized. All the various characteristics of Dharma, the sutras, and so forth do not appear as separate. Thus it is said: "The truth of no-differentiation . . ." (MV 2:17B).

The **specific things abandoned**: See the second level.

The **specific state of birth**: Most bodhisattvas on this level take rebirth as a divine monarch among the Delighting in Others' Manifestations[456] gods. They are skilled in bringing about realizations of the śrāvakas and pratyekabuddhas:

> Through this full consequence,
> they become kings of the Delighting in Others' Manifestations
> gods.
> They become great, outstanding Dharma masters
> with a genuine understanding of the [four] noble truths. RA 5:54

The **specific ability**: In one instant, a short moment, a small fraction of time, they can enter a hundred quadrillion meditative absorptions and so forth.

The Eighth Bodhisattva Level

Its **specific name** is the Unshakable.

The **specific etymology**: It is so called because it is unmoved by notions that either strive after characteristics or the absence of characteristics. Therefore:

> It is known as the Unshakable
> since it is unmoved by the two notions. MSA 21:37AB

The **specific thorough training**: This level is achieved through eight kinds of mastery, such as understanding the behavior of sentient beings and so forth. Therefore:

> Awareness of the mind of every being,
> love due to clear cognition . . . AA 1:66AB

The **specific practice**: Although bodhisattvas on this level practice all ten perfections in general, it is said that they place particular emphasis on that of aspirational prayers.

The **specific purity**: As explained previously, three causes make the roots of virtue of bodhisattvas on this level extremely pure and powerful:

> To give an example, were a fine piece of golden jewelry, made by a master goldsmith, to be worn on the head or the throat of a ruler of Jambudvīpa, it could not be surpassed by gold ornaments worn by other people. Likewise, the roots of virtue of eighth-level bodhisattvas are so utterly and perfectly pure that they cannot be excelled by those of śrāvakas, pratyekabuddhas, or bodhisattvas established on lower levels.[457]

The **specific realization**: On this level the space-like and concept-free nature of every phenomenon is realized. Therefore its bodhisattvas are not shocked and frightened by emptiness—the unborn. This is known as the achievement of forbearance concerning the unborn. Through this forbearance of the unborn nature of everything, they realize the nonexistence of increase and decrease and do not consider the really afflicted or the totally pure as either decreasing or increasing, respectively. Hence: "No increase, no decrease . . ." (MV 2:17C). It is also said that:

> This is also [the first of] the states with the four powers. MV 2:17D

The four powers are: (1) power over nonconceptuality, (2) power over very pure realms, (3) power over pristine awareness, and (4) power over actions.

Of these four, bodhisattvas on the eighth level have realized the first two powers, those of nonconceptuality and of very pure realms. Furthermore, it is said [in other scriptural sources] that those on the eighth level have achieved the ten powers, the powers over lifespan, mind, commodities, action, birth state, prayer, intentions, miracles, pristine awareness, and Buddhadharma.

The **specific things abandoned**: See the second level.

The **specific state of birth**: Most bodhisattvas on this level take rebirth as a divine monarch among the Brahma gods with power over an entire thousandfold world system. They are skilled in expounding the meaning of the śrāvaka and pratyekabuddha paths:

> The full consequence is to take birth
> as a Brahma god, lord of a thousandfold world systems.
> They are unsurpassed by śrāvakas and pratyekabuddhas
> in the exposition of the doctrines. RA 5:56

The **specific ability**: In one instant, a short moment, a small fraction of time, they can enter as many meditative absorptions as the number of particles in a quadrillion world systems and so forth.

The Ninth Bodhisattva Level

Its **specific name** is the Excellent Intelligence.

The **specific etymology**: It is so called because it is endowed with extremely fine intelligence, namely, clear and exact discernment. Therefore:

> That level is the Excellent Intelligence
> because of its good intelligence, clearly discerning. MSA 21:38AB

The **specific thorough training**: This level is achieved through twelve factors, such as infinite prayers and so forth. Therefore:

> The infinite number of prayers . . .
> and the knowledge of divine languages.[458] AA 1:68AB

The **specific practice**: Although bodhisattvas on this level practice all ten perfections in general, it is said that they place particular emphasis on that of the powers.

The **specific purity**: As explained previously, three causes make the roots of virtue of bodhisattvas on this level extremely pure and powerful:

> To give an example, were a fine piece of golden jewelry, made by a master goldsmith, to be worn on the head or throat of a universal monarch, it could be excelled neither by the pieces of jewelry worn by the kings of the various regions nor by those worn by any of the inhabitants of the four continents [of that world system]. Likewise, the roots of virtue of ninth-level bodhisattvas are so adorned with great pristine awareness that they cannot be excelled by those of śrāvakas, pratyekabuddhas, or bodhisattvas established on lower levels.[459]

The **specific realization**: Of the four powers [mentioned in the previous section], bodhisattvas at this ninth level realize the state of the *power of pristine awareness*, since they have achieved the four modes of perfectly clear, discerning knowledge. What are the four modes of perfectly clear, discerning knowledge? The *Ten Levels Sutra* explains:

> What are the four modes of clear discerning knowledge? They are constant possession of: perfectly clear discerning knowledge of Dharma, perfectly clear discerning knowledge of meanings, perfectly clear discerning knowledge of definitions, and perfectly clear discerning knowledge of teaching skill.[460]

The **specific things abandoned**: See the second level.

The **specific state of birth**: Most bodhisattvas on this level take birth as a divine monarch among the Brahma gods with power over a millionfold world system. They are able to answer all questions:

> The full consequence is to take birth
> as Brahma, lord of a millionfold world systems.
> In dispelling qualms from the minds of sentient beings,
> they are unsurpassed by arhats and the like. RA 5:56

The **specific ability**: In one instant, a short moment, a small fraction of time, they can enter as many meditative absorptions as there are pure particles in a million countless[461] buddhafields and so forth.

The Tenth Bodhisattva Level

Its **specific name** is the Cloud of Dharma.

The **specific etymology**: It is called the Cloud of Dharma because the bodhisattvas on that level are like a cloud that causes a rain of Dharma teachings to fall on beings, thereby washing away the fine dust of their afflictions. Alternatively, like clouds filling space, their meditative absorptions and the retention dhāraṇī they have attained pervade the entire space-like reality. Therefore:

> It is the Cloud of Dharma because like clouds,
> the two [meditative absorptions and dhāraṇis] pervade the space-
> like reality. MSA 21:38CD

The **specific thorough training**: [Unlike for the previous levels,] there is no presentation of this level in the *Ornament of Clear Realization*, but in the *Ten Levels Sutra* it says:

> O children of the victors! Up to the ninth level, bodhisattvas have thoroughly analyzed and do thoroughly analyze immeasurable aspects of knowledge with an investigatory intelligence.[462]

Through such statements, we see the teaching that this level is achieved through an empowerment of pristine awareness of omniscience due to ten thorough trainings. This tenth level is the "level empowered by omniscient pristine awareness." Why is it so called? Because, as the *Ten Levels Sutra* explains, the bodhisattvas on the tenth level are empowered with light by the buddhas of the ten directions. Further details can be found in that sutra. The *Precious Garland* also says:

> . . . because the bodhisattva is empowered
> by rays of light from the buddhas. RA 5:59CD

(This is the interpretation of Maitreya and that found in the commentaries of his tradition. It is said in the tantras that at the end of the tenth level, bodhisattvas receive empowerment from the buddhas of the ten directions and themselves become buddhas. These two views are in fact the same. Different questions attract different answers, but there is no contradiction between the two.)[463]

The **specific practice**: Although bodhisattvas on this level practice all ten perfections in general, it is said that they place particular emphasis on that of pristine awareness.[464]

The **specific purity**: As explained previously, three causes make the roots of virtue of bodhisattvas on this level extremely pure and powerful:

> To give an example, were a fine piece of golden jewelry to be made by a god skilled in crafts, who set it with the finest precious gems, and then worn on the head or throat of an empowered king of the gods, it could not be surpassed by any other jewelry of gods or humans. Likewise, the roots of virtue of tenth-level bodhisattvas are so adorned with great pristine awareness that they cannot be excelled by those of any ordinary beings, śrāvakas, pratyekabuddhas, or bodhisattvas on the ninth level and below.[465]

The **specific realization**: Of the four powers [mentioned above], bodhisattvas at this tenth level realize the state of the *power over actions*, since they accomplish the welfare of beings just as they wish, through every type of emanation.

The **specific things abandoned**: See the second level.

The **specific state of birth**: Most bodhisattvas on this level take birth as the king of the gods, Īśvara, with power over a billionfold world system. They are skilled in teaching the perfections to all sentient beings, śrāvakas, pratyekabuddhas, and bodhisattvas:

> The full consequence of this
> is to take birth as lord of the pure-realm[466] gods
> and as a mighty lord over domains
> of inconceivable pristine awareness. RA 5:60

The **specific ability**: In one instant, a short moment, a small fraction of time, they can enter as many meditative absorptions as there are pure particles in a thousand million million "countless" buddhafields and so forth. Furthermore, in one instant they can manifest from just one pore of their skin countless buddhas in the company of incalculable numbers of bodhisattvas. They can manifest as all sorts of beings—as gods, humans, and so forth. According to whatever is necessary for the training of those to be trained, they can teach Dharma by adopting the physical form of Indra, Brahma, Īśvara, universal guardians, monarchs, śrāvakas, pratyekabuddhas, or buddhas. In *Entering the Middle Way* it says:

> In one instant they can manifest,
> from a pore, perfect buddhas
> in the company of countless bodhisattvas
> and also gods, humans, and demigods. MA 11:9

This completes the explanation of the ten bodhisattva levels.

The fifth point describes the **level of buddhahood**, the final stage of the path. When the diamond-like meditative absorption arises, it eliminates simultaneously the obscurations to be removed by the path of cultivation, that is, any afflictions or knowledge obscurations that remain, comparable to the core.[467] The achievement of this level is described in *Bodhisattva Levels*:

> These levels are accomplished over the span of three countless cosmic eons. During the first great countless eon, [the bodhisattva] traverses the level of practice motivated by aspiration and achieves the state of the Joyous. Further, this is all achieved through constant effort, without which the achievement will not take place.
>
> In the second great cosmic eon, [the bodhisattva] transcends the Joyous and works through to the seventh level, the Far-Reaching, to achieve the eighth level, the Unshakable. This is precisely the way it happens because bodhisattvas of pure intention will definitely make these efforts.
>
> In the third great cosmic eon, [the bodhisattva] traverses the

> eighth and ninth levels and attains the tenth, Cloud of Dharma. Some apply themselves to this most diligently and thereby reduce many sub-eons of progress into one. Some even reduce many eons' work into one. But there are none who reduce the countless eons into one. It should be known in this way.[468]

This concludes the nineteenth chapter, explaining the spiritual levels, of this *Ornament of Precious Liberation, a Wish-Fulfilling Gem of Sublime Dharma.*

Part V. The Result

20. The Bodies of Perfect Buddhahood

To expound the line "The results are the bodies of perfect buddhahood":[469] When the paths and the levels have been completely traversed as described above, [the bodhisattva] becomes a perfect buddha within the three bodies (*kāya*), or "embodiments of enlightenment." Therefore it says in *Lamp for the Path to Awakening*:

> Buddhahood and enlightenment no longer remain distant. BP 59D

Buddhahood is described in terms of the following synopsis:

> **The bodies of a perfect buddha are described through seven points: their nature, etymology, aspects, presentation, definite number, characteristic properties, and particularities.**

The first point concerns the **nature of a truly perfect buddha.** It is described through its perfect purity[470] and perfect pristine awareness.

Its *perfect purity* means that all the affliction and knowledge obscurations, which were being eliminated during the paths and the levels, are completely eliminated subsequent to the diamond-like meditative absorption. Other obscurations, such as those impeding various meditative attainments, are subcategories of the two main obscurations and hence disappear with the elimination of those two.

As for the *perfect pristine awareness*, there are different views. Some say that buddhas have concepts as well as pristine awareness. Some say that buddhas do not have concepts yet do have pristine awareness, which knows everything clearly. Some say that the continuum of pristine awareness is broken. Some say that the Buddha has never possessed any such thing as pristine awareness. However, the authoritative texts of the sutras and treatises speak of the pristine awareness of the buddhas. Of the sutras, we find in the *Verse Summary of the Perfection of Wisdom*:

> Therefore, if you want to penetrate the supreme pristine awareness of the buddhas, trust in this, the mother of the conquerors.
> RS 7:7AB

The *Perfection of Wisdom in a Hundred Thousand Lines* says:

> A totally pure and perfect buddha has secured pristine awareness that knows everything without any obscuration.[471]

It also says in the twenty-first chapter of the same work:

> There is the pristine awareness of a perfect buddha. There is the turning of the wheel of Dharma. There is the bringing of beings to maturity.[472]

Many statements on pristine awareness are also to be found in other sutras. Of the treatises, we find, in the *Ornament of Mahayana Sutras*:

> You should know that just as when
> one sun ray shines all the others are shining too,
> so it is the case also
> with the pristine awareness of the buddhas. MSA 10:31

and

> The mirror-like pristine awareness
> is immovable and is the basis for
> the other three pristine awarenesses
> of equanimity, discernment, and activity. MSA 10:67

Buddha pristine awareness is also mentioned in other treatises. The opinion of those who say that buddhas possess pristine awareness is based on these authoritative texts. The following explains the way in which the buddhas possess pristine awareness. In brief, pristine awareness is twofold: (1) pristine awareness of the ways things are and (2) pristine awareness of things as manifold.

Of these, the *pristine awareness of the way things are* is the perception of the ultimate truth. For, as mentioned above, when through complete familiarity with suchness in the culmination of the diamond-like meditative absorption, every single conceptual elaboration pertaining to objectification has been severed, every form of mental activity has come to cease. As such the ultimate expanse free of conceptual elaboration and pristine awareness free of conceptual elaboration have merged into a single taste, indivisible like water poured into water or butter mixed into butter. So, like referring to seeing no form as "seeing empty space," the great wisdom devoid of any appearance had become the ground of all precious qualities. Therefore it is said:

> Like water poured into water,
> like butter mixed into butter,
> the knowable free of elaboration
> and pristine awareness free of elaboration
> are totally fused.
> It is this that is called *dharmakāya*
> and that is the essential nature of all the buddhas.[473]

and

> People talk of seeing space.
> Think about it and consider how they see space.
> The Tathāgatha taught that this is how to see phenomena.
> Such seeing cannot be expressed by any other example. RS 12:9

The *pristine awareness of things as manifold* is omniscience with respect to conventional, relative reality. All potential for obscuration has been destroyed by the diamond-like meditative absorption, and so there is great wisdom. Through its power, every aspect of the knowable throughout the three periods of time is seen and known, as clearly as if it were a fresh purple plum in the palm of the hand. The sutras speak of the buddhas' sublime awareness of what is relative in these terms:

> All the various causes of a single eye
> in a peacock's tail are unknowable
> by someone not omniscient, yet such knowledge
> is within the power of the Omniscient One. AK 1:92

Furthermore, the *Uttaratantra* says:

> With great compassion, as the knower of the world,
> having seen the world completely . . . RGV 2:53AB

When buddhas know and see as described above, it is not as though they perceive things as real. They see and know things as illusions. Thus it says in *Perfectly Gathering the Qualities [of Avalokiteśvara] Sutra*:

> An illusionist is not himself duped
> by his conjurations and thus,
> through his clear knowledge of what is happening,
> does not become attached to his illusory creations.
> Similarly, those skilled in perfect enlightenment
> know the three worlds to be like an illusion.[474]

In the *Meeting of Father and Son Sutra* it says:

> By remaining conscious of the fact
> that conjurations are but illusions,
> a magician will not fall under their spell.
> I pay homage and praise you, the omniscient ones,
> who regard all beings like this.[475]

Now, some hold the view that perfectly enlightened buddhas do possess the pristine awareness of the way things are—awareness of the ultimate truth—but do not possess the pristine awareness of things as manifold—awareness of the relative. Their point is not that there is something there to be known and that the buddhas are not aware of it but rather that, since there is nothing relative to be aware of in the first place, there could be no pristine awareness that is aware of it.

"Relative" or "conventional" reality is something that appears to immature beings conditioned by afflicted ignorance, as well to the three types of realized beings who are conditioned by ignorance that does not belong to the class of affliction. This is analogous to the appearance of falling hair and blurs to someone with impaired sight. Given that, following the diamond-like meditative absorption, a buddha has totally eliminated ignorance and thus "sees" suchness in the way someone "sees" nothing whatsoever, for a buddha this illusion of the relative is not present. This is analogous to the fact that, to those with unimpaired sight, there is no perception of falling hair or the blurs.

Therefore such appearances of the relative occur due to the power of ignorance and are posited only in relation to [the perspectives of] the worldly. In relation to buddhahood, they have no existence, and so there can be no buddha's pristine awareness that perceives them. Were the buddhas to possess a mind that contained relative appearances, then by definition, buddhas would themselves have to be deluded due to the manifestation of such deluded fields of experience. This is in contradiction to the scriptures, which state that the great victors are constantly in a state of meditative equipoise and so forth. (As it says, for instance, in the *Vast Manifestation Sutra*: "Totally pure and perfect buddhas are at all times in meditative equipoise."[476]) So those [with this view] say.

Of this, the proponent of the former viewpoint asserts the following. It is not the case that just by virtue of being a subsequent-meditation state it involves distraction and so forth. Therefore there is no contradiction with the scriptures such as the ones that state [that the buddhas] always remain in meditative equipoise. It is also incorrect to state a perception to be deluded simply because illusory objects appear to it. For although all the illusory phenomena that are the objects of others' illusions do appear [to the buddhas], the mind perceiving them recognizes all of it to be illusions. Furthermore, they dispel them, using them as a cause for the higher rebirth, purity, and liberation of beings. So how could there be delusion? Thus:

> When they are recognized as mere illusions,
> that which is not an illusion is perceived with certainty.[477]

Yet others say that there is no great logical harm in holding the relative as a valid object, provided one does not cling to it as real. And if anything is free of logical harm, even if the buddhas were to perceive it, there would be no delusion.

Those who hold the first view maintain that buddhas *do* possess *subsequent* pristine awareness, what is referred to as [pristine awareness of] things as manifold. Thus they say:

> The first, awareness of the way things are, is:
> undeluded, equipoise, and without mental activity.
> The next, awareness of the manifold, is:
> with appearance of delusion, subsequent knowledge, and mental activity.[478]

Those who hold the second view that buddhas *do not* possess the pristine awareness of things as manifold quote as their authority the *Infinite Means of Purification Sutra*:

> Having reached true and perfect buddhahood, the Tathāgata neither knows nor has in mind any phenomenon whatever. Why is this? Because there exists no objective reality whatsoever to be known.[479]

Furthermore, it is said:

> Some non-Buddhists say
> that you speak of going to liberation,
> yet when you have arrived at peace
> nothing remains, like something burned away.[480]

This concludes my review of the divergent standpoints around this particular issue.

A geshé's position on buddha pristine awareness is as follows.[481] The actual pure and perfect buddha is the dharmakāya. The very term *dharmakāya*—"embodiment of Dharma"—is applied to the exhaustion of all errors, and thus its nature is [defined] in opposition to errors. It is expressed in this way merely as a conventional reality. In actual fact, dharmakāya itself is unborn and free of conceptual elaboration.

Jetsun Milarepa's position is as follows.

> What we call pristine awareness is this very uncontrived awareness, beyond all such terms and ideas as "is" or "is not," "eternal" or "nothing." Therefore, no matter which terms are used to express it, there is no contradiction. Even if someone, with an ambition to become learned, were to ask the Buddha him-

> self [about this topic], I do not think there is something definite that he can say about it. Dharmakāya is beyond the intellect; it is unborn and free of conceptual elaboration. So do not ask me; observe your own mind. That is the way it is.[482]

Thus he does not uphold a standpoint in the [dichotomous] terms characterized above.

It says in the *Ornament of Mahayana Sutras*:

> Liberation is simply the exhaustion of error. MSA 7:2D

Thus a buddha is the dharmakāya, and since the dharmakāya is unborn and free of conceptual elaboration, it does not possess pristine awareness.

One might say that this [standpoint] contradicts the sutras that speak of twofold pristine awareness. In fact, it does not, for just as visual consciousness arises with the perception of the color blue and one says, "I see blue," so the pristine awareness that is the ultimate expanse is pristine awareness of the way things are, whereas the pristine awareness of the manifold is the relative aspect [of that same pristine awareness] when it is triggered by whatever manifests to [the deluded minds of] beings. This position is taught to be the most convenient approach to the topic.

Thus the very essence or the very nature of a buddha [can be viewed as] the most perfect purity and the most perfect pristine awareness. As is said in the *Uttaratantra*:

> Buddhahood is indivisible yet categorized
> in terms of its two qualities of purity,
> pristine awareness and relinquishment,
> like the sun and space. RGV 2:4

Also, it says in the *Ornament of Mahayana Sutras*:

> Those who, through vast purification, have absolutely triumphed
> over the obscurations that have been consistently present for
> such a long time—
> the afflictions and knowledge obscurations, along with their
> latent potentials—

and who possess the supreme good qualities through perfect transmutation: those are buddhas! MSA 10:12A–C

The second point is the **etymology** of *buddha*. Why *buddha*? The term *buddha* (Tib. *sangs rgyas*) is applied because they have awakened (*sangs*) from sleep-like ignorance and because the mind has fully expanded (*rgyas*) with respect to the two aspects of the knowable. As it says:

Woken from the slumber of ignorance
and mind fully expanded, hence *buddha*.[483]

The third point concerns **its aspects.** Buddhahood can be divided into three aspects, namely, its three bodies: dharmakāya, saṃbhogakāya, and nirmāṇakāya. It says in the *Sutra of Golden Light*:

All tathāgatas possess three bodies: the dharmakāya, the saṃbhogakāya, and the nirmāṇakāya.[484]

Someone might remark that some scriptures speak of two bodies, others of four bodies, and some of even five bodies. Although they are discussed as such, the bodies are all covered by this categorization in terms of three bodies. Thus the *Ornament of Mahayana Sutras* says:

Be aware that all the buddha bodies
are included within the three bodies. MSA 10:65AB

The fourth point is a **presentation** [of the bodies]. The dharmakāya is what buddha really is. The *Perfection of Wisdom in Eight Thousand Lines* says:

Do not view the Buddha as the form body. The Buddha is the dharmakāya.[485]

The *King of Meditation Sutra* says:

Do not view the King of Conquerors as the form body.[486]

The two form bodies are a consequence of the convergence of the following three factors: (1) the power of transmission of the dharmakāya, (2) the subjective experience of the spiritual trainees, and (3) one's past aspiration prayers. Were the form bodies due solely to the power of transmission of the ultimate expanse (*dharmadhātu*), the logical consequence would be that everyone would be effortlessly liberated, since the ultimate expanse pervades all beings. Were that the case, it would follow that all beings would come face to face with the buddhas. However, since this is not so, they do not come solely from the power of transmission of the ultimate expanse.

Were the form bodies to be solely due to the subjective experience of beings training on the path, buddhahood would be dependent on error, since to perceive something that is not there is an error. Also, since beings have been perceiving erroneously since time without beginning, all of them should already be buddhas. But this not the case either, so the form bodies are not just the subjective projections of beings still training.

Were the form bodies to be solely due to former prayers, then has a true and perfect buddha achieved power over prayer? If not, then that buddha has not reached omniscience. If a buddha has, then since his prayers are unbiased and for the benefit of all beings, the logical consequence would be for each and every being to be liberated. But this is not the case, so the form bodies do not come solely from former prayers.

Therefore the form bodies are a consequence of the combination of these three factors.

The fifth point explains the reasons for **a definite number**. There are three bodies, and this number is determined by necessity, inasmuch as there is dharmakāya as benefit for oneself and the two form bodies as benefit for others.

How does the dharmakāya represent *benefit for oneself*? Once the dharmakāya has been achieved, it is the basis for all other qualities, such as the [four] fearlessnesses, the [ten] powers, and so forth, which gather as though they had been summoned. Furthermore, even if someone has not achieved dharmakāya itself, those who aspire to dharmakāya, have a little realization of it, a partial realization, or nearly complete realization of it will have just a few qualities, many qualities, a great number of qualities, or an immeasurable amount of qualities, respectively:

The qualities arising from *aspiration* to dharmakāya are those of the meditative absorptions, clear cognitions, and all the superb qualities up to and including the highest worldly realization.[487]

The qualities emerging from a *little realization* of dharmakāya are all the qualities of purification, clear cognition, supernatural ability, and so forth of realized śrāvaka arhats.

The qualities emerging from a *partial realization* of dharmakāya are all the qualities of purification, meditative absorption, clear cognition, and so forth of realized pratyekabuddha arhats.

The qualities emerging from *nearly complete realization* of dharmakāya are the qualities of purification, meditative absorption, clear cognition, and so forth of bodhisattvas of the bodhisattva levels.

The two form bodies are presented in this way as *benefit for others,* inasmuch as there is the enjoyment body (*saṃbhogakāya*) that appears to pure disciples and the emanation body (*nirmāṇakāya*) that appears to impure disciples.

Thus there are definitely three bodies.

The sixth point describes the **characteristic properties of the three bodies.**

First, *dharmakāya* simply refers to the exhaustion of all error—the turning away from what is by nature delusory—once the meaning of emptiness (namely, the ultimate expanse) has been realized. However, as such, *dharmakāya* is simply a term representing a conceptual convention. In real essence, there is no dharmakāya whatsoever possessing true existence, either as dharmakāya, as characteristic properties of dharmakāya, or as anything that could serve as a basis for properties of dharmakāya. Since it is like that, this is how my guru Milarepa explained it.

Dividing it into its various aspects, dharmakāya has eight characteristic qualities—namely, being identical, profound, permanent, unitary, right, pure, lumionous, and linked to the enjoyment body. It is *identical* inasmuch as there are no differences among the dharmakāyas of the various buddhas. It is *profound* because it is difficult to realize, having nothing to do with conceptual elaboration. It is *permanent* because it is not composite; it is without coming into being or cessation; and it is without beginning, middle, or end. It is *unitary* because it is indivisible, the ultimate expanse [i.e., emptiness] and its pristine awareness being inseparable. It is *right* because it is without error, since it transcends the two extremes of underestimation and exaggeration. It is *pure* because it is free from the pollution of the three obscurations (namely, the afflictions and knowledge obscurations and the impediments to meditative attainment). It is *luminous clarity*. Free of conceptuality, it is focused on nonconceptual suchness. It is *linked to the enjoyment body*. It is the basis for the enjoyment body (*saṃbhogakāya*), which is the very expression of its vast qualities.

The *Uttaratantra* says:

> Beginningless, devoid of center and periphery, it is indivisible,
> without the two, free from the three, stainless, and
> nonconceptual—
> such is realized to be the nature of the ultimate expanse
> when seen by the yogi resting in meditative equipoise.
> RGV 2:38

The *Ornament of Mahayana Sutras* also says:

> Identical, the nature body (*svabhāvakāya*),
> subtle and linked with the enjoyment body (*saṃbhogakāya*).
> MSA 10:62AB

Second, the *enjoyment body* (*saṃbhogakāya*) also has eight characteristics—those of entourage, domain, form, marks, teaching, deeds, spontaneity, and absence of an own-being. The *entourage* with which it is spontaneously experienced is composed solely of bodhisattvas abiding in the ten bodhisattva levels. The *domain* in which it is experienced is that of the utterly pure buddhafields. The *form* or way in which it is experienced is in the form of illustrious Vairocana and so forth. The *marks* with which it is endowed physically are the thirty-two marks of excellence and the eighty adornments. The Dharma *teachings* through which it is perfectly experienced are solely that of the Mahayana. The enlightened activity that forms its *deeds* is to predict the future enlightenment of the bodhisattvas and so forth. Its *spontaneity* is that those deeds and so forth are all accomplished without any effort, occurring spontaneously as in the example of the supreme [wish-fulfilling] gems. Its *absence of own-being* is that even though it manifests various sorts of form, they are not its true nature. They are like the colors picked up in a crystal.

Thus the *Ornament of Mahayana Sutras* says:

Perfect experience: in every domain a complete entourage,
the place, the marks, the form,
the perfect use of Dharma teaching, and its deeds.
These are the various characteristics. MSA 10:61

Also, in the *Ornament of Clear Realization* it says:

That endowed with the thirty-two marks
and eighty adornments is known as
the enjoyment body of the Buddha
because it partakes of ["enjoys"] the Mahayana. AA 8:12

Third, the *emanation body* (*nirmāṇakāya*) also has eight principal characteristics—those of its basis, its cause, its domain, its duration, its character, its role of encouraging, its maturing function, and its liberating function. Its *basis* is the dharmakāya, [from which it emanates] without there being any movement. Its *cause* is tremendous compassion aspiring to benefit every single being. Its *domain* embraces both the very pure lands and quite impure ones. Its *duration* is that it endures, without interruption, for as long as the world endures. Its *character* is to manifest forms as the three types of emanation:

- *Creative emanations* endowed with outstanding skill in and mastery of a given art or craft, such as playing lute and so forth
- *Birth emanations* that take birth in various inferior bodies as specific types of existence, for example, as a hare
- *Supreme emanations* that manifest [the twelve deeds]—descent from Tuṣita Heaven, entering the mother's womb, and so forth, and eventually entering great peace

As it says in the *Ornament of Mahayana Sutras*:

Constantly manifesting as an artist,
a human birth, great enlightenment, and nirvana,
the Buddha's emanation body is
a great expression of liberation. MSA 10:64

As is said in the *Uttaratantra*:

Through emanations of various kinds,
he manifestly takes birth—(1) descends from Tuṣitā,
(2) enters the womb, and (3) is born.
(4) Skilled in all arts and crafts,
he (5) enjoys the company of his consorts,
(6) [renounces], (7) undergoes hardships,
(8) goes to the seat of enlightenment,
(9) vanquishes the armies of harmful forces,
(10) attains perfect enlightenment,
(11) turns the wheel of Dharma, and (12) passes away.
In all those realms, quite impure,
he shows these deeds for as long as worlds endure. RGV 2:54–56

The *role of encouraging* is that the emanation body makes ordinary, worldly beings long for and work toward whichever of the three types of nirvana corresponds to their mentality. The *maturing function* is that the emanation body brings to full spiritual maturity those already engaged in the path. The *liberating function* is that the emanation body frees from the fetters of existence those who have reached full maturity in virtue.

Thus it says in the *Uttaratantra*:

It causes worldly beings to enter the path of peace,
brings them to full maturity, and is that which gives rise to predictions. RGV 2:41AB

These are the eight characteristics of the emanation body. The *Ornament of Clear Realization* says:

The body that acts simultaneously
and in all sorts of ways to help beings
for as long as existence continues
is the unceasing emanation body of the Sage. AA 8:33

The seventh point concerns the **three particularities** of the buddha bodies: those of identity, permanence, and manifestation.

The *particularity of identity* is that the dharmakāya of all buddhas is identical, being inseparable from its support, the ultimate expanse. The enjoyment body of all buddhas is identical since its noble disposition is the same. The emanation body of all buddhas is identical because their activity is common. Therefore the *Ornament of Mahayana Sutras* says:

> These are identical because of
> their support, intention, and activity. MSA 10:66AB

The *particularity of permanence*: The dharmakāya is permanent by its very nature because, being the ultimate, its very identity is that which is without coming into being or ceasing. The enjoyment body is permanent through being continuous, inasmuch as the experience of Dharma that it manifests is uninterrupted. The emanation body is permanent insofar as its deeds are permanent. Although its manifestations disappear, it shows itself over and over again. Although that which manifests in correspondence to a certain need will cease, there is a functional permanence since it arises appropriately, without delay. The *Ornament of Mahayana Sutras* says:

> Permanence of nature,
> of uninterruptedness, and of continuity . . . MSA 10:66CD

The *particularity of manifestation*: The dharmakāya manifests through the purification of the knowledge obscuration that clouds the ultimate expanse. The enjoyment body manifests through the purification of the afflictions obscuration. The emanation body manifests through the purification of karmic obscurations.

This concludes the twentieth chapter, on the result—perfect buddhahood—of this *Ornament of Precious Liberation, a Wish-Fulfilling Gem of Sublime Dharma.*

Part VI. Enlightened Activities of the Buddhas

21. Enlightened Activities of the Buddhas

Here is explained the line "The activity is to nonconceptually fulfill the welfare of beings."[488] At first bodhicitta is developed, then the path is practiced, and finally the fruition, buddhahood, is achieved. Because all these goals have been pursued solely to eliminate beings' sufferings and ensure their happiness, you may wonder how in fact there can be any benefitting of beings when buddhahood is attained, since buddhas are without either conceptual activity or effort. There does nevertheless occur spontaneous and uninterrupted benefitting of beings, even though buddhas do not think or make effort. To explain this point, the following is the synopsis:

> **Enlightened activity is summed up in three points: the noble bodies of the buddhas, without deliberate thought, accomplish benefit for beings, and likewise do the magnificent speech and the noble mind.**

Examples of this nonconceptual performance of the welfare of beings—physically, verbally, and mentally—are given in the *Uttaratantra*:

> Like Indra, the divine drum, a cloud, and Brahma,
> like the sun and a precious wish-fulfilling jewel,
> like an echo, like space, and like the earth:
> such is [the activity of] the Tathāgata. RGV 4:13

First, we have examples of how the **noble forms** [or bodies] of the buddhas nonconceptually accomplish benefit for beings. The quotation "like the manifestation of Indra" gives the example of how the nonconceptualizing bodies can bring benefit to sentient beings. In this example, Indra, lord of the gods, dwells in his palace called the House of Victory in the company of a host of young goddesses. The palace is made of vaidūrya jewel[489] so pure and lustrous that Indra's reflected image appears on the walls and can be seen from the outside. Were humans living on Earth able to behold this image of Indra and his divine enjoyments in the heavens above them, they would long and pray to live like that. With such a goal in mind, they would make sincere efforts to be virtuous, and through such virtue they might be reborn in such a state after death. The vision that inspires them takes place without any effort of intention on the part of Indra.

In a similar way, those who have entered the path of highest good and who cultivate faith and similar virtues will see the forms of the perfect buddhas adorned with their special marks and signs; they will see them walking, standing, sitting, sleeping, teaching the Dharma, meditating, and accomplishing all sorts of miracles. As a result they will experience faith and yearn to attain such a state. To become like that, they will practice the virtues that are its cause: bodhicitta and all the other requisite practices. As a result, they will eventually become buddhas. The manifestation of the buddhas' form bodies takes place without any deliberate thought and without any movement [on the buddhas' part]. Thus it is stated:

> Just as, on the clear surface of vaidūrya jewel,
> there appears the reflected form of the lord of gods,
> so on the clear surface of beings' minds here
> appears the reflected form of the King of Conquerors. RGV 4:14

The line "like the divine drum" gives the example of how **the buddhas' speech** can accomplish the welfare of beings without forethought. In the example, a drumbeat sounds in the realm of the gods. It resounds as a result of the gods' former beneficial actions. The drumbeat does not have thought or intention, yet its sound conveys messages such as "All conditioned things are impermanent!" that alert the gods, who are inclined to neglect virtue in the present. Thus it is stated:

> Just as through the power
> of the gods' former virtue,
> the Dharma drum in the divine realms—
> without any thought, effort,
> location, mind, or form—
> alerts all the carefree gods over and over again

> with the words "impermanence," "suffering,"
> "no self," and "peace" . . . RGV 4:31–32

As in the example, it is without any effort or deliberation that the speech of the buddhas transmits suitable teachings to those who are ready. So it is stated:

> Likewise, without effort and so forth,
> the omnipresent embraces all beings, without exception,
> with the speech of the enlightened ones,
> teaching the Dharma to those who are ready. RGV 4:33

In the above way, the speech of the buddhas accomplishes the welfare of beings without any [need for] conscious deliberate thought.

The line "Like a cloud . . ." presents the analogy of how the **perfect mind** of the buddhas nonconceptually accomplishes the good of beings. During the monsoon, clouds gather effortlessly in the sky, and their rain, falling on the earth without any deliberation on the clouds' part, causes the growth of perfect crops and many other things to happen. It is stated:

> Just as from monsoon clouds
> a mass of water,
> the condition for plentiful crops,
> falls down to earth . . . RGV 4:42

In a similar way, the activity of the buddha mind, without requiring any deliberation, pours down the rain of Dharma onto beings training in virtue. Thus it is stated:

> Similarly, the clouds of great compassion
> without any need of deliberation,
> rain down the sublime teachings of the victorious ones
> and ripen crops of wholesomeness among beings. RGV 4:43

Thus the buddha mind accomplishes the welfare of beings without any need for conscious thought.

Regarding the words, "like Brahma . . . ," Brahma, lord of the gods, manifests his presence in all the heavens yet never leaves his own Brahma heaven. In a similar way, without ever moving from the dharmakāya, the buddhas manifest the twelve deeds and other similar emanations to those training in virtue, thereby bringing them benefit. So it is stated:

> Just as Brahma, without ever moving
> from the Brahma heaven,
> effortlessly shows his manifestations
> in all the other heavens,
> so also does a victorious one,
> without ever moving from the dharmakāya,
> effortlessly show his emanations everywhere
> to those whose karma makes them ready. RGV 4:53–54

In the example of the sun, the sun's rays, without any need for deliberation, cause lotuses and innumerable other kinds of flowers to blossom simultaneously. Similarly, without any thought or effort, the rays of the buddhas' teachings cause the lotuses that are the minds of infinitely varied disciples, with their different aspirations, to open toward that which is wholesome. Thus it is stated:

> Just as the sun, without any deliberation,
> through the simultaneous radiation of its sunbeams,
> brings the lotuses to full bloom
> and ripens other plants,
> so does the sun of the Buddha
> with the rays of his sublime teachings
> pour without any need for deliberation
> into the lotus-like beings training in virtue. RGV 4:59–60

Taking this example of the sun another way, just as the reflection of the sun appears simultaneously on all surfaces that are sufficiently clear and smooth, so does the Buddha appear simultaneously to all disciples of sufficiently pure inner disposition:

> In all the water vessels
> that are those pure disciples,

countless reflections of the buddha sun
appear simultaneously. RGV 4:62

In the example of the wish-fulfilling gem, just as a wish-fulfilling gem does not think yet effortlessly produces whatever is requested by the person who calls on it, so the goals corresponding to the various motivations of the śrāvakas and other disciples are accomplished because of the buddhas. Thus it is stated:

Just as a wish-fulfilling gem,
without thought and spontaneously,
completely fulfills the wishes
of those within its sphere of influence,
so also, on account of the wish-fulfilling buddha,
those of various motivations
hear different kinds of teachings,
without any deliberation [on the Buddha's part]. RGV 4:67–68

Similar to the above, there are three more examples—those of an echo, of space, and of the earth—showing how beings can be benefitted by the buddhas without requiring any conscious thought on their part.

This was the twenty-first chapter, on nonconceptual enlightened activity, of this *Ornament of Precious Liberation, a Wish-Fulfilling Gem of Sublime Dharma.*

* * *

This concludes this *Ornament of Precious Liberation, a Wish-Fulfilling Gem of Sublime Dharma*, progressively explaining the Mahayana path, composed by the physician Sönam Rinchen at the instigation of Darma Kyap and transcribed by the latter.

May whatever merit there be in your transcription
in terms of nonconceptual benefit for beings
through the wish-fulfilling sacred Dharma
help all beings attain supreme enlightenment. Virtue!

Notes

1. Gampopa's work was also translated by Khenpo Konchog Gyaltsen in 1998 with the same title, no doubt following the precedent set by Guenther. However, the Twelfth Tai Situpa made it very clear to the present translator that the *rin po che* ("precious") in the main title modifies "liberation" and not "ornament."
2. Some feel that the Mahāmudrā quotations in the wisdom chapter were not in Gampopa's original work, and some extensive research is under way at the time of writing, by a team of scholars under Khenpo Damchö Dawa, to clarify the exact evolution of the versions we have today.
3. This introduction, and particularly the comments here about the tenrim genre and Gampopa's Kadampa predecessors, owes a large debt to the introduction to *Stages of the Buddha's Teachings* (Boston: Wisdom, 2015), the volume where this translation previously appeared. That introduction was principally composed by David P. Jackson.
4. The following brief sketch of Gampopa's life is based mainly on Gö Lotsāwa's *Blue Annals*.
5. These four disciples who went on to found distinct Kagyü lineages were Lama Shang (1122–93), Karmapa Düsum Khyenpa (1110–93), Phakmodrupa (1110–70), and Barompa Darma Wangchuk (1127–94). For Peter Alan Roberts's overview of the development of the Kagyü school in Tibet and the doctrinal threads that underpin it, see the Tibetan Classics volume *The Mind of Mahāmudrā* (Boston: Wisdom, 2014).
6. The name Kagyü (*bka' brgyud*) is a shortened form of *bka' babs bzhi'i brgyud pa*, "lineage of the four transmissions of mastery," referring to the four key practices embodied in various ways in the different highest yoga tantra transmissions held by Tilopa.
7. Youthful Mañjuśrī—Mañjuśrī Kumārabhuta—is one of the names of the great bodhisattva Mañjuśrī. It signifies his status as a tenth-level bodhisattva: one of those who remain ever young, not "aging" into full buddhahood.
8. The Palpung edition has "When will delusion be fully clarified? It will be clarified when highest enlightenment is reached."
9. These boldface synopses are an important part of the text. They are memorized by students as a way of recollecting its subject matter. Each of the six headings in this opening synopsis constitutes a chapter of the book, with the exception of the fourth, which is spread over sixteen chapters.

10. The text says "lesser beings," but since that is comparing them with exalted beings, such as buddhas and realized bodhisattvas, the meaning is that they are regular, worldly beings.
11. *Samādhirājasūtra*, 32a7.
12. *Mahāparinirvāṇasūtra* (shorter version), 112a4.
13. *Mahāparinirvāṇasūtra* (longer version), 111b1.
14. Asaṅga's discussion of the six shortcomings and how the convergence of them deprives one of the enlightenment potential is found in his *Śrāvaka Levels* (*Śrāvakabhūmi*), 7b5. It is difficult to determine whether Gampopa is here citing from another source or versifying this same citation.
15. *Mahākaruṇāpuṇḍarīkasūtra*, 87a7.
16. The source of this quote has not been identified.
17. The source of this quote has not been identified.
18. Jambudvīpa in this context refers principally to India.
19. *Saddharmapuṇḍarīkasūtra*, 54b1.
20. Ibid., 75a3.
21. The term *bodhicitta*, or "thought of awakening," can be used to describe the aspiration of the Hinayana paths. When such is the case, the more familiar bodhicitta of the bodhisattva is known as *great bodhicitta*.
22. *Saddharmapuṇḍarīkasūtra*, 40b1.
23. These synonyms are very helpful in understanding the connotations of *rigs*, the Tibetan translation of the Sanskrit term *gotra*. It is a *potential* one is born with, if that term is seen through its meaning of "family," remembering that caste and profession were so closely linked to birth family. It is like a *seed*, containing from the outset the genetic information of its fruit; it is like the one prime *element* permeating all existence; and it is the *essential nature* of all things, once the veil of illusions has fallen.
24. This is the first mention of the two obscurations (*āvaraṇa*) in this text, the afflictions obscuration (*kleśāvaraṇa*) and the knowledge obscuration (*jñeyāvaraṇa*).
25. The Palpung edition has "a lack of care."
26. *Daśadharmakasūtra*, 167b7.
27. Ibid., 168a1.
28. Prajñākaramati, *Commentary on the Guide to the Bodhisattva Way of Life* (*Bodhicaryāvatārapañjikā*), 45b5.
29. The Tibetan *ngo tsha* signifies a personal sense of dignity that makes you ashamed of yourself for committing unworthy actions, whereas a respect for others (*khrel*) signifies being concerned about what others will think or say.
30. The Palpung and Beijing editions say, "This makes them unsuited for a vigorous quest for virtue."
31. Asaṅga, *Śrāvaka Levels* (*Śrāvakabhūmi*), 3b4.
32. The "actions of immediate consequence" are so called because they cause you to be reborn immediately in the lower realms after death, without passing through the intermediate state (*bardo*) as most people do.

33. "Others" here implies benefactors who help create appropriate material circumstances.
34. *Bodhisattvapiṭaka*, 67b5.
35. *Mahākaruṇāpuṇḍarīkasūtra*, 69a2.
36. *Gaṇḍavyūhasūtra*, 381a7.
37. *Host of Flowers Sutra* (*Kusumasaṃcayasūtra*), 302a7.
38. The term *puruṣa* had great significance in the other religions of India and was therefore a loaded term. This is the Buddhist way of appropriating it.
39. *Nāgas* are generally of serpentine form but possess powers that ordinary snakes do not. *Kiṃnaras* are half-human, half-horse beings. *Uragas*—literally, those that "slide on their bellies"—are one of the eight classes of spirits.
40. The source of this quote has not been identified.
41. *Daśadharmakasūtra*, 166a3.
42. *Avataṃsakasūtra*, *ka*, 90b5.
43. *Lalitavistarasūtra*, 49b5.
44. The desire realm (Skt. *kamadhātu*, Tib. *'dod khams*) is one of the three realms of existence (see glossary). It is often translated literally as "desire realm," on account of the Tibetan *'dod*, and it can be explained in that way—as a domain where beings have much desire. However, there is another explanation in which *'dod* is short for *'dod pa'i yon tan* ("fields of the senses"), since its beings' experiences are principally those of the five sense consciousnesses. Another translation would therefore be "sensorial realms."
45. The Tibetan term translated here is *dang ba*. The term literally connotes "clarity" but can also mean "joy," because a person has joyful admiration for the Three Jewels and so forth. When used in a more Vajrayana context of faith subsequent to clear realization that confirms the value of the Three Jewels, the term can also mean "lucidity," an explanation favored by the late Kalu Rinpoche.
46. Vasubandhu, *Abhidharmakośabhāṣya*, *ku*, 64a1.
47. *Ratnolkānāmadhāraṇīsūtra*, 63b5.
48. *Bodhisattvapiṭaka*, 186a1.
49. "Rely on" is used here to translate the Tibetan *bsten*, which could equally have been translated by "attend" in its traditional but perhaps less familiar meanings of "stay with," "pay heed to," "serve," and "look after."
50. *Aṣṭasāhasrikāprajñāpāramitā*, 216b1.
51. *Instructions for Liberation of Śrī Saṃbhava* is found in the *Flower Ornament Sutra* (*Avataṃsakasūtra*), *ā*, 286a5.
52. *Flower Ornament Sutra* (*Avataṃsakasūtra*), *ā*, 284b3.
53. *Instructions for Liberation of Upāsikā Acalā* is found in the *Flower Ornament Sutra* (*Avataṃsakasūtra*), *ā*, 36b3.
54. Indrabhūti, *Achieving Pristine Awareness* (*Jñānasiddhisādhanopāyikā*), 51a2.
55. *Gaṇḍavyūhasūtra*, *a*, 286a7.
56. Asaṅga, *Bodhisattvabhūmi*, 127a3.
57. *Gaṇḍavyūhasūtra*, *a*, 305a3.

58. Ibid., 343a2.
59. *Perfection of Wisdom in Eight Thousand Lines* (*Aṣṭasāhasrikāprajñāpāramitā*), 261a3.
60. The bodhisattva Sudhana was sent to King Anala to learn compassion, but when he arrived, he saw what seemed to be the king judging and punishing evildoers mercilessly. Thus he initially doubted the king's bodhisattva qualities. However, he listened to his inner voice and went to the king, who then took him to wonderful paradises and explained that he could manifest visions of the worst punishments or the greatest rewards in order to instill confidence in moral discipline in his subjects.
61. *Flower Ornament Sutra* (*Avataṃsakasūtra*), *ā*, 288b1.
62. These three "faults of the container" refer respectively to being unreceptive, nonretentive, or soiled by the afflictions.
63. *Flower Ornament Sutra* (*Avataṃsakasūtra*), *ā*, 285a2.
64. *Aṣṭasāhasrikāprajñāpāramitā*, 267b3.
65. This is the general synopsis for part IV of the text, and it covers the sixteen chapters to come, each of which has its own synopsis and sometimes consists of internal subchapters, each having its own synopsis. The first teaching mentioned here (on impermanence) is addressed below in the present chapter, the second teaching (on suffering and karma) is covered in chapters 5 and 6, the third teaching (on love and compassion) in chapter 7, and the fourth teaching (on the bodhisattva path) in chapters 8–19.
66. The four remedies that follow also reappear as headings below.
67. *Gaṇḍavyūhasūtra*, *ā*, 284b2.
68. *White Lotus of Great Compassion Sutra* (*Mahākaruṇāpuṇḍarīkasūtra*), 75a6.
69. *Vīradattagṛhapatiparipṛcchāsūtra*, 201b2.
70. *Lalitavistarasūtra*, 88a2.
71. *Eliminating Suffering* (*Śokavinodana*), 33a6.
72. Rishis, or "seers of truth" (Skt. *ṛṣi*, Tib. *drang srong*), were highly accomplished meditators of India, renowned for their supernatural abilities. In early times, the rishis and rishikas (female rishis) were poet-seers; in later times, their name came to mean those who spoke only the truth. Straightforwardness and truthfulness are conveyed by the Tibetan translation.
73. Aśvaghoṣa, *Eliminating Suffering* (*Śokavinodana*), 33a6.
74. Ibid., 33b3. The plantain has no heartwood. Sentient beings have no single enduring, central component guaranteeing life.
75. *Crown Jewel Dhāraṇī Sutra* (*Ratnaketudhāraṇīsūtra*), 211b3.
76. Ibid., 211b3.
77. The source of this citation has not been located.
78. In the original, this is attributed to the *Guide to the Bodhisattva Way of Life*, but the verse is actually found in the *Collection of Aphorisms*.
79. This is a reference to the various ways of disposing of a corpse according to the four elements and astrology. Although Gampopa attributes this quotation to Śāntideva, it is not found in the *Bodhicaryāvatāra*.
80. The source of this quote has not been located.

81. Yaśomitra, *Abhidharmakośaṭīkā*, 3b3.
82. *Karuṇāpuṇḍarīkasūtra*, 157b6.
83. The Beijing edition has 12,960 billion instead of 12,990 billion.
84. The Beijing edition has 103,680 billion instead of 100,680 billion.
85. The Beijing edition has 829,040 billion; Palpung has 825,400 billion.
86. The Beijing edition has 53,840,160 billion; Palpung has 51,840,160 billion.
87. In the *Lifespan Sutra* (*Āyuṣparyantasūtra*), 143b2.
88. *Basis of Vinaya* (*Vinayavastu*), 100b:3.
89. Koṭikarṇa ("Ten Million in the Ear") was so called because he was born with a divine jewel worth ten million ounces of gold set in his ear. He set out as a merchant to please his father but was abandoned by his servants and then lost in a desert, where he spent twelve years with various types of hungry spirits. They were lucid about the past actions that had caused their plight and gave him messages for the human realm, to which he returned. He became a monk under Mahākatyāyana, gaining deep realization. *Basis of Vinaya* (*Vinayavastu*), 251b3. A translation of this story appears in Rotman, *Divine Stories*, 39–70.
90. It is useful to know that the often-encountered "five hundred" in Buddhist texts actually is the ancient way of saying "many hundreds" and should not always be taken literally.
91. The source of this quote has not been identified.
92. *Nandagarbhāvakrāntinirdeśa*, 223b7.
93. The four modes of birth are spontaneous, from a womb, from an egg, or from heat and moisture.
94. It is not that the sperm and ovum are particularly impure compared to other bodily substances but that they form part of the thirty-six impure physical substances of which a human body is composed.
95. *Nanda's Abiding in the Womb* (*Nandagarbhāvakrāntinirdeśa*), 238a1.
96. *One Hundred Stories* (*Avadānaśataka*), 254a6.
97. *Nandagarbhāvakrāntinirdeśa*, 231b2.
98. *Lalitavistarasūtra*, 88b4.
99. Ibid., 88b5.
100. *Rājāvavādakasūtra*, 10b5.
101. In the longer *Great Passing into Nirvana Sutra* (*Mahāparinirvāṇasūtra*), *nya*, 302a3.
102. *Nandagarbhāvakrāntinirdeśa*, 228a5.
103. Although the text attributes this quotation to the *Meeting of Father and Son Sutra* (*Pitāputrasamāgamasūtra*), it is actually found in the *Questions of Pūrṇa Sutra* (*Pūrṇaparipṛcchāsūtra*), 171a5.
104. *Karmaśataka*, 106a7.
105. *Mahākaruṇāpuṇḍarīkasūtra*, 62b3.
106. Asaṅga, *Abhidharmasamuccaya*, 85a8.
107. The traditional way of describing karma—as "action, cause and effect"—shows an assumption that the consequences of an action are actually part and parcel of that action rather than something else that happens later due to the action.
108. The five actions that have immediate result at death (i.e., no intermediate state

but immediate rebirth in the worst realms) are parricide, matricide, killing an arhat, creating divisions in the Sangha, and injuring a buddha.

109. The truths of cessation and of the path are the third and fourth of the so-called noble truths, which are more accurately rendered the *four truths of the noble ones.*
110. The thorn-like view is a view that denies the long-term consequences of actions (karma) on their doer and only acknowledges their immediate consequences.
111. Asaṅga, *Abhidharmasamuccaya*, 89b6.
112. *Basis of Vinaya* (*Vinayavastu*), 41a1.
113. Asaṅga, *Abhidharmasamuccaya*, 89b6.
114. This quote is actually from the longer *Great Passing into Nirvana Sutra* (*Mahāparinirvāṇasūtra*), *nya*, 354a5.
115. *Surataparipṛcchāsūtra*, 181b7.
116. King Kṛkin had seven daughters with powerful karma due to their Dharma practice in former lives. This gave them radical feelings of renunciation. They refused all the royal benefits offered them by their father and eventually obtained his permission to leave palace life to practice Dharma. They later also refused the gifts of the god Indra, who offered them divine substances when he saw them dressed in rags and meditating assiduously in a charnel ground.
117. *Karmaśataka*, 16a3.
118. This quote is actually from the longer *Great Passing into Nirvana Sutra* (*Mahāparinirvāṇasūtra*), *ka*, 354a5.
119. The source of this quote has not been identified.
120. *Extensive Explanation of Root Vajrayana Downfalls* (*Vajrayānamūlāpattiṭīkā*), 16a5.
121. Ibid., 10b2.
122. *Akṣayamatinirdeśasūtra*, 132a3. "The forbearance accepting unborn phenomena" (*mi skye ba'i chos la bzod pa*), translated elsewhere also as "acceptance of unoriginated factors," is a bodhisattva's stable realization of emptiness.
123. *Aṣṭasāhasrikāprajñāpāramitā*, 139b4.
124. This canonical text, *Beginningless Time Sutra*, does not appear to exist in the Tibetan canon. However, the "Questions" chapter of the longer *Great Passing into Nirvana Sutra* does contain a version extremely similar to this quotation: *Mahāparinirvāṇasūtra*, *ta*, 11b4.
125. *Prayer of Excellent Conduct* (*Bhadracaryāpraṇidhāna*) is part of the *Flower Ornament Sutra* (*Avataṃsakasūtra*), *ā*, 361a6.
126. *Candraprabha Sutra* is one of several names for the *King of Meditation Sutra* (*Samādhirājasūtra*), 115b6. Gampopa himself is considered an incarnation of the Buddha's interlocutor in this sutra, Candraprabhakumāra.
127. In the ITC critical edition as well as the Tsipri edition, it reads "you will derive / hundredfold benefits from loving kindness." Here we have chosen to follow the reading of the Beijing and Palpung editions instead.
128. A former incarnation of Buddha Śākyamuni, the brahman Mahādatta was a wealthy prince whose heart was saddened by the poverty he saw in his land and by knowing the harmful thoughts and actions to which poverty gives rise. He set out

on an epic and arduous journey to collect wish-fulfilling gems powerful enough to dispel all the poverty in his world. His long quest bore fruit, and he was able to help innumerable beings due to his loving concern for their happiness. This story is found in chapter 3 of the *Sage and Fool Sutra* (*Damamūkanāmasūtra*), 223a3.

129. King Bāla Maitreya was another former incarnation of Buddha Śākyamuni. His loving mind and prayers were so strong that it protected his subjects from flesh-eating demons. Five such rakṣas, very hungry because of this, came to him to plead their case. He gave them his own flesh and blood. The strong karmic connection created by this selfless act led them eventually to meet him again and again, finally becoming Kauṇḍinya and the four other ascetics who were Śākyamuni's meditation companions before his enlightenment and subsequently among the first to receive his teachings. *Sage and Fool Sutra* (*Damamūkanāmasūtra*), chapter 12, 155b4.
130. The source of this quote has not been identified.
131. *Perfectly Gathering the Qualities* [*of Avalokiteśvara*] *Sutra* (*Dhamasaṃgītisūtra*), 84a6.
132. Ibid., 84a7.
133. The *Sutra of the Tathāgata's Secrets* has not been found. However, this quotation was found in the *Enlightenment of Vairocana* (*Vairocanābhisaṃbodhi*), 143a5.
134. Engaged (*'jug pa*) bodhicitta is also sometimes rendered as "practice bodhicitta" in this translation.
135. The Beijing and Palpung texts add "for there to be practice [bodhicitta]."
136. This fuller explanation is found in chapter 1, on the essence of buddhahood.
137. *Great Sutra of the Supreme Victory* (*Dhvajāgranāmamahāsūtra*), 267a3.
138. *Mañjuśrīvikrīḍitasūtra*, 237a1.
139. Ibid., 237a2.
140. *Mahāparinirvāṇasūtra* (longer version), *nya*, 120a7.
141. The "four stages of result" are stream-enterer, once-returner, nonreturner, and arhat.
142. *Detailed Explanation of the Uttaratantra* (*Mahāyānottaratantraśāstravyākhyā*), Toh 4025 Tengyur, sems tsam, *phi*, 84b7.
143. *Mahāmokṣasūtra*, 229a3.
144. See glossary. The idea here is that these actions are performed without perceiving any of the elements involved—object, agent, or act—to possess self-entity.
145. This is a gloss of the word *buddha*.
146. Tib. *chos kyi dbyings kyi rjes su song ba*, conveys the idea of sharing the nature of the dharmadhātu, or flowing from the dharmadhātu.
147. *Anavataptanāgarājaparipṛcchāsūtra*, 250a7.
148. The view of the "perishable composite" (*'jig tshogs*, *satkāya*) is the misconception that self as an individual truly exists. The term refers to mistaken views of one's own existence and identity as real conceived on the basis of the perishable aggregates (*skandha*), one's body and mind.
149. *Mahāparinirvāṇasūtra* (longer version), *nya*, 120a5.
150. Ibid.

151. In Buddhist scriptures, a *tīrthika* is a proponent of one of the non-Buddhist philosophical schools. I have translated the Tibetan *mu stegs pa* as "the misguided," following the Kagyü-lineage explanation for this term, which is far from the oft-used "heretic," as they are truly devoted to a spiritual path that has many beneficial elements.

152. *Mahāparinirvāṇasūtra* (longer version), *nya*, 120a6.

153. In itself, and as the basis for all the other precepts, taking refuge is a cause of great merit, since the karmic power of a vow such as refuge acts continuously, even in sleep.

154. The temporary lay precepts (*bsnyen gnas*, *upavāsatha*) are eight precepts observed for twenty-four-hour periods on special occasions: not to kill, steal, lie, have sex, take intoxicants, eat after the appointed time (usually noon), wear adornments, sing or dance, or use high seats or beds.

155. The names of these seven levels in Sanskrit are respectively *bhikṣu*, *bhikṣuṇī*, *śrāmaṇera*, *śikṣamāṇā*, *śrāmaṇerikā*, *upāsaka*, and *upāsikā*.

156. Asaṅga, *Bodhisattvabhūmi*, 74b7.

157. Sthiramati, *Detailed Exposition of the Ornament of Mahayana Sutras* (*Sūtrālaṃkāravṛttibhāṣya*), 53b1.

158. Ibid. The "meditative concentration vow" (*dhyānasaṃvara*) is the conceptual and artificial dedication of the mind needed to develop profound absorption. It requires discipline. When it bears fruit, the "untainted vow" (*anāsravasaṃvara*), natural to the state of meditative concentration itself, supplants the artifice, which need no longer be maintained.

159. The text here lists this twentieth bodhicitta as resembling an "echo" (*sgra brnyan*), but in Gampopa's explanation below, it is given as "melodious sound" (*sgra snyan*). The spellings in Tibetan are very close. As the Sanskrit here is *ānandokti*, *sgra snyan* is the better choice.

160. The paths of seeing and cultivation are defined differently by Gampopa here than in the later chapters dedicated to the phases of the path (chapter 18) and the bodhisattva levels (chapter 19). The more usual allocation of the path of seeing to the first bodhisattva level alone is here extended up to the seventh level, while the path of cultivation is confined to the nondual eighth through tenth levels.

161. *Dhāraṇī* (Tib. *gzungs*) here refers to the ability to associate many things to a key trigger, such as a syllable, and the way this leads to retention of knowledge and experience. In higher phases of the path, simply uttering, and remaining within, the key trigger can spontaneously activate one's accumulated knowledge and experience.

162. *Saṃdhinirmocanasūtra*, 34b7.

163. Ibid.

164. Ibid.

165. Sthiramati, *Sūtrālaṃkāravṛttibhāṣya*, 54a7.

166. Asaṅga, *Abhidharmasamuccaya*, 95b4.

167. Asaṅga, *Bodhisattvabhūmi*, 7b3.

168. In the *Marvelous Array Sutra* (*Gaṇḍavyūhasūtra*), *a*, 361a6.

169. *Daśadharmakasūtra*, 168a1.
170. Asaṅga, *Bodhisattvabhūmi*, 9a3.
171. Ibid., 82a7.
172. Ibid., 83b2.
173. Śāntideva, *Śikṣāsamuccaya*, 9b1.
174. The Tibetan *bshags pa* is commonly rendered as "confession." Besides the obvious drawbacks of immediate associations with Roman Catholic confession, this does not seem to convey the practical meaning of *bshags pa*, which has a root sense of disencumbering, freeing, and cleansing oneself of past errors and their consequences. In its full form in Tibetan, this term is preceded by *mthol lo*, meaning "to evoke." Thus *mtho lo bshags* means bringing past misdeeds to mind in a skillful way so as to free the mind of their sullying power. Classically, this is done by using four powers (see below), such as remorse and resolution, each of which contribute to the overall meaning of *bshags pa*.
175. Mahāmudrā (Tib. *phyag rgya chen po*), the central teaching and practice of the Kagyü tradition, is both meditation on and realization of the true nature of the mind. The meditation can be done with tantric visualization practice, which is what "meditation of the deities' forms" refers to in this sentence.
176. The source of this quote has not been identified.
177. *Susthitamatidevaputraparipṛcchāsūtra*, 300a3.
178. *Siṃhanādasūtra*, 103b6.
179. *Mahāparinirvāṇasūtra* (longer version), *nya*, 305b1.
180. Ibid., 305b2.
181. *Caturdharmanirdeśasūtra*, 59b1.
182. *Vīradattagṛhapatiparipṛcchāsūtra*, 201b6.
183. Ibid., 201b7.
184. In the *Sage and Fool Sutra* (*Damamūkanāmasūtra*), 253b4.
185. There are several versions of this well-known story. For a fuller account, see Gombrich's "Who Was Aṅgulimāla?" in his *How Buddhism Began*, 135ff.
186. For more on Udayana, Nanda, and Ajātaśatru, see notes 198, 200, and 204 below.
187. Asaṅga, *Abhidharmasamuccaya* chap. 1, 19b4.
188. A *Treasury of the Tathāgatas* is not to be found in the Tibetan canon, but this quote appears in Śāntideva, *Compendium of Trainings* (*Śikṣāsamuccaya*), 96a7.
189. Kamalaśīla, *Diamond Cutter Sutra Commentary* (*Vajracchedikāṭīkā*), 226b7.
190. *Subāhuparipṛcchātantra*, 126b6.
191. *Puṣpakūṭadhāraṇī*, 160b2.
192. The chapter mentioned has not been identified, but this statement is found in Śāntideva's *Śikṣāsamuccaya*, 97a7.
193. *Vinayavastu*, 125a2.
194. *Mahāparinirvāṇasūtra* (longer version), *nya*, 304b5.
195. Ibid., 305b5.
196. Toh 555, 44b4.
197. Ibid.
198. Story from *Basis of Vinaya* (*Vinayavastu*) verse 14, 120b1. Udayana's mother

brought him up alone. To prevent his having an illicit liaison with a neighbor, she locked him in his room. Overcome by rage, he killed his mother. His overwhelming remorse eventually led him to become a Buddhist monk, though he was later expelled from the Sangha. By that time he had become very devout and learned. As a layman, he built and sponsored retreats for monks. At death he was reborn immediately in hell, but through his good deeds he swiftly migrated to the god realms, where he practiced well and progressed.

199. *Nanda's Abiding in the Womb* (*Nandagarbhāvakrāntinirdeśa*), 205b2.

200. Nanda was the Buddha's nephew and heir to a throne. He was enthralled with his wife's beauty and talents and, more generally, was an extreme romantic. Even when he became a monk, his mind was constantly distracted by romantic thoughts and attachment. The Buddha took him to both heaven and hell, to show the future rebirths he would gain if he continued to think and act through passion and self-centeredness. Terrified by the prospect of his future, he deeply resolved to forsake his mind's clinging. He eventually became an arhat. His story comprises one of the most celebrated works of Sanskrit literature: Aśvaghoṣa's *Saundarananda*. See Linda Covill's translation in *Handsome Nanda* (New York: New York University Press, 2007).

201. *Sūkarikāvadāna*, 290b6. In this story, a god who is nearing the end of his life is in agony, for he sees he is about to be reborn in the womb of a pig in the city of Rājagṛha. Śakra, king of the gods, comes upon him and encourages him to take refuge in Buddha, Dharma, and Sangha. The god does so and is instead reborn in Tuṣita Paradise. See Rotman, *Divine Stories*, 325–28.

202. *Mahāparinirvāṇasūtra* (longer version), *nya*, 120a6.

203. *Gaṇḍavyūhasūtra*, *a*, 310a4 and 310a7.

204. Ajātaśatru was monarch of a kingdom in central India. His father, Bimbisāra, was a patron of the Buddha and also a highly advanced Buddhist who had attained the state of stream-enterer. Ajātaśatru was drawn into several harmful actions by Devadatta, the Buddha's jealous cousin. One of them was an assassination attempt on the Buddha. Another was the killing of Bimbisāra. Having committed two of the five "evils of no reprieve," Ajātaśatru became covered with foul-smelling boils and was destined to go straight to hell at death. He sought refuge in the Buddha and managed to purify his misdeeds, mainly through the power of practicing bodhicitta. His story is in the longer *Great Passing into Nirvana Sutra* (*Mahāparinirvāṇasūtra*), *ta*, 199b4.

205. Cited in Śāntideva, *Śikṣāsamuccaya*, 97a4.

206. From the *Sutra Describing the Qualities of the Buddhafield of Mañjuśrī* (*Mañjuśrībuddhakṣetraguṇavyūhasūtra*), 279a7.

207. The following readings of the *Bhadrakalpikasūtra* owe a particular debt to Peter Skilling for his careful analysis and suggestions.

208. *Bhadrakalpikasūtra*, *ka*, 316b5.

209. Ibid., 289a4.

210. Ibid., 296a6. The Sanskrit Vijṛmbhitagāmī for *bsgyings ldan bzhud* is speculative.

211. This entire passage of the actual ceremony of conferring the bodhisattva vows is from the moral discipline chapter of Asaṅga's *Bodhisattva Levels* (*Bodhisattva-*

bhūmi, 83a4). For an alternative translation, see Mark Tatz, *Asanga's Chapter on Ethics*, 61.

212. Asaṅga, *Bodhisattvabhūmi*, 7b6.
213. Ibid., 8a3.
214. Some Buddhist texts describe the end of our universe through destruction by various waves of elements, including seven successive burnings. This is the disintegration of the fire element, i.e., the release of its remaining latent energy.
215. Asaṅga, *Bodhisattvabhūmi*, 8a1.
216. *Vīradattagṛhapatiparipṛcchāsūtra*, 202b6.
217. Ibid.
218. *Gaṇḍavyūhasūtra*, *a*, 309b6.
219. Asaṅga, *Bodhisattvabhūmi*, 7b7. The "two extremes" here are the extremes of samsara and nirvana—being imprisoned within samsaric existence controlled by karma and affliction or falling into the meditative absorption of a solitary peace of personal nirvana.
220. Ibid., 97b4. A *defeat* (*pham pa*, *pārājika*) is a complete breakage by a monk or nun of one of the four root prātimokṣa precepts (no killing, lying, stealing, or sexual intercourse). "Great involvement" is committing any of the four offenses analogous to the grounds of defeat wherein (a) the bodhisattva makes a regular practice of it, (b) generates not the slightest sense of shame and embarassment, (c) is pleased with and glad of it, and (d) has a view for its good qualities. If one or more of these are missing, then the degree of involvement is characterized as being lesser or medium. For Asaṅga's discussion of these points, see Tatz, *Asanga's Chapter on Ethics*, 64–65.
221. Asaṅga, *Yogācārabhūmiviniścayasaṃgrahaṇī*, 38b6.
222. Śāntideva, *Śikṣāsamuccaya*, 99a7.
223. See note 220 above for these offenses and involvements.
224. Candragomin, *Twenty Verses on the Bodhisattva Vow* (*Bodhisattvasaṃvaraviṃśaka*) verse 8, 166b5. This verse lists four different ways of dealing with infraction of the bodhisattva vow. If the vow has been broken due to either the loss of the aspiration bodhicitta or through the commitment of any of the four offenses with great involvement, one then needs to retake the vow afresh. If the infraction consists of committing any of the four offenses with a medium involvement, one then needs to declare it and purify it in the presence of at least three people. For the rest, by which the author means the commitment of any of the four offenses with a lesser involvement, one then needs to rectify this by purifying it in the presence of a single person. Finally, if the infraction consists of violating any of the secondary precepts with or without manifest afflictions present in one's mind, one can then purify it within one's own mind, as if taking one's own mind as the witness.
225. *Anavataptanāgarājaparipṛcchāsūtra*, 208b4.
226. This seemingly shocking statement probably refers to śrāvakas and pratyekabuddhas who are deeply absorbed in the bliss of meditative concentrations, where the sense gates are oblivious to input and the mind is so absorbed in its own peace that it is oblivious to everything else.

227. The source of this quote has not been identified.
228. *Marvelous Array Sutra* (*Gaṇḍavyūhasūtra*), *a*, 309b1.
229. Ibid., 311b2.
230. Ibid., 310b4–5.
231. Ibid., 310b2.
232. The four means of gathering beings are four ways a Dharma master gathers a following: through generosity (especially of Dharma), pleasing speech, appropriate conduct, and actions consistent with the teachings.
233. Vasubandhu, *Sambhāraparikathā*, 173b2.
234. Atiśa, *Ritual Order for Bodhicitta and Vows* (*Cittotpādasaṃvaravidhikrama*), 246a3. Many contemporary masters attribute these words to Buddha Śākyamuni three cosmic eons ago, when he first gave rise to bodhicitta.
235. *Kāśyapaparivartasūtra*, 120a6.
236. Ibid., 120b3.
237. This means telling lies for self-interest. Lies that may save others from harm, and lies in other altruistic instances, may be the most appropriate thing a bodhisattva could do (Khenchen Thrangu Rinpoché).
238. In the Tibetan original, there is a parenthetical sentence immediately following this sentence that reads: "Chengawa and Jayulwa speak of Mahayana virtuous actions, while Gya Yöndak says that it is the same for any virtuous action, be it that of the Mahayana or the Hinayana. In the case of engaging in giving, for example, the act as well as the agent becomes good if one has been engaged in a giving." It is unclear whether this annotation is part of the original or was added by a subsequent editor.
239. *Subāhuparipṛcchāsūtra*, 154a6.
240. "Environment" is to be taken here in the widest sense of people, life circumstances, and places.
241. This, and the following etymologies, are those of the Sanskrit terms for the perfections. *Dāna*, the Sanskrit for generosity, comes from a root meaning "to sweep away," the implication being that it sweeps away greed and clinging. Coolness was a sought-after quality in hot India, and the relief of *śīla* (moral discipline) is compared to the shade of a cool tree in contrast to the searing summer heat of the passions. There is not a precise match in English for the broad uses of the word *kṣānti* (forbearance) as understood in Buddhism. *Forbearance* with the etymology of "to bear"—to cope with difficulty—comes perhaps closer than the commonly found "patience." Similarly, no single English term seems to translate the various implications of the Sanskrit *vīrya*, which means "energetic," "efficient," or "courageous"—all relevant meanings (see chapter 15 on diligence below). The Tibetan *brtson 'grus* means "industrious diligence." The etymology of "diligence" takes us to the Latin *diligere*, denoting a sense of joy (the same root as "delight"), and to find joy in Dharma lies at the heart of this perfection and leads automatically to industrious perseverance.
242. Often translated as the "other shore," which would imply that samsara is itself a shore rather than the dangerous ocean to which it is so often compared.

243. *Vinayavastu*, 256a6. See the summary of Śroṇa Koṭikarṇa's story in note 89 above.
244. Ibid., 256b7.
245. *Bodhisattvapiṭaka*, 61a3.
246. *Ratnameghasūtra*, 12a7.
247. *Gṛhapatyugraparipṛcchāsūtra*, 264b5.
248. Asaṅga, *Bodhisattvabhūmi*, 61b4.
249. Ibid., 63b5.
250. Ibid., 73a6.
251. Ibid., 65b3.
252. Ibid., 66a1.
253. There is the following in a parenthetical passage in the Tibetan original, perhaps added by a later editor: "The *Precious Garland* says: 'Should poison benefit someone, / then poison should be given. / If it is not beneficial to the person, / even the best food should not be given. // It is said that chopping off a finger / bitten by a poisonous snake is beneficial; / the Buddha taught that even unpleasant things / should be done if they benefit others.'" RA 3:63–64.
254. A.k.a. *Sutra of the Absorption that Gathers All Merit* (*Sarvapuṇyasamuccayasamādhisūtra*), 85a5.
255. *Sutra of the Absorption that Gathers All Merit* (*Sarvapuṇyasamuccayasamādhisūtra*), 83b7.
256. Asaṅga, *Bodhisattvabhūmi*, 71b7.
257. Asaṅga, *Abhidharmasamuccaya*, 16a1.
258. Asaṅga, *Bodhisattvabhūmi*, 72a7.
259. *Kāśyapaparivartasūtra*, 125b4.
260. Asaṅga, *Bodhisattvabhūmi*, 72b1.
261. A.k.a. *King of Meditation Sutra* (*Samādhirājasūtra*), 85b7.
262. *Saddharmapuṇḍarīkasūtra*, 106a3.
263. *King of Meditation Sutra* (*Samādhirājasūtra*), 106a4.
264. *Sāgaramatiparipṛcchāsūtra*, 110b7.
265. Ibid., 111b1.
266. *Bodhisattvapiṭaka*, 60b6.
267. Asaṅga, *Bodhisattvabhūmi*, 65b1.
268. *Akṣayamatinirdeśasūtra*, 107a1.
269. Śāntideva, *Śikṣāsamuccaya*, 2b6.
270. *Ratnacūḍaparipṛcchāsūtra*, 215b2.
271. Asaṅga, *Bodhisattvabhūmi*, 73b6.
272. Ibid., 65b2.
273. *Śīlasaṃyuktasūtra*, 127b2.
274. Ibid.
275. A.k.a. *King of Meditation Sutra* (*Samādhirājasūtra*), 89a5.
276. This quotation does not seem to be from the *Meeting of Father and Son Sutra* but from the sutra that immediately follows it in the Kangyur, i.e., the *Questions of Pūrṇa Sutra* (*Pūrṇaparipṛcchāsūtra*), 187b4.
277. Ibid.

278. *Śīlasaṃyuktasūtra*, 127a7.
279. Asaṅga, *Bodhisattvabhūmi*, 74a3.
280. Ibid., 74b7.
281. A.k.a. *Sutra of the Absorption that Gathers All Merit* (*Sarvapuṇyasamuccayasamādhisūtra*), 87b6.
282. Of the above, 1 through 5 are root downfalls associated with a monarch, and 1 through 4, along with 6, are those associated with a minister.
283. The text says "forbearance of emptiness." This is a stage of attainment of emptiness meditation in which one is able to withstand the truth of it.
284. Śāntideva, *Śikṣāsamuccaya*, 43a5. Numbering here has been added for clarity.
285. Candragomin, *Bodhisattvasaṃvaraviṃśaka* verses 6–7, 166b4.
286. Ibid. verse 9, 166b46.
287. Asaṅga, *Bodhisattvabhūmi*, 75a1.
288. Ibid., 79a3.
289. This quotation was not found in the *Clouds of Jewels Sutra*, but it occurs in the *Sutra Encouraging Nobler Intention* (*Adhyāśayasaṃcodanasūtra*), 145b1.
290. A.k.a. *King of Meditation Sutra* (*Samādhirājasūtra*), 85b4.
291. *Sarvadharmāpravṛttinirdeśasūtra*, 274b4.
292. *Adhyāśayasaṃcodanasūtra*, 142a5.
293. *Pitāputrasamāgamasūtra*, 162a5.
294. *Sutra Encouraging Nobler Intention* (*Adhyāśayasaṃcodanasūtra*), 147a4. Quoted also in Śāntideva, *Śikṣāsamuccaya*, 65a2.
295. Ibid.
296. The cross-reference is to the section on enhancing generosity in the preceding chapter (see pages 164–65).
297. Asaṅga, *Bodhisattvabhūmi*, 101a4.
298. *Bodhisattvapiṭaka*, 84a4.
299. A.k.a. the *Sutra of the Absorption that Gathers All Merit* (*Sarvapuṇyasamuccayasamādhisūtra*), 88b5.
300. Ibid., 89a3.
301. *Bodhisattvapiṭaka*, 98b2.
302. Ibid., 98b3.
303. Although our author attributes this quotation to the *Meeting of Father and Son Sutra*, it is actually from the sutra that immediately follows it in the Dergé Kangyur, i.e., the *Questions of Pūrṇa Sutra* (*Pūrṇaparipṛcchāsūtra*), 170b5.
304. Were one less literal, the definition of forbearance provided here could be translated as "to be able to cope with anything."
305. Asaṅga, *Bodhisattvabhūmi*, 101b7.
306. Ibid., 102b2.
307. Ibid., 103b7.
308. Ibid., 105a5.
309. Ibid., 107a3.
310. *Sāgaramatiparipṛcchāsūtra*, 40a5.
311. The Sanskrit *satkāya* was freely rendered into Tibetan as *'jig tshogs*, which refers to

the five aggregates and their nature as being both perishable (*'jig*) and composite (*tshogs*). Each aggregate can be mistaken for a lasting and/or unitary self, as "me" or "mine." And with four types of mistaken approaches to any of these five, one ends up with the twenty major aberrant views of personhood (*satkāyadṛṣṭi*), or as sometime rendered from the Tibetan, "view of the transitory collection."

312. Vasubandhu, *Commentary on the Ornament of Mahayana Sutras* (*Sūtrālaṃkārabhāṣya*), 201b5.
313. *Sāgaramatiparipṛcchāsūtra*, 40a7.
314. *Pūrṇaparipṛcchāsūtra*, 187b5.
315. This is not verbatim, but the meaning is that found in Asaṅga's *Abhidharmasamuccaya*, 49a1.
316. Vasubandhu, *Sūtrālaṁkārabhāṣya*, 201b5.
317. *Sutra on Moral Discipline* (*Śīlasaṃyuktasūtra*), 127a4.
318. *Bodhisattvapiṭaka*, 116a7.
319. *Varmavyūhanirdeśasūtra*, vol. 1, 76a6.
320. *Akṣayamatinirdeśasūtra*, 105b7.
321. Asaṅga, *Bodhisattvabhūmi*, 107b3.
322. *Ratnameghasūtra*, 20b2.
323. *Vajraketusūtra.*
324. Asaṅga, *Bodhisattvabhūmi*, 110b6.
325. (1) Clairvoyance, (2) clairaudience, (3) knowledge of others' minds, (4) knowledge of past and future lives and transmigrations, and (5) knowledge of miraculous abilities. Sometimes also included is (6) the ability to overcome imperfections.
326. *Dharmasaṃgītisūtra*, 42a6.
327. The three types of enlightenment refer to the arhat states of śrāvakas and prateyakabuddhas and to buddhahood.
328. Asaṅga, *Bodhisattvabhūmi*, 111a2.
329. *Adhyāśayasaṃcodanasūtra*, 143b2.
330. A.k.a. *King of Meditation Sutra* (*Samādhirājasūtra*), 16a2.
331. *King of Meditation Sutra* (*Samādhirājasūtra*), 16a3.
332. Ibid., 16a5.
333. Ibid., 93b7.
334. Ibid., 98a3.
335. *Gṛhapatyugraparipṛcchāsūtra*, 279b2.
336. Whatever the original Indian sutra alluded to, with these two references to bears, the terms were translated into Tibetan as the generic bear (*dom*), famous for its savagery, and the bear of the north (*dred*), famous for its stupidity.
337. This is a reference to (1) loving kindness focused on sentient beings, (2) loving kindness focused on the nature of things, and (3) loving kindness with no objective reference. See page 90.
338. *Śālistambasūtra*, 116a4.
339. The dependent origination of external phenomena and the environment is not discussed here in this text.
340. "Formations" (Skt. *saṃskāra*, Tib. *'du byed*). This term is often translated as

"compositional factors," "compounded phenomena," or "mental formations." Since neither the Sanskrit nor the Tibetan contains a reference to mind, and since mentioning mind creates certain problems, I have omitted "mental." The second link of dependent origination can also be explained in several ways. Sometimes it refers to the immediate coming into being of the notion of self, then other, and so on. At other times it refers to the whole backlog of conditioning that one has at any given moment: a person's karmic formations from past conditioning.

341. *Rice Shoot Sutra* (*Śālistambasūtra*), 116a7.
342. There are four modes of birth: from an egg, from a womb, spontaneous, and from ambient conditions.
343. Nāgārjuna, *Pratītyasamutpādahṛdayakārikā*, 46b2.
344. "Tainted" in the context of karma means tainted by dualistic concepts, be it virtuous or nonvirtuous karma.
345. *Flower Ornament Sutra* (*Avataṃsakasūtra*), *kha*, 222b2.
346. *Rice Shoot Sutra* (*Śālistambasūtra*), 116b4.
347. At the heart of the Kagyü lineage lie two major streams of transmission. The first, referred to here, is that of the Mahāmudrā meditations of Saraha, passed down via a lineage including Maitripa and Marpa and here referred to under one of its other names, Innate Union (*lhan cig skyes sbyor*, *sahajayoga*). The other stream of transmission is that of the Six Practices of Nāropa, which conveys the quintessence of the father, mother, and nondual tantras.
348. This entire paragraph is absent in the Palpung edition of the text. It seems that, unless we treat this paragraph as part of the parenthetical annotation, its inclusion interrupts the flow of the text.
349. Asaṅga, *Bodhisattvabhūmi*, 111a5.
350. Ibid., 113a4.
351. *Akṣayamatinirdeśasūtra*, 170a7.
352. *Vimalakīrtinirdeśasūtra*, 201b1.
353. *Anavataptanāgarājaparipṛcchāsūtra*, 228b3.
354. *Gayāśīrṣasūtra*, 290a1.
355. Asaṅga, *Abhidharmasamuccaya*, 48b3.
356. "Creative skill" is used here for the Tibetan *bzo ba rig pa*. This is often translated as "arts and crafts," yet covers the much wider scope of all knowledge of how things come into being. The field so often translated as "medicine" also has a broader sense: it is the knowledge of how to act on any causal processes to prevent or reduce the harm they would normally cause.
357. *Saptaśatikāprajñāpāramitā*, 197b6.
358. In the critical Tibetan edition, the Beijing edition, as well as the Tsipri edition, there is the following reading: "What then are the two kinds of self or mind? . . . What is the self or mind of persons?" In these editions, in these two instances, *self-entity* (*bdag*) is equated with *mind* (*sems*), thus giving rise to a somewhat awkward reading of the text. Here, we have chosen to follow the reading of the Palpung edition.
359. This is reference to the etymology of *dharma*, the root *dhṛ* of which gives a sense

of "holding," "possessing." Thus each distinct phenomenon known by the mind has its own characteristics.

360. This passage is a summary of well-rehearsed arguments found in the Perfection of Wisdom literature. It consists of a minute examination of the successive moments of time of a supposed creation and an exploration of the very notion of "cause": one thing disappearing and another occurring.
361. Vasubandhu, *Viṃśatikā*, 3b3.
362. *Avataṃsakasūtra*, *kha*, 220b4.
363. *Laṅkāvatārasūtra*, 165a6.
364. Ibid., 165a5.
365. This parenthetical sentence appears as an annotation, written in a small font, embedded in the original Tibetan text.
366. Literally, "Does it have the three times?"
367. *Kāśyapaparivartasūtra*, 139a2.
368. *Dam pa'i chos yongs su 'dzin pa'i mdo*. The source of this quote has not been identified.
369. *Dharmatāsvabhāvaśūnyatācalapratisarvālokasūtra*, 172b3.
370. This is not verbatim but based on Tilopa's *Treasury of Dohas* (*Dohakoṣa*), 136b2.
371. *Dharmadhātuprakṛtyasambhedanirdeśasūtra*, 143a3.
372. *Song of an Inexhaustible Treasure of Instruction* (*Dohakoṣopadeśagīti*), 29a4.
373. *Laṅkāvatārasūtra*, 180b3.
374. *Song of an Inexhaustible Treasure of Instruction* (*Dohakoṣopadeśagīti*), 29a4.
375. *Kāśyapaparivartasūtra*, 132b1.
376. *Trisaṃvaranirdeśaparivarta*, Toh 45 Kangyur, dkon brtsegs, *ka*, 130b1.
377. *Instructions on Madhyamaka* (*Madhyamakopadeśa*), 95b5. This entire quotation from Atiśa is missing in the Palpung edition of the text.
378. *Brahmaviśeṣacintiparipṛcchāsūtra*, 33b3.
379. The *Precious Space Jewel Sutra* (*Nam mkha' rin po che'i mdo*) source of this famous quotation has not been identified. But the verse appears, among other places, in AA 5:21 and RGV 1:154.
380. *Suvikrāntavikramiparipṛcchāsūtra*, 23a5.
381. *Sgra can 'dzin gyis yum la bstod pa*. Although this verse homage to the *Perfection of Wisdom* attributed to the Buddha's son Rāhula is well known, its exact source in the canonical texts remains unidentified.
382. The Tibetan for what is translated here as "natural settled state" is archaic: *rnal du dbab pa*. Although the word meaning of this was defined by later Tibetan translators as "abiding within its own natural dominion, untroubled by harm from what is other," the actual meaning of this and many other specialized Mahāmudrā terms is reserved for the correct moment of meditative intimacy between guru and disciple, as it is beyond words and concepts. In this case both *rnal* and *dbab* have "pointed out" meanings revealed by the actions and presence of the master.
383. *Saptaśatikānāmaprajñāpāramitā*, 204a5.
384. The Palpung edition of the text does not have this sentence.
385. This translation of this famous six-point instruction from Tilopa follows the

traditional meaning more than a strictly literal interpretation. The traditional explanation sets them into a time context as follows: "Not dwelling on [the past], not intending [about the future], not analyzing [the present, in terms of 'being' in the present]."

386. A scriptural source of this and the previous quote from Tilopa has not been identified. Some pith advice belongs to the intimate instructions handed down orally (*man ngag*) and was only committed to writing generations after its originator.
387. Although our author ascribes this quote to Nāgārjuna, most probably the verse is from Saraha's *Treasury of Spiritual Songs* (*Dohakoṣagīti*), 74b3.
388. The source of this quote ascribed to Nāgārjuna has not been identified.
389. The source of this quote from Śavaripa has not been identified.
390. The source of this quote has not been identified.
391. *Treasury of Spiritual Songs* (*Dohakoṣagīti*) verse 16, 71b2.
392. *Song of Seeing Dharmadhātu* (*Dharmadhātudarśanagīti*) verses 2–3, 255a1.
393. The source of this quote has not been identified.
394. *Saptaśatikānāmaprajñāpāramitā*, 186a3.
395. The Tibetan verb *sgom pa* (Skt. *bhāvanā*) has been translated here and in the following quotations as "cultivate," so as to remain close both to its etymology and its relevant meaning. "Cultivating" means putting into practice again and again. The following chapters, on the stages of the path and in particular on the fourth one known as "cultivation" (*sgom*), reveal it clearly to be the continued application, in all circumstances, of the emptiness insight gained at the previous, third, stage and not at all confined to formal meditation sessions in general or to meditating on a particular topic, as this section has already made clear. The term has often been translated as "to meditate" due to its meaning in other contexts.
396. *Aṣṭasāhasrikāprajñāpāramitā*, 167b5.
397. Ibid., 111b2.
398. *Advice on Cheating Death* (*Mṛtyuvañcanopadeśa*), 133b1.
399. *Dharmasaṃgītisūtra*, 68b5.
400. Atiśa, *Penetrating the Two Truths* (*Satyadvayāvatāra*), 72a6. Gampopa refers to *Satyadvayāvatāra* as the *Shorter Text on Middle Way Two Truths*.
401. *Samādhirājasūtra*, 26b2.
402. *Spyod pa'i de kho na nyid*, **Caryātattva*. The source of this quote has not been identified.
403. *De kho na nyid bstan pa'i mdo*. The sutra that is the source of this quote has not been found.
404. *Mahāsamayavaipulyasūtra*, 287b5. Intriguingly, a large part of the text, starting from this point up to the section relating to the signs of having cultivated wisdom (p. 245), is missing in the Palpung edition. This variance represents a significant difference between the texts, especially since the section missing in the Palpung edition deals specifically with an important standpoint of the simultaneist (*gcig bcar ba*) approach to the path—that all key elements of the path to buddhahood are embodied within the single practice of understanding the nature of your mind.

405. *Gtsug tor chen po'i mdo.* The source of this quote has not been identified.
406. Approximation of *Mahāyānaprasādaprabhāvanasūtra*, 32b6.
407. *Sarvadharmāpravṛttinirdeśasūtra*, 294a5.
408. *Daśacakrakṣitigarbhasūtra*, 138b2.
409. Ibid., 139b5.
410. *Anavataptanāgarājaparipṛcchāsūtra*, 250a6.
411. *Sems bskyed chen po mdo.* This sutra has not been identified.
412. *Hevajratantra*, 6a7.
413. *Sarvabuddhasamayoga*, 152a6. The term *yoga* means "fusion" or "union." In the lines cited here, the term refers to a union with the deity during the completion stage of tantra, while "the yogi" here is the tantric meditator.
414. *Vajraśekharatantra*, 155b1.
415. *Amṛtaguhyatantrarāja*, 234b6.
416. *Vajrasamādhidharmākṣara*, 125b7, but not identical to Gampopa's quote.
417. *Brahmaviśeṣacintiparipṛcchāsūtra*, 58a2.
418. *Daśacakrakṣitigarbhasūtra*, 224a6.
419. Ibid., 225b2.
420. Ibid., 226b2.
421. Ibid., 227b4.
422. A *Precious Space Sutra* has not been identified, but this quote is found in Nāgārjuna's *Five Stages* (*Pañcakrama*).
423. *Pitāputrasamāgamasūtra*, 99b3.
424. *Amṛtaguhyatantrarāja*, 234b7.
425. *Las rnam par dag pa'i mdo.* This quotation is given by Vimalamitra as coming from the *Great Liberation Sutra*, in his *Meditating on Nonthought, Penetrating Simultaneity* (*Sakṛtprāveśikanirvikalpabhāvanārtha*), 13b1.
426. *Susthitamatidevaputraparipṛcchāsūtra*, 12b1.
427. *Daśacakrakṣitigarbhasūtra*, 120b3.
428. *Rab tu mi gnas pa'i rgyud.* This sutra has not been identified.
429. *Treasury of Spiritual Songs* (*Dohakoṣagīti*), 71b.
430. *Amṛtaguhyatantrarāja*, 234b2.
431. *Jñānālokālaṃkāra*; *Ye shes snang ba rgyan gyi mdo.* This quotation does not appear in present versions of this sutra.
432. *Mahāsaṃbhārodayatantra*, 309b3.
433. The source of this quote has not been established.
434. Atiśa, *Lamp for the Summary of Conduct* (*Caryāsaṃgrahapradīpa*), 313a5.
435. *Saptaśatikānāmaprajñāpāramitā*, 203b7.
436. As is explained below in the text, the "heat" here is metaphorical and has nothing to do with an experience of heat during meditation. The metaphor is one of approaching a blaze, such as a bonfire, and reaching that initial point where the heat can be felt. The "blaze" referred to is that of pristine awareness.
437. Literally, "qualities without needing to train" or "qualities of the phase of no-more learning." These spontaneous qualities are contrasted to the previous four phases of the path, where effort and training are needed for qualities to arise.

438. *Ten Levels Sutra* (*Daśabhūmikasūtra*), *kha*, 120a2.
439. The list of various trainings needed for mastery of this and the following nine bodhisattva levels are to be found in Maitreya's *Ornament of Clear Realization* and its commentaries.
440. *Ten Levels Sutra* (*Daśabhūmikasūtra*), *kha*, 182b5.
441. Ibid., 182a5.
442. These three factors are important in their own right and often cited as the activities of great bodhisattvas. Reference will be made back to this list of three in the following nine levels.
443. *Ten Levels Sutra* (*Daśabhūmikasūtra*), *kha*, 183a2.
444. The usual number is eighty-eight, based on Maitreya's *Ornament of Clear Realization*. Eighty-two could have been an early slip, by Gampopa himself or by a copyist or woodblock carver, that has been reproduced ever since.
445. *Ten Levels Sutra* (*Daśabhūmikasūtra*), *kha*, 126a5.
446. Ibid., 125a6.
447. Ibid., 193a4.
448. "And so forth" refers back to the list of twelve specific abilities mentioned for the first bodhisattva level, the only difference being in their numbers. For instance, on the first level, it was a hundred, on the second level a thousand, on the third ten thousand, and so on.
449. *Ten Levels Sutra* (*Daśabhūmikasūtra*), *kha*, 201a7.
450. Ibid., 208b7.
451. Ibid., 215b6.
452. MV 2:16d. "Ten sorts of sameness" refers to a list found in the *Ten Levels Sutra* where, in presenting the emptiness of all phenomena, the sutra identifies two basic kinds of sameness—the sameness of all phenomena with respect to their absence of inherent existence and the sameness of all phenomena with respect to their absence of signs. These two are then explained further in terms of eight kinds of sameness.
453. As long as samsara or nirvana seem real, separate from and different from each other, the mind falls into the general "impurity" of being sway to concepts. The profound wisdom of this sixth level reveals mind's innate and pristine purity, and this automatically dispels such dualistic elaborations.
454. *Ten Levels Sutra* (*Daśabhūmikasūtra*), *kha*, 215a5.
455. Ibid., 236a2.
456. Tib. *dbang sgyur* or *gzhan 'phrul dbang byed*, Skt. *paranirmitavaśavartin*. These gods are the highest within the desire realm and exercise dominion over others' manifestations for their own enjoyment.
457. *Ten Levels Sutra* (*Daśabhūmikasūtra*), *kha*, 247b3.
458. The twelve factors as listed in the *Ornament of Clear Realizations* are, in addition to the two listed in the text, (3) possessing a steadfast confidence, (4) being conceived in an excellent womb, (5) being of excellent caste, (6) being of excellent family lineage, (7) having excellent parents, (8) having excellent retinue, (9) possessing excellent birth, (10) attaining excellent renunciation,

(11) being endowed with an excellent site, such as with the presence of a bodhi tree, and (12) bearing excellent higher qualities.

459. *Ten Levels Sutra* (*Daśabhūmikasūtra*), *kha*, 257b6.

460. Ibid., 254b1.

461. "Countless" is the last of the series of names that ancient India had for each multiple of ten, from 100 up to 10^{51}. This extraordinary range of names was needed for comparing differences in lifespan and so forth in the various levels of the cosmos.

462. *Ten Levels Sutra* (*Daśabhūmikasūtra*), 261b2.

463. This passage is in reduced print in the Tsipri xylograph, which is the basis of the critical Tibetan edition produced for the *Library of Tibetan Classics* series. To indicate this, we have presented it within parentheses. This entire parenthetical paragraph is not found in the Palpung edition, which suggests the possibility that it could be a later addition by an editor.

464. *Ten Levels Sutra* (*Daśabhūmikasūtra*), *kha*, 274b1.

465. Ibid., 273b6.

466. The higher five of the seventeen form-realm paradises are known as the "pure realms," not to be confused with pure lands of buddhas. The highest of those heavens is Akaniṣṭha, or Supreme.

467. "Core" is used here in contrast to the skin and flesh of the fruit, which are used as examples in lower levels.

468. Asaṅga, *Bodhisattvabhūmi*, 184b3.

469. This is the fifth line of the six-line topical summary presented by the author in the opening section of the text on page 12.

470. The Tibetan *spangs pa* literally means "abandon," "renunciation," or "shedding." However, to translate this important point as such would be misleading, suggesting deliberate actions of renunciation, of letting go. Such imagery is too gross for what happens here. In this section, we are looking at the end result of a very fine and thorough process of *purification* that has been going on throughout the bodhisattva levels, using the most refined meditation.

471. *Śatasāhasrikāprajñāpāramitā*, *'a*, 343b3.

472. Ibid., 333a7.

473. Although Gampopa does not name the source of this quote, these lines can be found in the Ngok Loden Sherap's *A Letter Entitled "Droplets of Nectar,"* p. 709, line 6.

474. *Dharmasaṃgītisūtra*, 43b4.

475. *Pitāputrasamāgamasūtra*, 111a3.

476. *Lalitavistarasūtra*. This sentence is in small font in the Tibetan original, indicating it to be an embedded annotation; it is missing in the Palpung edition.

477. The source of this quote has not been identified.

478. Ngok Loden Sherap, *Letter Entitled "Droplets of Nectar,"* p. 709, line 7.

479. *Anantamukhapariśodhananirdeśaparivartasūtra*, 49b7.

480. Udbhaṭasiddhasvāmin, *Praise of the Excellence* [*of the Buddha*] (*Viśeṣastava*), 3b6.

481. Although it is clear by the usage of the term *geshé* that it is referring to a Kadampa master, who that specific master is remained undetermined.

482. Most probably the author is here citing his teacher Milarepa's oral teaching, not a specific text.
483. Candrakīrti, *Seventy Stanzas on Going for Refuge* (*Triśaraṇasaptatī*), 251a2.
484. *Suvarṇaprabhāsottamasūtra*, Toh 556, 164b1.
485. *Aṣṭasāhasrikāprajñāpāramitā*, 277b3.
486. *Samādhirājasūtra*, 62a7.
487. The final stage of the path of application, just prior to transition into the ārya state.
488. This is the final line of the six-line topical summary presented by the author in the opening section of the text on page 12.
489. *Vaidūrya* has been translated as "lapis lazuli" and as "beryl." Khenchen Thrangu Rinpoché explains that it is in fact a gem found only in the god realms.

Glossary

Abhidharma (*chos mngon pa*). The collection of scripture containing systematic works explicating the elements of existence.

absorptions. *See* eight absorptions.

afflictions (*nyon mongs, kleśa*). Dissonant mental states, both thoughts and emotions, that have their root in ignorance and that disturb the person from deep within. The classical Abhidharma texts list six root afflictions—attachment, aversion, pride, afflicted doubt, ignorance, and afflicted views—and twenty afflictions that are derivative of these root afflictions.

aggregates (*phung po, skandha*). *See* five aggregates.

antidote (*gnyen po, pratipakṣa*). Just as specific medicines are seen as antidotes for specific illnesses, so specific mental states such as courage and compassion are identified as antidotes to specific mental ills. The Tibetan term *gnyen po* is sometimes translated "aid" or "remedy" as well.

arhat (*dgra bcom pa*). In Sanskrit, a term of respect (literally, "worthy," "venerable," "respectable," etc.), in Tibetan it was rendered with a different etymology as "foe destroyer." An arhat has eliminated all the afflictions and has thus attained nirvana.

ārya (*'phags pa*). *See* noble one.

aspiration bodhicitta (*smon pa'i sems bskyed, praṇdihicitta*). *See* bodhicitta.

aspiration prayer (*smon lam, praṇidhāna*). A solemn oath or vow, such as that of a bodhisattva, that creates a karmic seed for future attainment.

Blessed One (*bcom ldan 'das, bhagavān*). Traditional epithet of the Buddha. An ancient Indian term of high respect used for spiritual masters.

bodhicitta (*byang chub kyi sems*, and *sems bskyed, cittotpāda*, "producing the intention"). The "thought of awakening," an altruistic resolve to attain buddhahood for the benefit of all beings. Bodhicitta is characterized by an *objective*, the full awakening of buddhahood, and a *purpose*, the fulfillment of others' welfare. *Relative bodhicitta* refers to this altruistic resolve, whereas *ultimate bodhicitta* refers to a direct realization of the emptiness of the fully awakened mind. *Aspiration bodhicitta* is the wish to attain the genuine thought of awakening, whereas *engaged bodhicitta* is the actual training in the thought of awakening by way of the six perfections.

bodhisattva (*byang chub sems dpa'*). A person who has cultivated bodhicitta and is on the Mahayana path to buddhahood.

bodies of buddhahood (*sku, kāya*). The five bodies of buddhahood are: (1) the emanation body (*sprul sku, nirmāṇakāya*), (2) the enjoyment body (*longs sku, saṃbhogakāya*), (3) the Dharma body (*chos sku, dharmakāya*), and (4–5) the ultimate-nature body (*ngo bo nyid kyi sku, svabhāvakāya*), which consists of two facets of the Dharma body—a buddha's mind purified of all defilements and the natural purity of that mind that is its emptiness.

buddhafield (*sangs rgyas kyi zhing, buddhakṣetra*). The expanse of specific, enlightened experience proper to a particular buddha, just like the kingdom of a monarch.

Cittamātra (*sems tsam*). The philosophical "mind only" school, also known as Yogācāra ("school of yoga practice") or Vijñānavāda ("doctrine of consciousness"). As the name indicates, the school maintains that external phenomena are a function of the mind, and its adherents advocate a meditative union (*yoga*) with the essential nature of the mind. The school was founded by Asaṅga (fourth century), who received these doctrines from Maitreya. The Cittamātra is one of two main streams of Mahayana Buddhism along with Madhyamaka.

compassion (*snying rje, karuṇā*). A mental state that wishes for others to be free from suffering. In its highest form, *compassion* is a synonym for great compassion (*snying rje chen po*)—a universal, nondiscriminatory compassion that wishes all beings to be free of suffering.

conceptual elaborations (*spros pa, prapañca*). *See* discursive thought; free of all conceptual elaborations.

conqueror (*rgyal ba, jina*). Traditional epithet of a fully awakened buddha.

defiling aggregates of personality. *See* five aggregates.

desire realm (*'dod khams, kāmadhātu*). One of the three realms of existence. Its beings' experiences are principally those of the five sense consciousnesses, whether the lower rebirths of hell beings, hungry ghosts, and animals, or the higher rebirths of humans and gods. This is contrasted with the mental consciousness, which produces the meditative experiences of the form and formless realms. *See also* three realms of existence.

dhāraṇī (*gzungs*). A verbal device, similar to a mantra, that encapsulates the meaning of longer Dharma texts, aiding in retention and integration. Can be longer or as short as a single syllable.

dharmadhātu (*chos kyi dbyings*). The ultimate expanse, sphere of reality, or mode of being, of things.

dharmakāya (*chos sku*). One of the embodiments of buddhahood. Dharmakāya (literally, "truth body" or "buddha body of reality") refers to the ultimate reality of a buddha's enlightened mind—unborn, free of the limits of conceptual elaborations, empty of intrinsic existence, naturally radiant, beyond duality, and spacious like the sky. The other two buddha bodies, the enjoyment body (*longs sku, saṃbhogakāya*) and the emanation body (*sprul sku, nirmāṇakāya*), are progressively grosser bodies that arise from the basic dharmakāya nature. Thus the two latter embodiments are referred to collectively as a buddha's "form body" (*gzugs sku, rūpakāya*). *See also* bodies of buddhahood.

dharmatā (*chos nyid*). Translated as "reality," "the nature of things," or "universal essence," the Sanskrit term and its Tibetan equivalent refer to the ultimate mode of being of things. As such, the term is often used as a synonym for *emptiness* and *suchness*.

discursive thought (*rtog pa'i spros pa, kalpanāprapañca*). Conceptual elaborations. The opposite of *nondiscursive awareness*.

eight absorptions. The four meditative concentrations (*dhyāna*) and the four meditative attainments (*samāpatti*).

eight freedoms (*dal ba, kṣaṇa*). These are freedom from eight unfavorable conditions, enabling a human being to practice the Buddhist doctrine: (1) not holding wrong views, (2) not being born in a barbaric land, (3) not being born in a region where no buddha has appeared, (4) not being born as an idiot or mute, and not having become (5) a hell being, (6) a hungry ghost, (7) an animal, or (8) a god.

eight worldly concerns (*'jig rten chos brgyad, aṣṭalokadharma*). Gain and loss, pleasure and pain, praise and blame, and fame and infamy.

eightfold path of the noble ones (*'phags pa'i lam yan lag brgyad pa, āryāṣṭāṅgamārga*). The eightfold path consists in: (1) right view (2) right thought, (3) right speech, (4) right action, (5) right livelihood, (6) right effort, (7) right mindfulness, and (8) right meditation.

emanation body (*sprul sku, nirmāṇakāya*). One of three (or five) bodies of buddhahood. *See* bodies of buddhahood; dharmakāya; form body.

emptiness (*stong pa nyid, śūnyatā*). According to the Perfection of Wisdom sutras, all things and events, including our own existence, are devoid of any independent, substantial, and intrinsic reality. This emptiness of intrinsic existence is phenomena's ultimate mode of being—the way phenomena actually are. The second-century master Nāgārjuna was the earliest systematic proponent of the theory of emptiness, and his writings provide the philosophical foundation of the Madhyamaka school of the Mahayana tradition. Seeing emptiness, the ultimate nature of all things, is the indispensable gateway to liberation and enlightenment.

engaged bodhicitta (*'jug pa'i sems bskyed, prasthānacitta*). *See* bodhicitta.

enjoyment body (*longs spyod rdzogs pa'i sku, saṃbhogakāya*). *See* bodies of buddhahood; dharmakāya; form body.

five aggregates (*phung po lnga, skandha*). Form, feeling, discernment, formations, and consciousness, which together are our basis for erroneously imputing the existence of a self.

five paths (*lam lnga, pañcamarga*). The paths of (1) accumulation, (2) application, (3) seeing, (4) cultivation, and (5) complete accomplishment.

form body (*gzugs sku, rūpakāya*). A collective term for two of the bodies of buddhahood—the enjoyment body (*longs sku, saṃbhogakāya*) and the emanation body (*sprul sku, nirmāṇakāya*). *See also* bodies of buddhahood; dharmakāya.

formless realm (*gzugs med kyi khams, arūpadhātu*). *See* three realms of existence.

four bases of magical powers (*caturṛddhipāda, rdzu 'phrul gyi rkang pa bzhi*). These four elements of the thirty-seven factors conducive to awakening are prerequisites to acquiring magical power and spiritual success. These are the meditative absorptions of aspiration (*chanda*), diligence (*vīrya*), intention (*citta*), and analysis (*mīmāṃsā*).

four foundations of mindfulness (*dran pa nyer bzhag bzhi, catuḥ-smṛtyupasthāna*). A series of meditations consisting in mindfulness, or recollection, of four different objects: (1) the body, (2) feelings, (3) mind, and (4) phenomena.

four fearlessnesses (*mi 'jigs pa bzhi, caturvaiśāradya*). Fearlessness with respect to (1) the perfect fulfillment of the powers, (2) the perfect fulfillment of the abandonments, (3) revealing the obstacles, and (4) revealing the path to definite freedom. These are qualities of an enlightened buddha.

four immeasurables (*tshad med bzhi, caturapramāṇa*). (1) Immeasurable compassion, (2) immeasurable loving kindness, (3) immeasurable sympathetic joy, and (4) immeasurable equanimity.

four impediments. *See* four remedies.

four means of attraction (*bsdus ba'i dngos po bzhi, saṃgrahavastu*). (1) Giving what is immediately needed (such as material goods), (2) using pleasant speech, (3) giving sound spiritual advice, and (4) living in accord with what you teach. These four factors are the primary means by which a bodhisattva attracts others and enhances their minds (whereas the six perfections are the primary factors for developing and enhancing the bodhisattva's own mind).

four meditative attainments (*snyoms 'jug bzhi, samāpatti*). The four meditative absorptions of the formless realm (or sphere): (1) infinite space, (2) infinite consciousness, (3) nothingness, and (4) neither ideation nor nonideation (i.e., the pinnacle of existence).

four meditative concentrations (*bsam gtan bzhi, dhyāna*). The four meditative absorptions of the form realm. These so-called first, second, third, and fourth concentrations are deepening levels of concentration and precede the four meditative attainments.

four perfect endeavors (*yang dag par spong ba bzhi, catvāri samyakprahāṇāni*). Literally, four "restraints" (*prahāṇāni*), these four elements of the thirty-seven factors conducive to awakening are understood as endeavors (*pradhānāni*) by the commentarial tradition. They are reliquishing nonvirtues, avoiding new nonvirtues, generating virtues, and further developing virtues.

four powers (*stobs bzhi, caturbala*). The four key elements necessary for successful shedding of harmful deeds through purification: (1) the power of the support, which refers to the objects of refuge, such as the Three Jewels; (2) the power of remorse; (3) the power of applying the remedy, the actual purification rite; and (4) the power of the resolve to not commit the harmful act again.

four remedies (*gnyen po bzhi, pratipakṣa*). These four remedy the four impediments: (1) meditation on impermanence, which remedies attachment to the experiences of this life; (2) meditation on the defects of samsara and on actions and their consequences, which remedies attachment to worldly well-being in general; (3) meditation on love and compassion, which remedies attachment to the well-being of meditative peace; and (4) the teachings concerning the cultivation of bodhicitta, which remedies ignorance of how to attain buddhahood.

free of all conceptual elaborations (*spros bral, niṣprapañca*). An important quality of ultimate reality in the Madhyamaka school. *See also* discursive thought.

gandharva (*dri za*). A class of beings, a kind of lesser god, that often appear as celestial musicians in classical Indian literature and may dwell in forests. The Tibetan word literally means "smell eater."

Hinayana (*theg dman, hīnayāna*). From the perspective of Mahayana, the "lesser vehicle" teachings and practices expounded by the Buddha in his initial turning of the

Dharma wheel. It sets as its ideal the nirvana of an arhat. Philosophically, it is prone to realism, as expressed in two major schools, Vaibhāṣika and Sautrāntika. From the Tibetan point of view, Hinayana is foundational but is superseded by the Buddha's later Mahayana and Secret Mantra Vehicle teachings.

hungry spirit (*yi dwags, preta*). Beings whose karma is too good for rebirth in the hells but too bad for rebirth as a demigod. They are subject to various torments of extreme deprivation and craving, suffering in particular from hunger and thirst because their bellies are huge but their throats are as thin as the eye of a needle. It is said that rebirth as a hungry spirit can be caused by emotions such as stinginess or envy.

insight (*lhag mthong, vipaśyanā*). An advanced meditative state in which the meditator has successfully attained physical and mental pliancy as a result of having applied analytic meditation on a basis of *tranquility* (*śamatha*). Sometimes the term is also used to embrace all analytic (as opposed to absorptive) meditation practices.

loving kindness (*byams pa, maitrī*). A mental factor wishing others to achieve happiness.

Madhyamaka (*dbu ma*). A school of Mahayana Buddhism founded on the teachings of Nāgārjuna (second century). This school is named after its philosophical "middle way" between absolute assertion or negation of the existence of phenonema. It is called "middle" because it distances itself from any "extreme" notions, Buddhist or non-Buddhist. Phenonema exist only in a conditioned way and do not have an inherent nature of their own; in that sense, they are described as being "empty" or "void" (*śūnya*) from the perspective of ultimate truth.

Mahāmudrā (*phyag rgya chen po*). Literally, "great seal," this is meditation practice aimed at direct realization of emptiness by way of looking at the nature of one's own mind. The name is applied both to the result and to the techniques of meditation that lead to that result. The Mahāmudrā lineage originated in India with Saraha and continued in Tibet predominantly in the Kagyü school.

mantra (*gsang sngags*). A ritual incantation of Sanskrit syllables connected to a particular deity or text. "Mantra" is also a synonym for tantra, especially in the usage "secret mantra."

māra (*bdud*). A term for various evils that afflict beings, namely, the four māras of the aggregates (*skandha*), afflictions (*kleśa*), death (*mṛtyu*), and seductive pleasure (*devaputra*). Māra is also frequently personified as a devil-like tempter.

meditative absorption (*ting nge 'dzin, samādhi*). Single-pointed absorption or focus of the mind on a chosen object. In the Abhidharma taxonomy of mental factors, the term refers to a mental factor whose primary function is to ensure the stability of the mind. This mental factor is part of a group of mental factors present in all unmistaken cognition. *Meditative absorption* can also refer to a specific advanced meditative state, such as the direct single-pointed realization of emptiness. *See also* eight absorptions.

meditative attainments (*snyoms 'jug, samāpatti*). *See* four meditative attainments.

meditative concentration (*bsam gtan, dhyāna*). The subject of the fifth of the six perfections. *See also* four meditative concentrations.

moral discipline (*tshul khrims, śīla*). Adherence to ethical codes.

nāga (*klu*). *Nāga* is a name given to a wide-ranging class of beings, generally of serpentine form but possessing powers that ordinary snakes do not have. The range goes from the animal realm through to the divine realms, with the more elevated types living in palaces and guarding fortunes, much like dragons. They tend to be associated with the water element.

nature of things (*chos nyid*). One possible translation for *dharmatā*, reality, which in other contexts is translated as "true nature" or "universal essence." *See also* dharmatā.

nirvana (*mya ngan las 'das pa, nirvāṇa*). Liberation from *samsara*, and hence the extinction of suffering.

noble one (*'phags pa, ārya*). A being on the path who has gained direct realization of the truth of emptiness on the path of seeing. Noble ones are contrasted with ordinary beings, whose understanding of the truth remains bound by language and concepts.

obscurations (*sgrib pa, āvaraṇa*). *See* two obscurations.

ordinary people or **beings** (*so so'i skye bo, pṛthagjana*). Those who have not yet attained the state of an ārya, or noble one (*'phags pa*), such as those on the first two of the five paths.

path of accumulation (*tshogs lam, saṃbhāramārga*). The first of the five paths, an overarching scheme mapping the full path to enlightenment. For the Mahayana practitioner, this path begins with the generation of bodhicitta, and what is accumulated is the merit, knowledge, and meditative stability necessary to pursue the higher attainments.

path of application (*sbyor lam, prayogamārga*). The second in the five-path scheme, it consists of four progressively more refined realizations about the nature of reality, preparing one for the direct realization on the path of seeing. The four levels are called heat, the peak, fearless acceptance, and highest worldly realization.

path of complete accomplishment (*mthar phyin pa'i lam, niṣṭhāmārga*). The fifth and final path in the five-path scheme, sometimes called the *path of no more training* (*mi slob lam, aśaikṣamārga*) in contrast to the lower "training" paths, where further development is still required.

path of cultivation (*sgom lam, bhāvanāmārga*). The fourth path in the five-path scheme, where the afflictions are eradicated through a process of purification, and where the Mahayana practitioner eradicates the two obscurations by traversing the ten bodhisattva stages.

path of seeing (*mthong lam, darśanamārga*). The third path in the five-path scheme, where the ordinary being becomes an ārya through seeing ultimate reality directly in meditative equipoise (*samāhita*) and has a direct realization of the four truths of an ārya, the so-called four noble truths.

perfection of diligence (*brtson 'grus kyi pha rol tu phyin pa, vīryapāramitā*). The fourth of the six perfections.

perfection of generosity (*sbyin pa'i pha rol tu phyin pa, dānapāramitā*). The first of the six perfections.

perfection of meditative concentration (*bsam gtan gyi pha rol tu phyin pa, dhyānapāramitā*). The fifth of the six perfections.

perfection of moral discipline (*tshul khrims kyi pha rol tu phyin pa, śīlapāramitā*). The second of the six perfections.

perfection of forbearance (*bzod pa'i pha rol tu phyin pa, kṣāntipāramitā*). The third of the six perfections.

perfection of wisdom (*shes rab kyi pha rol tu phyin pa, prajñāpāramitā*). The sixth of the perfections that lie at the heart of the practice of the bodhisattva. The term refers also to a class of Mahayana scriptures that outlines the essential aspects of meditation on emptiness and their associated paths and resultant states.

prātimokṣa vows (*so sor thar pa,*). The precepts of "individual liberation" are one of the three sets of vows (the others being bodhisattva vows and tantric vows), those concerned primarily with restraining outward activity. Described typically in seven categories for seven different types of practitioners, they include the levels of monastic discipline and the vows for lay Buddhists.

pratyekabuddha (*rang sangs rgyas*). Literally, a "solitary realizer" or "self-enlightened one," a pratyekabuddha is an adept who seeks liberation on the basis of autonomous practice. *See also* śrāvaka.

precious human existence (*dal 'byor, kṣaṇasampad*). Rebirth under favorable conditions, possessing the eight freedoms and the ten endowments (*'byor ba*) for practicing the Dharma.

pristine awareness (*ye shes, jñāna*). Often contrasted with ordinary consciousness (*rnam shes, vijñāna*), *pristine awareness* refers to a buddha's fully awakened wisdom and also the uncontaminated knowledge of the noble ones that is characterized by the direct realization of emptiness.

relative bodhicitta (*kun rdzob sems bskyed*). *See* bodhicitta.

samsara (*'khor ba, saṃsāra*). The perpetual cycle of birth, death, and rebirth caused by karma and the emotional afflictions. Freedom from samsara, or cyclic existence, is characterized as *nirvana* (the extinction of suffering). But in the Mahayana, both are considered extremes to be avoided.

self-entity (*bdag* or *bdag nyid, ātman*). This refers to the illusions that minds can create about two main areas of "things" (*dharma*), believing them to have ultimate existence in their own right. Were such to be possible, a thing would not depend on other things for its existence but would exist innately. The two main areas of such projected belief are (1) that perceiving persons exist ultimately (individual self-entity), and (2) that perceived phenomena exist ultimately (phenomenal self-entity). A more detailed presentation of how the various Buddhist traditions treat the relative and ultimate existence of things is found in their treatises on emptiness.

six perfections (*phar phyin drug, ṣaḍpāramitā*). These are: (1) generosity, (2) moral discipline, (3) forbearance, (4) diligence, (5) meditative concentration, and (6) wisdom.

śrāvaka (*nyan thos*). An ordained follower of the Buddha whose primary spiritual objective is to attain liberation from samsara. The Sanskrit term and its Tibetan equivalent are sometimes translated as "hearer" (which stays close to the literal meaning) or "disciple." Śrāvakas, who seek liberation through listening to others' instruction, are often paired with pratyekabuddhas, who seek liberation on the basis of autonomous practice.

suchness (*de bzhin nyid, tathatā*). The reality of things as they are; often used as a synonym for *emptiness*. *See also* dharmatā.

supramundane (*'jig rten las 'das pa, lokottara*). A spiritual category that relates to the transcendental, that is, to life or people freed from the faults of samsara. The opposite of worldly or mundane.

tantra (*rgyud*). A highly advanced system of thought and meditative practice wherein the very aspects of the resultant states of buddhahood are brought into the path right from the start. Unlike the practices of general Mahayana, engagement in the meditative practices of tantra requires prior initiation into the teachings. The term *tantra* can also refer to the literature or tantric texts that expound these systems of thought and practice. Often the term is used as a shorthand for Tantrayana or Vajrayana, where it is contrasted with the Sutra Vehicle or Perfection Vehicle.

ten directions (*phyogs bcu*). The four cardinal directions, their intermediaries, plus up and down.

ten nonvirtues (*mi dge ba bcu, daśa-akuśala*). Killing, stealing, sexual misconduct, lying, slander, prattle, harsh speech, covetous thoughts, harmful thoughts, and wrong views.

ten powers (*stobs bcu, daśabala*). Ten powers that are possessed by buddhas, namely, the powers of knowing (1) what is lawfully appropriate or inappropriate, (2) the fruitional effects of karma, (3) the diverse aspirations of sentient beings, (4) the diverse mental dispositions, (5) the level of mental faculties of sentient beings, (6) the paths that lead to all destinations, (7) the concentrations, liberating paths, meditative stabilizations, and absorptive states, (8) the states of sentient beings' past lives, (9) the future deaths and rebirths of sentient beings, and (10) the cessation of all contaminants.

ten virtues (*dge ba bcu, daśa-kuśala*). Abstaining from the ten nonvirtues.

three bodies of buddhahood (*sku gsum, trikāya*). (1) The emanation body (*nirmāṇakāya, sprul sku*), (2) the enjoyment body (*saṃbhogakāya, longs sku*), and (3) the Dharma body (*dharmakāya, chos sku*). *See also* bodies of buddhahood; dharmakāya.

three realms of existence (*khams gsum, tridhātu*). The three realms are those of (1) the desire realm (*kāmadhātu*), which includes the six types of rebirth from the hell beings up to the devas, (2) the form realm (*rūpadhātu*), which is characterized by states of meditative concentration, and (3) the formless realm (*arūpadhātu*), where beings with no physical form abide in highly refined meditative states for tens of thousands of eons.

three spheres of activity (*'khor gsum, trimaṇḍala*). The three key elements of an action—namely, the object of the action, the agent of the act, and the act itself—that together form the basis of grasping at the substantial reality of actions and events.

three trainings (*bslab pa gsum, triśikṣā*). The trainings in moral discipline, meditative absorption, and wisdom.

tīrthika (*mu stegs pa*). A proponent of one of the non-Buddhist Indian philosophies.

tranquility (*zhi gnas, śamatha*). Literally, "calm abiding," a meditative state in which the meditator has attained a physical and mental pliancy derived from focusing the mind. It is characterized by stable single-pointed attention on a chosen object with all mental distractions calmed. Tranquility is an essential basis for cultivating *insight* (*vipaśyanā*). Sometimes the term is applied to the actual meditative practice that leads to the state of tranquility.

two accumulations (*tshogs gnyis, saṃbhāradvaya*). The preparatory amassing of meritorious acts (*punya*) and of sound knowledge (*jñāna*), without whose completion buddhahood is impossible.

two obscurations (*sgrib pa gnyis, āvaraṇa*). The afflictions obscuration and the knowledge obscuration. The knowledge obscuration (*jñeyāvaraṇa, shes bya'i sgrib pa*) consists of the subtle residue of dualistic thinking and obstructs perfect wisdom and omniscience; it is only abandoned by buddhas. It is much finer than the afflictions obscuration (*kleśāvaraṇa, nyon mongs pa'i sgrib pa*), which consists of the mental poisons, such as anger, desire, confusion, pride, and jealousy, along with their innate tendencies, which are abandoned by arhats upon attaining nirvana. *See also* afflictions.

two truths (*bden pa gnyis, satyadvaya*). Relative (or conventional) truth (*kun rdzob bden pa, saṃvṛtisatya*) and ultimate (or absolute) truth (*don dam bden pa, paramārthasatya*). According to the Madhyamaka school, ultimate truth refers to emptiness—the absence of intrinsic existence of all phenomena. In contrast, relative truth refers to the empirical aspect of reality as experienced through perception, thought, and language.

ultimate (*don dam, paramārtha*). The opposite of relative or conventional (*kun rdzob*).

ultimate bodhicitta (*don dam sems bskyed*). *See* bodhicitta.

ultimate expanse (*chos kyi dbyings*). *See* dharmadhātu.

ultimate truth (*don dam bden pa, paramārthasatya*). *See* two truths.

universal essence (*chos nyid*). *See* dharmatā.

universal monarch (*'khor los sgyur ba'i rgyal po, cakravartin*). Literally, "wheel turner." One of the best worldly incarnations possible, these soveriegns have seven exceptional attributes (such as a perfect queen, minister, and so on), including a wheel that, somewhat like a flying saucer, is their means of transport across the world systems they govern. There are four types of universal monarchs, denoted by their iron, copper, silver, or golden wheels.

Vaibhāṣika (*bye brag smar ba*). "Particularists" is one possible transation for this Hinayana school. They hold the external universe to be composed of indivisible particles and the mind to be a series of indivisible instants of awareness. Their name means "Followers of the *Great Treatise* (*Mahāvibhāṣa*)."

vajra (*rdo rje*). The vajra is the ultimate weapon wielded by the god Indra. It can destroy anything, yet nothing can destroy it. This is a famous metaphor for the eternal buddha mind.

wisdom (*shes rab*, *prajñā*). The Sanskrit term and its Tibetan equivalent can also be translated as "discerning wisdom" (or "insight") or as "intelligence," depending on context. In the Abhidharma taxonomy of mental factors, *prajñā* refers to a specific mental factor that helps evaluate the properties or qualities of an object. The term can refer simply to intelligence or mental aptitude. In the context of the Mahayana path, *prajñā* refers to the wisdom aspect of the path, consisting primarily of profound insight into the emptiness of all phenomena. It is also the name of the sixth perfection.

yakṣa (*gnod sbyin*). A broad range of beings, mainly spirits, some belonging to the hungry spirits realm and others, more elevated, to the god realms. Their Tibetan name literally means "harm doers," and this is often the case. However, it is also applied to the gods of wealth and to some of the four guardians of the Heaven of the Four Great Kings.

Yogācāra. *See* Cittamātra.

Bibliography

As was the case for the Tibetan edition of the text published by the Institute of Tibetan Classics (ITC), three xylographic editions have been consulted for this translation. The main reference was the Tsipri edition, but the Palpung and Beijing were also consulted. See details in abbreviations below.

Abbreviations

AA	Maitreya, *Ornament of Clear Realization* (*Abhisamayālaṃkāra*).
AK	Vasubandhu, *Treasury of Higher Knowledge* (*Abhidharmakośa*).
BCA	Śāntideva, *Guide to the Bodhisattva Way of Life* (*Bodhicaryāvatāra*).
Beijing	The modern edition of Gampopa's *Ornament of Precious Liberation*, found as volume 20 in the *Gangs can rig brgya'i sgo 'byed lde mig* series (Beijing: Mi rigs dpe skrun khang, 1987–97).
BP	Atiśa, *Lamp for the Path to Awakening* (*Bodhipathapradīpa*).
ITC	Institute of Tibetan Classics, *Bstan pa la 'jug pa'i rim pa ston pa'i gzhung gces btus*, by Dge bshes Dol pa, Sgam po pa Bsod nams rin chen, and Sa pan Kun dga' rgyal mtsan; introduction by Thupten Jinpa; Bod kyi gtsug lag gces btus 10 (New Delhi: Institute of Tibetan Classics, 2009).
MA	Candrakīrti, *Entering the Middle Way* (*Madhyamakāvatāra*).
MMK	Nāgārjuna, *Fundamental Verses on the Middle Way* (*Mūlamadhyamaka-kārikā*).
MSA	Maitreya, *Ornament of Mahayana Sutras* (*Mahāyānasūtrālaṃkāra*). Chapter numbers follow the Tibetan translation, which divides the first Sanskrit chapter into two.
MV	Maitreya, *Clear Differentiation of the Middle and Extremes* (*Madhyāntavibhāga*).
P	Peking edition of the Tibetan *Tripiṭaka*, reprinted under the supervision of Ōtani University, Kyoto, Daisetzu T. Suzuki et al., eds., vols. 1–168 (Tokyo–Kyoto: Tibetan Tripitaka Research Institute, 1955–61).
Palpung	Dergé edition of Gampopa's *Ornament of Precious Liberation* from Palpung Monastery. See reference in bibliography under Gampopa below.
PV	Dharmakīrti, *Thorough Exposition of Valid Cognition* (*Pramāṇavarttika*).
RA	Nāgārjuna, *Precious Garland* (*Ratnāvalī*).
RGV	Maitreya, *Uttaratantra* (*Ratnagotravibhāga Mahāyānottaratantraśāstra*).

RS	*Verse Summary of the Perfection of Wisdom* (*Ratnaguṇasaṃcayagāthā*).
ŚI	Candragomin, *Letter to a Student* (*Śiṣyalekha*).
SU	Nāgārjuna, *Letter to a Friend* (*Suhṛllekha*).
Toh	The Tibetan *Tripiṭaka*, Dergé edition, as described in H. Ui et al., eds., *A Complete Catalogue of the Tibetan Buddhist Canon* (Sendai, Japan: Tohoku University, 1934).
Tsipri	The version of Gampopa's *Ornament of Precious Liberation* from the former Tsipri (Rtsib ri) printing house in southwestern Tibet, the woodblocks of which have been preserved in Solukhumbu Monastery of northern Nepal.
UV	*Collection of Aphorisms* (*Udānavarga*).

Works Cited by the Author

Kangyur (Canonical Scriptures)

Advice to a King Sutra. Rājāvavādakasūtra. Rgyal po la gdams pa'i mdo. Toh 221, mdo sde, *dza* 78a1–84b4.

Ākāśagarbha Sūtra. Nam mkha'i snying po'i mdo. Toh 260, mngo sde, *za* 264a4–283b2.

Akṣayamati Sutra. Akṣayamatinirdeśasūtra. Blo gros mi zad pas bstan pa'i mdo. Toh 175, mdo sde, *ma* 79a1–174b7.

Attention to Mindfulness Sutra. Smṛtyupasthānasūtra. Dam pa'i chos dran pa nye bar gzhag pa'i mdo. Toh 287, mdo sde, *ya* 82a1–*sha* 229b7.

Basis of Vinaya. Vinayavastu. 'Dul ba gzhi. Toh 1, 'dul ba, *ka* 1b1–*nga* 302a5.

Bodhisattva Collection. Bodhisattvapiṭaka. Byang chub sems dpa'i sde snod. Toh 56, dkon brtsegs, *kha* 255b1–*ga* 205a7.

Candraprabha Sutra. See *King of Meditation Sutra.*

Clouds of Jewels Sutra. Ratnameghasūtra. Dkon mchog sprin gyi mdo. Toh 231, mdo sde, *wa* 1b1–112b7.

Collection of Aphorisms. Udānavarga. Ched du brjod pa'i tshoms. Toh 326, mdo sde, *sa* 209a1–253a7.

Crown Jewel Dhāraṇī Sutra. Ratnaketudhāraṇīsūtra. 'Dus pa chen po rin po che tog gi gzungs gyi mdo. Toh 138, mdo sde, *na* 187b3–277b7.

Diamond Meditative Absorption Scripture. Vajrasamādhidharmākṣara. Rdo rje'i ting nge 'dzin gyi chos kyi yi ge. Toh 135, mdo sde, *na* 122a1–144b2.

Enlightenment of Vairocana. Vairocanābhisambodhi. Rnam snang mngon byang. Toh 494, rgyud, *tha* 151b2–260a7; P 126, rgyud, *tha* 115b2–225b2.

Flower Ornament Sutra. Avataṃsakasūtra. Phal po che (*Sangs rgyas phal po che'i mdo*). Toh 44, phal chen, *ka–a*.

Gayāśīrṣa Hill Sutra. Gayāśīrṣasūtra. Ga ya mgo'i ri kyi mdo. Toh 109, mdo sde, *ca* 285a1–292a7.

Good Eon Sutra. Bhadrakalpikasūtra. Bskal pa bzang po'i mdo. Toh 94, mdo sde, *ka* 1b1–340a5.

Great Liberation Sutra. Mahāmokṣasūtra. Thar pa chen po'i mdo. Toh 264, mdo sde, *'a* 210a1–264a1.

Great Passing into Nirvana Sutra (longer version). *Mahāparinirvāṇasūtra. Mya ngan las 'das pa'i mdo.* Toh 119, mdo sde, *nya* 1b1–ta 339a7.
Great Passing into Nirvana Sutra (shorter version). *Mahāparinirvāṇasūtra. Mya ngan las 'das pa'i mdo.* Toh 120, mdo sde, *tha* 1b1–151a4.
Great Sutra of the Supreme Victory. Dhvajāgramahāsūtra. Mdo chen po rgyal mtshan dam pa. Toh 293 Kangyur, mdo sde, *sha* 265b4–267a7.
Heap of Flowers Dhāraṇī. Puṣpakūṭadhāraṇī. Me tog brtsegs pa'i gzungs. Toh 886, gzungs 'dus, *e* 159b1–161b3.
Hevajra Tantra. Kye'i rdo rje'i rgyud. Toh 417, rgyud, *nga* 1b1–30a3.
Host of Flowers Sutra. Kusumasaṃcayasūtra. Me tog gi tshogs gyi mdo. Toh 266, mdo sde, *'a* 288a1–319a6.
Infinite Means of Purification Sutra. Anantamukhapariśodhananirdeśaparivartasūtra. Sgo mtha' yas pa rnam par sbyong ba bstan pa'i le'u kyi mdo. Toh 46, dkon brtsegs, *ka* 45b1–99b7.
Jewel Lamp Dhāraṇī Sutra. Ratnolkānāmadhāraṇīsūtra. Dkon mchog ta la la'i gzungs zhes bya ba'i mdo. Toh 145, mdo sde, *pa* 34a4–82a3, and Toh 847, gzungs, *'e* 3b6–54b7.
Kāśyapa Chapter Sutra. Kāśyapaparivartasūtra. 'Od srungs kyis zhus pa'i mdo. Toh 87, dkon brtsegs, *cha* 119b1–151b7.
King of Meditation Sutra. Samādhirājasūtra. Ting nge 'dzin rgyal po'i mdo. Toh 127, mdo sde, *da* 1b1–170b7. Also known as the *Candraprabhasūtra.*
King of Secret Nectar Tantra. Amṛtaguhyatantrarāja. Gsang ba 'dud rtsi'i rgyud kyi rgyal po. Toh 401, rgyud, *ga* 233a5–235a5.
Lifespan Sutra. Āyuṣparyantasūtra. Tshe'i mtha'i mdo. Toh 307, mdo sde, *sa* 139a4–145b3.
Lion's Roar Sutra. Siṃhanādasūtra. Byams pa'i seng ge'i sgra chen po'i mdo. Toh 67, dkon brtsegs, *ca* 68a1–114b7.
Lotus Sutra. Saddharmapuṇḍarīkasūtra. Dam pa'i chos padma dkar po zhes bya ba theg pa chen po'i mdo. Toh 113, mdo sde, *ja* 1b1–180b7.
Marvelous Array Sutra. Gaṇḍavyūhasūtra. Sdong po bkod pa'i mdo. Chapter 45 of the *Flower Ornament Sutra.*
Meeting of Father and Son Sutra. Pitāputrasamāgamasūtra. Yab dang sras mjal ba'i mdo. Toh 60, dkon brtsegs, *nga* 1b1–168a7.
Nanda's Abiding in the Womb. Nandagarbhāvakrāntinirdeśa. Dga' bo mngal du 'jug pa bstan pa'i mdo. Toh 57, dkon brtsegs, *ga* 205a7–236b7.
One Hundred Stories (of Great Deeds). Avadānaśataka (short for *Pūrṇapramukhāvadānaśataka*). *Gang po la sogs pa'i rtogs pa brjod pa brgya pa.* Toh 343, mdo sde, *ām* 1b1–286b7.
One Hundred [Stories] about Karma. Karmaśataka. Las brgya tham pa. Toh 340, mdo sde, *ha* 1b1–*a* 128b7.
Perfection of Wisdom in Eight Thousand Lines. Aṣṭasāhasrikāprajñāpāramitā. Shes rab kyi pha rol tu phyin pa brgyad stong pa. Toh 12, sher phyin, *ka* 1b1–286a6.
Perfection of Wisdom in a Hundred Thousand Lines. Śatasāhasrikāprajñāpāramitā. Shes rab kyi pha rol tu phyin pa stong phrag brgya pa. Toh 8, sher phyin *ka–'a.*
Perfection of Wisdom in Seven Hundred Lines. Saptaśatikāprajñāpāramitā. Shes rab kyi

pha rol tu phyin pa bdun brgya pa. Toh 24, sher phyin, *ka* 148a1–174a2, and Toh 90, dkon brtsegs, *cha* 182b6–209b7.

Perfectly Gathering the Qualities [of Avalokiteśvara] Sutra. Dharmasaṃgītisūtra. Chos yang dag par sdud pa'i mdo. Toh 238, mdo sde, *zha* 1b1–99b7.

Prayer of Excellent Conduct. Bhadracaryāpraṇidhāna. Bzang po spyod pa'i smon lam gyi rgyal po. Toh 1095, gzungs 'dus, *waṃ* 262b5–266a3. Also part 4 of the *Flower Ornament Sutra.*

Questions of Brahma Viśeṣacinti Sutra. Brahmaviśeṣacintiparipṛcchāsūtra. Tshangs pa khyad par sems kyi zhus pa. Toh 160, mdo sde, *ba* 23a1–100b7.

Questions of the Layman Ugra Sutra. Gṛhapatyugraparipṛcchāsūtra. Khyim bdag drag shul can gyis zhus pa'i mdo. Toh 63, dkon brtsegs, *nga* 257a7–288a4.

Questions of the Layman Vīradatta Sutra. Vīradattagṛhapatiparipṛcchāsūtra. Khyim bdag dpas byin gyis zhus pa'i mdo. Toh 72, dkon brtsegs, *ca* 194a1–240b1.

Questions of Nāga King Anavatapta Sutra. Anavataptanāgarājaparipṛcchāsūtra. Klu'i rgyal po ma dros pas zhus pa'i mdo. Toh 156, mdo sde, *pha* 206a1–253b7.

Questions of Nārāyaṇa Sutra. See *Sutra of the Absorption that Gathers All Merit.*

Questions of Pūrṇa Sutra. Pūrṇaparipṛcchāsūtra. Gang pos zhus pa'i mdo. Toh 61, dkon brtsegs, *nga* 168b1–227a6.

Questions of Ratnacūḍa Sutra. Ratnacūḍaparipṛcchāsūtra. Gtsug na rin po ches zhus pa'i mdo. Toh 91, dkon brtsegs, *cha* 210a1–254b7.

Questions of Sāgaramati Sutra. Sāgaramatiparipṛcchāsūtra. Blo gros rgya mtsho zhus pa'i mdo. Toh 152, mdo sde, *pha* 1b1–115b7.

Questions of Subāhu Sutra. Subāhuparipṛcchāsūtra. Lag bzangs kyis zhus pa'i mdo. Toh 70, dkon brtsegs, *ca* 154a1–180b7.

Questions of Subāhu Tantra. Subāhuparipṛcchātantra. Dpung bzang gis zhus pa'i rgyud. Toh 805, rgyud 'bum, *wa* 118a1–140b7.

Questions of Surata Sutra. Surataparipṛcchāsūtra. Nges pas zhus pa'i mdo. Toh 71, dkon brtsegs, *ca* 181a1–193b7.

Questions of the Devaputra Susthitamati Sutra. Susthitamatidevaputraparipṛcchāsūtra. Lha'i bu blo gros rab gnas kyis zhus pa'i mdo. Toh 80, dkon brtsegs, *ca* 285a1–*cha* 27a4.

Rice Shoot Sutra. Śālistambasūtra. Sa lu'i ljang ba'i mdo. Toh 210, mdo sde, *tsha* 116b2–123b1.

Sage and Fool Sutra. Damamūkanāmasūtra. 'Dzangs blun zhes bya ba'i mdo. Toh 341, mdo sde, *a* 129a1–298a7.

Story of the Sow. Sūkarikāvadāna. Phag mo'i rtogs brjod. Toh 345, mdo sde, *am* 289b2–291a7.

Sutra of the Absorption that Gathers All Merit. Sarvapuṇyasamuccayasamādhisūtra. Bsod nams thams cad bsdus pa'i ting nge 'dzin gyi mdo. Toh 134, mdo sde, *na* 70b2–121b7.

Sutra Adorning the Brilliance of Pristine Awareness. Jñānālokālaṃkārasūtra. Ye shes snang ba'i rgyan rgyi mdo. Toh 100, mdo sde, *ga* 276a1–305a7.

Sutra Definitely Elucidating the Noble Intention. Saṃdhinirmocanasūtra. Dgongs pa nges par 'grel pa'i mdo. Toh 106, mdo sde, *ca* 1b1–55b7.

Sutra Describing the Qualities of the Buddhafield of Mañjuśrī. Mañjuśrībuddhakṣetra-guṇavyūhasūtra. 'Jam dpal gyi sangs rgyas kyi zhing gi yon tan bkod pa'i mdo. Toh 59, dkon brtsegs, *ga* 248b1–297a3.

Sutra Encouraging Nobler Intention. Adhyāśayasaṃcodanasūtra. Lhag pa'i bsam pa bskul ba'i mdo. Toh 69, dkon brtsegs, *ca* 131a7–153b7.

Sutra on Excellently Nurturing Faith in the Mahayana. Mahāyāna-prasādaprabhāvanasūtra. Theg pa chen po la dad pa rab tu sgom pa'i mdo. Toh 144, mdo sde, *pa* 6b6–34a3.

Sutra on the Full Development of Great Realization. Mahāsamayavaipulyasūtra. Rtogs pa chen po yongs su rgyas pa'i mdo. Toh 265, mdo sde, *'a* 264a1–287b7.

Sutra on Going to Laṅka. Laṅkāvatārasūtra. Lang kar gshegs pa'i mdo. Toh 107, mdo sde, *cha* 56a1–191b7.

Sutra of Golden Light. Translated from Chinese. *Gser 'od dam pa mchog tu rnam par rgyal ba'i mdo.* Toh 555, rgyud, *pa* 19a1–151a7. Also *Suvarṇaprabhāsottamasūtren-drarājasūtra. Gser 'od dam pa mdo sde'i dbang po'i rgyal po.* Toh 556, rgyud, *pa* 151b1–273a7.

Sutra on the Indivisibility of the Dharmadhātu. Dharmadhātuprakṛtyasambhedanirdeśa-sūtra. Chos kyi dbyings kyi rang bzhin dbyer med pa bstan pa'i mdo. Toh 52, dkon brtsegs, *kha* 140b1–164a5.

Sutra of the Play of Manjuśrī. Mañjuśrīvikrīḍitasūtra. 'Jam dpal rnam par rol pa'i mdo. Toh 96, mdo sde, *kha* 217a1–241b7.

Sutra Requested by Suvikrāntavikrami. Suvikrāntavikramiparipṛcchāsūtra. Rab kyi rtsal gyis rnam par gnon pas zhus pa'i mdo. Toh 14, shes rab sna tshogs, *ka* 20a1–103b7.

Sutra on Moral Discipline. Śīlasaṃyuktasūtra. Tshul khrims yang dag par ldan pa'i mdo. Toh 303, mdo sde, *sa* 127a2–127b7.

Sutra Teaching the Four Qualities. Caturdharmanirdeśasūtra. Chos bzhi bstan pa'i mdo. Toh 249, mdo sde, *za* 55a5–59b7.

Sutra Teaching the Nonorigination of All Things. Sarvadharmāpravṛttinirdeśasūtra. Chos thams cad 'byung ba med par bstan pa'i mdo. Toh 180, mdo sde, *ma* 267a1–296a6.

Sutra Teaching the Wearing of Armor. Varmavyūhanirdeśasūtra. Go cha'i bkod pa bstan pa'i mdo. Toh 51, dkon brtsegs, *kha* 70b1–140a7.

Tantra of the Arising of the Supremely Blissful. Mahāsaṃvārodayatantra. Dpal bde mchog 'byung ba'i rgyud. Toh 373, rgyud, *kha* 265a1–311a6.

Teachings of Vimalakīrti Sutra. Vimalakīrtinirdeśasūtra. Dri ma med par grags pas bstan pa'i mdo. Toh 176, mdo sde, *ma,* 175a1–239b7.

Ten Dharmas Sutra. Daśadharmakasūtra. Chos bcu pa'i mdo. Toh 53, dkon brtsegs, *kha* 164a6–184b6.

Ten Levels Sutra. Daśabhūmikasūtra. Sa bcu pa'i mdo. Chapter 31 of the *Flower Ornament Sutra.*

Ten Wheels of Kṣitigarbha Sutra. Daśacakrakṣitigarbhasūtra. 'Dus pa chen po las sa'i snying po'i 'khor lo bcu pa'i mdo. Toh 239, mdo sde, *zha* 100a1–241b4.

Three Vows Chapter. Trisaṃvaranirdeśaparivarta. Sdom pa gsum bstan pa'i le'u kyi mdo. Toh 45, dkon brtsegs, *ka* 1b1–45a7.

Union with All the Buddhas. Sarvabuddhasamayoga. Sangs rgyas thams cad dang mnyam par sbyor ba mkha' 'gro ma sgyu ma bde ba'i mchog. Toh 366, rgyud, *ka* 151b1–193a6.

Unwavering Suchness Sutra. Dharmatāsvabhāvaśūnyatācalapratisarvālokasūtra. Chos nyid rang gi ngo bo stong pa nyid las mi g.yo bar tha dad par thams cad la snang ba'i mdo. Toh 128, mdo sde, *da* 171a1–174b4.

Vajra Peak Tantra. Vajraśekharatantra. Rdo rje rtse mo'i rgyud. Toh 480, rgyud, *nya* 142b1–274a5.

Vajra Victory Banner Sutra. Vajraketusūtra. Rdo rje rgyal mtshan gyi mdo. Toh 30 Kangyur, shes rab sna tshogs, *ka* 178b6–179a7.

Vast Manifestation Sutra. Lalitavistarasūtra. Rgya cher rol pa'i mdo. Toh 95, mdo sde, *kha* 1b1–216b7.

Verse Summary of the Perfection of Wisdom. (*Prajñāpāramitā-*) *Ratnaguṇasaṃcayagāthā. Shes rab kyi pha rol tu phyin pa sdud pa tshigs su bcad pa.* Toh 13, sher phyin, *ka* 1b1–19b7.

White Lotus of Compassion Sutra. Karuṇāpuṇḍarīkasūtra. Snying rje pad ma dkar po'i mdo. Toh 112, mdo sde, *cha* 129a1–297a7.

White Lotus of Great Compassion Sutra. Mahākaruṇāpuṇḍarīkasūtra. Snying rje chen po'i pad ma dkar po'i mdo. Toh 111, mdo sde, *cha* 56a1–128b7.

Tengyur (Canonical Treatises)

Asaṅga. *Bodhisattva Levels, from the Yogic Conduct Levels. Bodhisattvabhūmi* (short for *Yogācārabhūmau Bodhisattvabhūmi*). *Byang chub sems dpa'i sa* (short for *Rnal 'byor spyod pa'i sa las byang chub sems dpa'i sa*). Toh 4037, sems tsam, *wi* 1b1–213a7.

———. *Compendium of Higher Knowledge. Abhidharmasamuccaya. Chos mngon pa kun las btus pa.* Toh 4049, sems tsam, *ri* 44b1–120a7.

———. *Detailed Explanation of the Uttaratantra. Mahāyānottaratantraśāstravyākhyā. Theg pa chen po'i rgyud bla ma'i bstan bcos kyi rnam par bshad pa.* Toh 4025, sems tsam, *phi* 74b1–129a7.

———. *Establishing Summaries of the Levels of Yogic Practice. Yogācārabhūmiviniścayasaṃgrahaṇī. Rnal 'byor spyod pa'i sa rnam par gtan la dbab pa bsdu ba.* Toh 4038, sems tsam, *zhi* 1a1–127a4.

———. *Śrāvaka Levels, from the Yogic Conduct Levels. Śrāvakabhūmi* (short for *Yogācārabhūmau Śrāvakabhūmi*). *Nyan thos kyi sa* (short for *Rnal 'byor spyod pa'i sa las nyan thos kyi sa*). Toh 4036, sems tsam, *dzi* 1a1–195a7.

Aśvaghoṣa (a.k.a. Mātṛceṭa). *Eliminating Suffering. Śokavinodana. Mya ngan bsal ba.* Toh 4177, spring yig, *nge* 33a2–34a3.

Atiśa (Dīpaṃkaraśrījñāna). *Instructions on Madhyamaka. Madhyamakopadeśa. Dbu ma'i man ngag.* Toh 3929, dbu ma, *ki* 95b1–96a7.

———. *Lamp for the Path to Awakening. Bodhipathapradīpa. Byang chub lam gyi sgron ma.* Toh 3947, dbu ma, *khi* 238a6–241a4, and Toh 4465, jo bo'i chos chung, *gi* 1b1–4b4.

———. *Lamp for the Summary of Conduct. Caryāsaṃgrahapradīpa. Spyod pa bsdus pa'i sgron ma.* Toh 3960, dbu ma, *khi* 312b3–313a7.

———. *Penetrating the Two Truths. Satyadvayāvatāra. Bden pa gnyis la 'jug pa.* Toh 3902, dbu ma, *a* 72a3–73a7, and Toh 4467, jo bo'i chos chung, *pho* 5b3–6b5.

———. *Ritual Order for Bodhicitta and Vows. Cittotpādasaṃvaravidhikrama. Sems bskyed pa dang sdom pa'i cho ga'i rim pa.* Toh 3969, dbu ma, *gi* 245a2–248b2.

———. *Song of Seeing Dharmadhātu. Dharmadhātudarśanagīti. Chos kyi dbyings lta ba'i glu.* Toh 2314, rgyud, *shi* 254b7–260b5.

Candragomin. *Letter to a Student. Śiṣyalekha. Slob ma la springs pa'i spring yig.* Toh 4183, spring yig, *nge* 46b3–53a6.

———. *Twenty Verses on the Bodhisattva Vow. Bodhisattvasaṃvaraviṃśaka. Byang chub sems dpa'i sdom pa nyi shu pa.* Toh 4081, sems tsam, *hi* 166b1–167a5.

Candrakīrti. *Entering the Middle Way. Madhyamakāvatāra. Dbu ma la 'jug pa'i tshig le'ur byas pa.* Toh 3861, dbu ma, *'a* 201b1–219a7.

———. *Seventy Stanzas on Going for Refuge. Triśaraṇasaptatī. Gsum la skyabs su 'gro ba bdun cu pa.* Toh 3971, dbu ma, *gi* 251a1–253b2.

Dharmakīrti. *Thorough Exposition of Valid Cognition. Pramāṇavārttika. Tshad ma rnam 'grel gyi tshig le'ur byas pa.* Toh 4210, tshad ma, *che* 94b1–151a7.

Indrabhūti. *Achieving Pristine Awareness. Jñānasiddhisādhanopāyikā. Ye shes grub pa zhes bya ba'i sgrub thabs.* Toh 2219, rgyud, *wi* 36b7–60b6.

Kamalaśīla. *Diamond Cutter Sutra Commentary. Vajracchedikāṭīkā. 'Phags pa shes rab kyi pha rol tu phyin pa rdo rje gcod pa'i rgya cher 'grel pa.* Toh 3817, mdo 'grel, *ma* 204a1–267a7.

Maitreya. *Clear Differentiation of the Middle and Extremes. Madhyāntavibhāga. Dbus dang mtha' rnam par 'byed pa.* Toh 4021, sems tsam, *phi* 40b1–45a6.

———. *Ornament of Clear Realization. Abhisamayālaṃkāra. Mngon rtogs rgyan.* Toh 3786, shes phyin, *ka* 1b1–13a7.

———. *Ornament of Mahayana Sutras. Mahāyānasūtrālaṃkāra. Theg pa chen po mdo sde'i rgyan.* Toh 4020, sems tsam, *phi* 1a1–39a4.

———. *Uttaratantra (Ratnagotravibhāga Mahāyānottaratantraśāstra). Rgyud bla ma (Theg pa chen po rgyud bla ma'i bstan bcos).* Toh 4024, sems tsam, *phi* 54b1–73a7.

Mañjuśrīkīrti. *Extensive Explanation of Root Vajrayana Downfalls. Vajrayānamūlāpattiṭīkā. Rdo rje theg pa'i rtsa ba'i ltung ba'i rgya cher bshad pa.* Toh 2488, rgyud 'grel, *thi* 197b7–231b7.

Nāgārjuna. *Five Stages. Pañcakrama. Rim pa lnga pa.* Toh 1802, rgyud, *ngi* 45a5–57a1.

———. *Fundamental Verses on the Middle Way. Mūlamadhyamakakārikā. Dbu ma rtsa ba'i tshig le'ur byas pa shes rab.* Toh 3824, dbu ma, *tsa* 1a1–19a6.

———. *Letter to a Friend. Suhṛllekha. Bshes pa'i spring yig.* Toh 4182, spring yig, *nge* 40b4–46b3.

———. *Precious Garland. Ratnāvalī. Dbu ma rin chen phreng ba.* Toh 4158, spring yig, *ge* 107a1–126a4.

———. *Verses on the Essence of Dependent Origination. Pratītyasamutpādahṛdayakārikā. Rten cing 'grel par 'byung ba'i snying po'i tshig le'ur byas pa.* Toh 3836, mdo 'grel, *tsa* 146b2–146b7.

Prajñākaramati. *Commentary on the Guide to the Bodhisattva Way of Life. Bodhicaryāvatārapañjikā. Byang chub kyi spyod pa la 'jug pa'i dka' 'grel.* Toh 3872, mdo 'grel, *la* 41b1–288a7.

Śāntideva. *Compendium of Trainings. Śikṣāsamuccaya. Bslab pa kun las btus pa.* Toh 3940, dbu ma, *khi* 3a2–194b5.

———. *Guide to the Bodhisattva Way of Life. Bodhicaryāvatāra. Byang chub sems dpa'i spyod pa la 'jug pa.* Toh 3871, dub ma, *la* 1b1–40a7.

Saraha. *Song of an Inexhaustible Treasure of Instruction. Dohakoṣopadeśagīti. Mi zad pa'i gter mdzod man ngag gi glu zhes bya ba.* Toh 2264, rgyud, *zhi* 28b6–33b4.

———. *Treasury of Spiritual Songs. Dohakoṣagīti. Do ha mdzod kyi glu.* Toh 2224, rgyud, *wi* 70b5–77a3.

Sthiramati. *Detailed Exposition of the Ornament of Mahayana Sutras. Sūtrālaṃkāravṛttibhāṣya. Mdo sde'i rgyan gyi 'grel bshad.* Toh 4034, sems tsam, *mi* 1a1–*tsi* 266a7.

Tilopa. *Treasury of Dohas. Dohakoṣa. Do ha mdzod.* Toh 2281, rgyud, *zhi* 136a4–137b6.

Udbhaṭasiddhasvāmin. *Praise of the Excellence [of the Buddha]. Viśeṣastava. Khyad par du 'phags pa'i bstod pa.* Toh 1109, bstod tshogs, *ka* 1a1–4b7.

Vāgīśvarakīrti. *Advice on Cheating Death. Mṛtyuvañcanopadeśa. 'Chi ba bslu ba'i man ngag.* Toh 1748, rgyud, *sha* 118b7–133b3.

Vasubandhu. *Commentary on the Ornament of Mahayana Sutras. Sūtrālaṃkārabhāṣya. Mdo sde'i rgyan gyi bshad pa.* Toh 4026, sems tsam, *phi* 129b1–260a7.

———. *Commentary on the Treasury of Higher Knowledge. Abhidharmakośabhāṣya. Chos mngon pa'i mdzod kyi bshad pa.* Toh 4090, mngon pa, *ku* 26b1–*khu* 95a7.

———. *A Discussion of Accumulation. Sambhāraparikathā. Tshogs kyi gtam.* Toh 4166, spring yig, *ge* 173b1–175a4.

———. *Treasury of Higher Knowledge. Abhidharmakośa. Chos mngon pa'i mdzod kyi tshig le'ur byas pa.* Toh 4089, mngon pa, *ku* 1a1–25a7.

———. *Twenty Stanzas. Viṃśatikā. Nyi shu pa'i tshig le'ur byas pa.* Toh 4056, sems tsam, *shi* 3a4–4a2.

Vimalamitra. *Meditating on Nonthought, Penetrating Simultaneity. Sakṛtprāveśikanirvikalpabhāvanārtha. Cig car 'jug pa rnam par mi rtog pa'i bsgom don.* Toh 3910, dbu ma, *ki* 6b1–13b4.

Yaśomitra. *Commentary on the Treasury of Higher Knowledge. Abhidharmakośaṭīkā. Chos mngon pa'i mdzod kyi 'grel bshad.* Toh 4092, mngon pa, *gu* 1b1–*ngu* 333a7.

Tibetan Works

Ngok Loden Sherap (Rngog Blo ldan shes rab, 1059–1109). *A Letter Entitled "Droplets of Nectar." Spring yig bdud rtsi'i thigs pa.* In *Bka' gdams gsung 'bum phyogs bsgrigs*, vol. 1. Chengdu: Sichuan Publishing House, 2006.

Works Cited by the Translator

Covill, Linda, trans. *Handsome Nanda by Ashvaghosha.* New York: New York University Press, 2007.

Döndrup Gyaltsen (Don grub rgyal mtshan), ed. *Treasury of Gems: Selected Anthology of the Well-Uttered Insights of the Teachings of the Precious Kadam Tradition. Legs par bshad pa bka' gdams rin po che'i gsung gi gces btus nor bu'i bang mdzod.* Bir, India: D. Tsondu Senghe, 1985.

Drolungpa Lodrö Jungné (Gro lung pa Blo gros 'byung gnas, fl. late eleventh to early twelfth century). *Great Tenrim. Bstan rim chen mo* (short for *Great Treatise on the Stages of the Doctrine. Bde bar gshegs pa'i bstan pa rin po che la 'jug pa'i lam gyi rim pa rnam par bshad pa*). Xylograph, Bihar Research Society, Patna.

Gampopa Sönam Rinchen (Sgam po pa Bsod nams rin chen, 1079–1153). *Ornament of Liberation. Thar rgyan* (short for *Dam chos yid bzhin gyi nor bu thar pa rin po che'i rgyan zhes bya ba theg pa chen po'i lam gyi bshad pa*). Thimphu, 1985.

Gö Lotsāwa Shönu Pal ('Gos Lo tsā ba Gzhon nu dpal, 1392–1481). *The Blue Annals. Deb ther sngon po.* Śata-Piṭaka Series 212. New Delhi: International Academy of Indian Culture, 1974. For an English translation, see Roerich, *The Blue Annals.*

Gombrich, Richard F. *How Buddhism Began: The Conditioned Genesis of the Early Teachings.* New Delhi: Munishiram Manoharlal Publishers, 2002.

Guenther, Herbert V., trans. *The Jewel Ornament of Liberation* by Gampopa. London: Rider, 1959. Reprinted Boulder: Shambhala, 1971.

Gyaltsen, Khenpo Konchog, trans. *The Jewel Ornament of Liberation: The Wish-Fulfilling Gem of the Noble Teachings by Gampopa.* Edited by Ani K. Trinlay Chödron. Ithaca: Snow Lion, 1998.

Jinpa, Thupten. "Introduction" (in Tibetan). In *Bstan pa la'jug pa'i rim pa ston pa'i gzhung gces btus,* by Dge bshes Dol pa, Sgam po pa bsod nams rin chen, and Sa pan kun dga' rgyal mtsan. Bod kyi gtsug lag gces btus 10. Sarnath: Institute of Tibetan Classics, 2009. (Volume abbreviated ITC.)

Roberts, Peter Alan, trans. *The Mind of Mahāmudrā: Advice from the Kagyü Masters.* Boston: Wisdom Publications, 2014.

Roerich, George N. *The Blue Annals.* Delhi: Motilal Banarsidass, 1976.

Rotman, Andy, trans. *Divine Stories: Divyāvadāna*, vol. 1. Boston: Wisdom Publications, 2008.

Tatz, Mark, trans. *Asanga's Chapter on Ethics with the Commentary of Tsong-kha-pa, The Basic Path to Awakening.* Studies in Asian Thought and Religion 4. Lewiston and Queenston, NY: Edwin Mellen Press, 1986.

Thrangu Rinpoche, Khenchen. *Life and Teachings of Gampopa.* Auckland, New Zealand: Zhyisil Chokyi Ghatsal Trust, 2004.

Index

Megharava Buddha, 132
merit, 39, 124, 164, 204, 217, 237–38, 295, 325
accumulation of, 29, 69, 107, 134, 138–41, 147–48, 154
and external world, 222
and wisdom, 117, 148
of making offerings, 93, 119–20
See also virtue
method. *See* skillful means
middle way, 225, 229–30, 324
Milarepa, 1, 3–5, 11, 64, 280–81, 284, 318n482
mind, 2, 20, 32, 58, 64–65, 75, 78, 81, 84, 92–95, 151, 153–54, 176, 179, 207–8, 248, 254
and forbearance, 181–82, 184–85
and giving, 157, 159–60, 162, 165
for enlightenment, 112, 114, 116, 119–21, 132–33, 138–40, 247
mastery of, 211–13
nature of, 4, 243–44
nonexistence of, 219–27, 230–32
of buddhas and bodhisattvas, 19, 41–42, 138–39, 147–48, 240, 261–62, 266–68, 279–82, 291–93
one-pointed, 84, 201, 204, 324–25, 328
purification of, 143, 148–49, 177, 239–40
seclusion of, 201, 204–5
settling of, 27, 135, 171, 192–93, 199–204, 233–35, 237, 241–42, 245
See also insight; tranquility
Mind Only. *See* Yogācāra
mindfulness, 234, 248–50, 321–22. *See also* four foundations of mindfulness
miracles, 41, 267, 292, 311n325
misguided. *See* tīrthikas
moral discipline, 33, 42, 108–9, 136–38, 239, 241, 243, 325–28
and five paths, 250
of amassing virtue, 171, 174, 179
of buddhas and bodhisattvas, 119
of restraint, 138, 171–74
of working for the welfare of others, 171, 174–78
perfection of, 112, 151–54, 169–79, 181, 191, 217, 258, 263, 326
purification of, 178
three kinds of, 139, 151
violations of, 257
mother, 69–71, 90–92, 95–96, 186, 207
Mother of the Conquerors. See *Perfection of Wisdom in Eight Thousand Lines*
motivation, 44, 101, 104, 109–10, 121, 137, 157–58, 160–62, 210, 271, 295

N

nāgas, 30, 179, 299n39, 324
Nāgārjuna, 4, 75, 115, 119, 213–14, 220, 234, 322, 324
Nanda, 126, 128, 130, 306n200
Nanda's Abiding in the Womb, 68, 70–71, 74–75
Nāropa, 4–5, 43, 211, 312n347
nature body, 285, 320
nihilist views, 228–29, 232
ninefold technique of meditating on death, 52–56
nirmāṇakāya. See emanation body
nirvana, 17–19, 101, 105, 130–31, 176, 235, 243, 286–87, 319, 324–25, 329
and dependent origination, 206, 209–210
and samsara, 2, 11, 113, 136, 229–30, 263, 307n219, 316n453, 327
as far shore, 40, 153
for oneself, 89
nature of, 219, 230–33
nonabiding, 165, 216–17
See also enlightenment; liberation
noble one, 60, 102–3, 113, 243, 248–50, 325, 327
Noble Tree Sutra, 54
non-Buddhists. See tīrthikas
nonexistence, refutation of, 226–29
nonhuman beings, 25–26
nonreturner, 59, 303n141
nonvirtue, 26, 30, 32, 78–82, 85–86, 121–22, 129, 194, 207, 248, 328. *See also* ten virtuous and ten nonvirtuous actions
Nyukrumpa, 3

O

obscurations, 20, 38, 40, 123, 166, 250,

About the Contributors

KEN HOLMES studied in Dharamsala before joining Samye Ling in Scotland, the first Tibetan monastery in the West, in 1971. There, he and his wife Katia have devoted the past forty-five years to researching, translating, publishing, and teaching the practice and study texts of Tibetan Buddhism. As the center's director of studies, Ken spends much of the year teaching at Samye Ling's branches in Europe and Africa. Previous publications include *Maitreya on Buddha Nature*; an earlier translation (with Katia) of the *Ornament of Precious Liberation* found in this volume; *Karmapa*; and a novel, *Tibet or Not Tibet* (in French).

GESHE THUPTEN JINPA was trained as a monk at the Shartse College of Ganden Monastic University, South India, where he received the Geshe Lharam degree. Jinpa also holds a BA in philosophy and a PhD in religious studies, both from Cambridge University, England. Jinpa has been the principal English-language translator for His Holiness the Dalai Lama for over two decades and has translated and edited numerous books by the Dalai Lama. Jinpa's own publications include, in addition to translations featured in *The Library of Tibetan Classics*, *Self, Reality, and Reason in Tibetan Philosophy*, *Essential Mind Training*, as well as *A Fearless Heart: How the Courage to be Compassionate Can Transform Our Lives*. He is president of the Institute of Tibetan Classics in Montreal, an adjunct professor at McGill University, and chair of the Mind and Life Institute.

What to Read Next from Wisdom Publications

The Mind of Mahāmudrā
Advice from the Kagyü Masters
Translated and Introduced by Peter Alan Roberts

"Quite simply, the best anthology of Tibetan Mahāmudrā texts yet to appear."—Roger R. Jackson, Carleton College, author of *Tantric Treasures*

Essential Mind Training
Translated and Introduced by Thupten Jinpa

"With the current rise of positive psychology, in which researchers are seeking a fresh vision of genuine happiness and well-being, this volume can break new ground in bridging the ancient wisdom of Buddhism with cutting-edge psychology."—B. Alan Wallace, author of *The Attention Revolution*

Wisdom of the Kadam Masters
Translated and Introduced by Thupten Jinpa

"Thupten Jinpa shines as an interpreter of classical Buddhism for our times. In *Wisdom of the Kadam Masters* he shows how these pithy sayings from long ago offer anyone sound principles for living a meaningful, fulfilling, and happy life."—Daniel Goleman, author of *Emotional Intelligence*

Stages of the Buddha's Teachings
Three Key Texts
Dölpa, Gampopa, Sakya Pandita
Translated by Ulrike Roesler, Ken Holmes, David P. Jackson

Stages of the Buddha's Teachings presents three extraordinary explanations of the complete path to enlightenment.

Mahāmudrā and Related Instructions
Core Teachings of the Kagyü Schools
Peter Alan Roberts

"This collection is a treasury of 'great seal' teachings from the most renowned gurus of the Mahamudra lineage, each text precious beyond compare. Every page exudes freshness of realization, holding the keys to our own personal awakening."—Judith Simmer-Brown, Naropa University, author of *Dakini's Warm Breath*

A Song for the King
Saraha on Mahamudra Meditation
Khenchen Thrangu Rinpoche
Edited by Michele Martin

"A lively commentary [on] a poetic classic of Buddhist literature. Editor Michele Martin has supplemented Thrangu Rinpoche's lucid commentary with notes and appendices that make the book as accessible for novices as it is rewarding for experienced practitioners and scholars."—*Buddhadharma*

Essentials of Mahamudra
Looking Directly at the Mind
Khenchen Thrangu Rinpoche

"Makes the practice of mahamudra, one of the most advanced forms of meditation, easily accessible to Westerners' everyday lives. A wonderful way of bringing us to the path."—*Mandala*

Mahāmudrā
The Moonlight— Quintessence of Mind and Meditation
Dakpo Tashi Namgyal
Translated by Lobsang P. Lhalungpa
Foreword by His Holiness the Dalai Lama

"Has helped numerous serious Dharma students. It is excellent that the second edition is now being brought out."—His Holiness the Dalai Lama

About Wisdom Publications

Wisdom Publications is the leading publisher of classic and contemporary Buddhist books and practical works on mindfulness. To learn more about us or to explore our other books, please visit our website at wisdompubs.org or contact us at the address below.

Wisdom Publications
199 Elm Street
Somerville, MA 02144 USA

We are a 501(c)(3) organization, and donations in support of our mission are tax deductible.

Wisdom Publications is affiliated with the Foundation for the Preservation of the Mahayana Tradition (FPMT).